WITH
MACARTHUR
IN JAPAN

By Ambassador WILLIAM J. SEBALD
with RUSSELL BRINES

WITH
MACARTHUR
IN JAPAN

A Personal History of the
Occupation

W · W · NORTON & COMPANY · INC · New York

To Edith

Contents

Illustrations

9

The Soviet Delegation to the Allied Council for Japan, headed by Lt. General Kuzma Derevyanko, walking out of the Council.

Ambassador Sebald addressing the graduating class of Saint Joseph's College, Yokohama.

His Imperial Highness Prince Takamatsu and John Foster Dulles.

The final discussion between John Foster Dulles and General MacArthur before Dulles' departure from Haneda Airport.

General MacArthur as Commander in Chief, United Nations Command, turning over the city of Seoul to President Syngman Rhee.

General MacArthur returning from a visit to the Korean battlefront.

General MacArthur departing for the Wake Island meeting with President Truman.

General MacArthur returning to Tokyo from the Wake Island meeting with President Truman.

A group of Japanese leaders at a reception to meet John Foster Dulles.

John Foster Dulles, Prime Minister Yoshida, and Ambassador Sebald.

General Matthew B. Ridgway with his senior commanders near the front line in Korea.

The command post of the 23rd Regimental Combat Team near Inje, Korea.

The signing of the Administrative Agreement between the U.S. and Japan.

General and Mrs. MacArthur leaving Japan.

Foreword

THE OCCUPATION OF JAPAN, between 1945 and 1952, was one of those unique developments which so rarely occur in a nation's history. It was an unprecedented attempt by the victorious Allies of the Pacific War, and principally the United States, to remake an entire people as a means of preventing another violent Asian conflict. The results, both good and bad, are clearly visible in today's Japan.

As the senior civilian official in the Occupation hierarchy, I was for a number of years in a position to observe events and to play an active role in implementing policy in Japan. This book is primarily my account of that period. It is also the story of the late General Douglas MacArthur as I saw him during an unusual and prolonged working relationship. Whatever the shortcomings of this Allied experiment, it was wise that MacArthur was appointed the Supreme Commander for the Allied Powers. No American has wielded such vast power over a foreign country with the wisdom and restraint of this victorious general. MacArthur became not only the symbol of the Occupation; to the Japanese people he *was* the Occupation.

The past was definite prologue to Japan's postwar years, and some knowledge of it is helpful in understanding the events of the Occupation. For this reason I have sketched into this story a number of scenes from my two previous periods of service in Japan. The first, beginning in 1925, brought me as a young United States Navy language officer to a country marked by peace and quiet, order and friendliness. During the thirties, while practicing law in Kobe, I observed the growth of nationalism and rampant imperialism which led to Pearl Harbor and to Japan's inevitable collapse. In less than one generation, from 1925 through 1951, the Japanese actually lived through a complete epoch. They moved swiftly from relative tranquillity to war and defeat and back to stability; from temporary military triumph to hunger and despair, then to revived vitality and confidence.

Japanese history teaches, however, that all this was the norm. Rebellion and war, turbulence and peace are deeply rooted in Japanese society. It is also evident that this long-suffering, remarkable people has developed self-discipline to an unbelievable extent. Were it otherwise, the Occupation, with its discordant pressures, might well have failed.

Against this background I have reconstructed the aspects of the Occupation with which I was directly involved in an attempt to add fresh insight to a historical period of continuing significance. In recounting these events I have drawn liberally upon a journal which I kept faithfully over the years. Quotations attributed to the principal characters are literal contemporary entries as they appear in the journal. The interpretations and conclusions are my own, of course, except where otherwise specified.

Russell Brines has contributed valuable background material accumulated during his service as a newspaper correspondent in Japan between 1939 and 1941 and, again, from 1945 to 1951. For the last five years of this period, he was chief of bureau of The Associated Press in Tokyo and was present at many of the events described in this book.

W.J.S.

Washington, D.C.
January 15, 1965

WITH
MACARTHUR
IN JAPAN

1

War's End

ON THAT CHILL AFTERNOON in mid-October, 1945, Washington was fretful and uncertain. A sense of futility hung heavy over its military offices, and spread to all of us still trapped within them. Armed combat in the Pacific had been over for two months, and the tidal wave of returning troops—Operation Magic Carpet— was well under way. Although important work still remained to be done, the tasks seemed minor and meaningless without the goad of war.

This feeling was particularly strong in what had been the headquarters of the Commander in Chief, United States Navy, until its technical demise through a reorganization on October 10, 1945. COMINCH, as it had been known, was located in the Navy Department Building on Constitution Avenue; a grim and somewhat ugly intruder among the classic architectural beauties of that boulevard. But the headquarters had created its own particular kind of beauty, a wartime command operation geared as delicately as a watch. Now this fine organization was being systematically destroyed.

By order, operations were ending with dispatch, and whole offices lost their personnel overnight. Men who had fought this peculiar Washington war together suddenly disappeared, without farewell. This was the Navy's way, yet the loss was always felt.

My office was the Pacific Section of the Combat Intelligence Division, F-22. On this particular afternoon only a half dozen of us remained on duty, busy with the details of working ourselves out of a job. There were last-minute accountings and inventories to be completed, and final reports to be written. The work and the afternoon dragged on.

Writing a summation of intelligence techniques, I reflected that peace had made an intelligence officer perhaps the most unemployable reject from the war, at least temporarily. In that period of sudden international trust, who wanted a man who had served for three years as chief evaluator of "enemy combat information pertaining to Japanese naval, air, economic and political strength, dispositions, capabilities and intentions"? The future did not necessarily bother me, for I was a lawyer and could always resume practice. But the future, to say the least, was blank and uninviting.

The buzzer on my desk barked suddenly, "Commander Sebald, on one," the WAVE clerk announced.

"Hello, this is Bill Turner, at State," the caller said. I greeted him affably, for William T. Turner was an old friend, who had been a fellow Japanese language officer in Japan during the mid-twenties. He was Japanese desk officer in the State Department, and for once the right man was in the right job.

"I'll come to the point quickly," Bill continued. "As you know, we're gathering the staff for the Occupation of Japan. Would you be interested in a job with the acting political adviser, as an adviser in Japanese law?"

"I don't know, Bill," I replied. "I hadn't thought of it."

"You're just the man for the job," Bill said. "In fact, we don't know anyone else who has practiced law in Japan and who also speaks the language."

"Well, I'll certainly think it over."

"Fine," he said. "I'll send you a memo on it."

This was a rather curious way to start a new career, as a diplomat. Bill Turner's proposal opened the way for me to become the chief political officer in the Occupation, the top State Department position in Japan. Ultimately this led to my becoming ambassador to Burma and Australia. Diplomacy was the furthest prospect from my mind at the time. A graduate of Annapolis, I had been a naval officer on two occasions. My second career had been the law. And now I was about to enter a new and exacting profession.

The promised letter from the State Department arrived the next day, and immediately sharpened the need for swift decision. The letter was specific. It read:

We are advised that the Office of the Political Adviser to the Supreme Commander for the Allied Powers in Tokyo is in urgent need of a qualified expert in Japanese law. The suggestion has been made that you might be available for this position if you feel that it is to your liking. Please inform me of your reaction to this matter as soon as possible as the matter is of some urgency.

General MacArthur already had established his headquarters in Tokyo, as the Supreme Commander, and the swift and dramatic reforms decreed by General MacArthur's headquarters in Japan were well under way. It was, to be sure, a military occupation imposed upon a thoroughly defeated nation, and the General's edict was law. Yet, sooner or later, the political changes which the American authorities were attempting to weave into the fabric of Japanese society had to be reconciled with the complicated maze of Japanese laws. I had struggled for some years with these laws and had translated several codes into English.

JAPAN HAD BECOME an inalienable part of my life since, almost on impulse, I had applied twenty years earlier for assignment as a naval Japanese language officer. I had studied and married there in the pleasant twenties, and had returned in the harsher thirties, when the government fell under the control of the militarists. Like many other foreigners who had known the sunshine of the mercurial Japanese character, I had expected and dreaded the Pearl Harbor attack; then felt the wound personally when it finally occurred.

Hearing of the attack, almost as it was happening, from a frenzied radio account in Washington, I rejected it instinctively. Then the announcer repeated the bulletin, more calmly, and insisted that it was genuine.

"Edith!" I called.

My wife appeared from the kitchen and stood silent, tears running down her cheeks. Then she nodded slowly and despairingly. Edith had been born in Japan, the daughter of an English father and a Japanese mother. Although married to a native American, she was legally without nationality, as our peculiar naturalization laws at that time denied her citizenship.

We remained silent, for there was nothing really to say, while the radio continued its melancholy report.

Finally, I cleared my throat. "I must go back into the Navy."

"Of course, you must," she replied quickly, "I knew you would."

That was all. Within an hour, I called an old friend from the U.S. Naval Academy, Commander Arthur H. McCollum. Mac was in charge of the Far Eastern Division of the Office of Naval Intelligence. I had followed his career closely, although I had been out of the Navy for eleven years, having resigned to study law and to take over the Japanese practice of my father-in-law upon his death. After ending my second residence in Japan in 1939, I had been practicing law in Washington.

Without preliminaries, I asked Mac if he had any use for me.

"By all means," he said quickly, in his soft Alabama drawl. "Come to my office tomorrow and we'll see how to get you back to where you belong as promptly as possible."

I first rejoined the Navy as a civilian. This was only an expedient until the completion of processing would permit a formal commission. Sworn in as an agent on December 15, I went to work immediately, handling some of the vital security information for which I was being cleared by hard-working FBI operatives.

My first job reflected the breath-taking scope and complexity of the Navy's effort to hold back Japanese sea power while recovering its own strength from the tragedy of Pearl Harbor. Each morning I digested scores of dispatches from throughout the world, condensing them into a single report for the director of Naval Intelligence, Rear Admiral Theodore S. Wilkinson. The report was to be on his desk at 8 A.M., promptly. Consequently, I had to leave my home, at the edge of Washington, at 4 A.M., traveling through the fitfully sleeping city, to read each day's installment of the dramatic story before dawn. In the quiet office, under the harsh glare of the lights, with the tobacco smoke and the tension of the previous day still present, I saw the frustrations and the apprehensions and the small triumphs of commanders throughout the Pacific. The messages were cryptic and often prosaic, but the facts created a daily record of quiet heroism.

Adequate intelligence requires an extensive organization, well-trained and well-knit, and a vast outlay of money. It is imperative for every major power to maintain such an organization constantly in being. For the United States, faced by powerful enemies since the rise of Hitler and the Japanese militarists in the thirties, the necessity always has been great, although not always widely recognized. From the viewpoint of cost accounting, there may be waste in such a system; and moralists often deplore the necessity for espionage. Yet a single fact, bought with money or, perhaps, with an agent's life, may save thousands of American lives in a momentary crisis of combat.

It was not until after Pearl Harbor, amid the frenzy of recovery and retaliation, that we acquired the funds and the men to assemble the necessary information about our enemy and the battlefields on which he had chosen to fight us.

As the war plunged into 1942 it became apparent in our sensitive office that the conflict would be prolonged. I had hoped for eventual assignment to sea duty, preferably in the Pacific, and this desire grew stronger as the indefinite duration of hostilities became clearer. But, obviously, a civilian could not be assigned aboard ship. My papers had disappeared into the vast void of Washington, and my commission was held up until they reached the appropriate offices for concurrence. So I traced my file, office by office, and by expediting the Washington procedure, I was sworn in as a lieutenant commander in the Reserves on March 23, 1942. Later, at home, Edith produced my World War I ribbon, earned through service as a midshipman at Annapolis during the summer of 1918. She pinned it on my blouse as if it had been a Congressional Medal of Honor. I was back in the Navy at last.

Necessity greatly altered the intelligence organization which had been maintained in peacetime. The need for faster, better, and more complete information became increasingly apparent. This resulted in the establishment of a Combat Intelligence Division within COMINCH headquarters. The division was known as F-2, and its two sections were designated as F-21 for Atlantic operations and F-22 for the Pacific. I was assigned to organize and to head the Pacific section, effective July 1, 1943.

As the great American war machine drove ever closer to Japan and began direct air and sea bombardment of the islands once believed invulnerable from forcign assault, I began to think more frequently of the smiling villages and the gentle people which form the backbone of that nation. The people had been enslaved by fanatical and arrogant militarists and a relative handful of their supporters; then had been driven into a war which the country as a whole neither wanted nor was equipped to fight. By early 1945 it was apparent Japan had lost the war, but until its military leaders chose to accept reality—and there was no indication when they would—the merciless pounding would continue.

In June of that year, Vice Admiral Charles M. Cooke, the Chief of Staff, asked me this difficult question: Given a continuation of the intense pressures then being maintained, would Japan surrender and, if so, when? The islands were being raked by increasingly severe air attacks, including devastating fire bomb raids on crowded cities, and by the naval gunfire of ships close inshore. For the most part, Japanese defenses were ineffective.

At that time there was considerable opinion in American command levels, particularly the Army, that the only way to end the war was to conquer Japan and completely to destroy its fighting capability. After analyzing the problem in great detail, however, I answered Admiral Cooke by predicting that, under continued air and sea assault, the surrender of Japan could be expected within sixty days, without invasion. This assessment turned out to be almost literally correct, but I never knew what happened to it.

My prediction was based partly on the logic of the situation but primarily upon an assessment of the Japanese people. Militarily, Japan could by that time have fought nothing but a battle of position, a losing defensive war. This would have been costly to Allied forces, but it would have meant the utter destruction of the nation itself. Japan's navy was completely destroyed. Oil was so scarce that no sustained operations of movement, by any branch of the service, could be conducted. The merchant marine was gone. The nation's economy was paralyzed by air attack and by the shortage of raw materials. The cream of the Japanese Army was dead, and the air force was reduced to suicidal Kamikaze tactics.

As for the people themselves, the sources of evaluation were more difficult to pinpoint. Historically, the Japanese pattern has been to seek methods of changing or ending a set course of action when disaster is the only alternative. In this tradition, it was reasonable to expect the current Japanese leaders to reach a collective decision to seek peace, if this could be done in a manner which they considered honorable and which, therefore, saved "face." The dominant problem at that time in the minds of the Japanese leaders, it appeared, was to end the war without permanently disgracing the Japanese race. They were not ready to accept the "unconditional surrender" which had been proclaimed as American policy. But perhaps a slight concession by the Allies would provide them with a face-saving escape from the hopeless conflict.

The Japanese masses, no doubt, would follow their leaders, but they already had given clear indication they would prefer to follow them toward peace. Despite regimentation and the extreme nationalism created by the war, Japanese had fled their bombed cities in sufficient numbers so that military production was crippled.

I expected peace to come with startling suddenness, but through the collective decision of the leaders, not through popular revolt. In retrospect, it seems that, in fixing a specific time for my prediction, I was gambling more upon the ability of Allied authorities to recognize and adjust to this situation than upon any initiative by the Japanese leaders.

A second question, which has continued to haunt the postwar world, arose in our headquarters during the hectic early summer of 1945. Admiral Cooke, who had legitimately earned his nickname of "Savvy," asked me abruptly one day whether the heavy attacks on Japanese cities, then under way, were in the best interests of the United States.

"Well, sir," I replied, "it seems to me that if we continue to insist upon unconditional surrender we will find that wholesale destruction is necessary to end the war."

The Admiral made no direct comment on this evaluation. Bent over his desk, he thought a moment, while continuing to sign an enormous stack of papers. Then, between interruptions from several clamoring telephones, he outlined his ideas. The wartime honeymoon with the Soviets, he said, would end quickly when the war was won. The United States then might face an aggressive Soviet Russia and might need all the allies it could find. The defeat of Japan would leave a vacuum of power in Asia, which the United States should make plans to fill. It was possible, the Admiral added, that in the not too distant future Japan would become an ally against Russia. In that case, the United States would have to rebuild much of what it was destroying in the defiant islands.

Harassed and hurried, Admiral Cooke ended the conversation

by directing me to prepare a study of the probable course of action to be expected from the Soviets as soon as hostilities ceased.

Our study, based upon historical precedent, concluded that, at least, the West could expect a Communist offensive of infiltration and steady pressure after the war. This estimate also disappeared into the files. But the point is that serious attention to the political future was being given in Navy headquarters months before the Japanese surrender, even though relentless prosecution of the military campaigns was of predominant concern.

As peace continued to erode this fine military organization and as, one by one, my own staff disappeared into civilian anonymity, my desire to be of further service grew stronger. This was the decisive reason for finally accepting Bill Turner's offer to go to Occupied Japan. Twenty years of direct and indirect contact and years of study of Japan's language, history, and culture had given me unique knowledge of Japan and its people. This knowledge, I decided, should be available where it was most needed.

Inevitably, I reviewed my experiences in this fascinating country, as well as the recent history with which I had become thoroughly familiar since my first arrival in Japan in 1925.

2

The Old Japan

IN 1925 THERE WAS no visible evidence that Japan was about to begin an imperialist policy which eventually led to Pearl Harbor. Imperialism was brewing in the minds of Japanese militarists, but their ambitions had not burst into the open. Instead, the nation was in the twilight of serenity; the last years of an internal harmony which has not yet been restored. Constitutional government was being practiced, with relative success. The country as a whole was comparatively prosperous, in the aftermath of World War I. That conflict had enabled Japan to achieve her major ambition of being accepted as a world power. Grave internal maladjustments existed, but they were repressed rigorously beneath the mask of conformance imposed by tradition.

So the Japan I first saw was the storybook country which, for too long, became the stereotype in the West: the land of sculptured mountains, manicured rice paddies and picturesquely stunted pine trees. Yet, to a young lieutenant, junior grade, bound for his first big adventure as a Japanese language officer, there were impressive sights, indeed. I clung to the rail of the old *President Monroe* as it nudged through the sea on that hot July 24, 1925, fascinated by the panorama.

We berthed in Kobe, with satisfaction that the voyage from San Francisco had been accomplished in twenty days. In the pre-

24

air age time itself had helped perpetuate Japan's remoteness. This was a nation still perched on the edge of the world, literally.

I stayed that first night at the foreign-style Oriental Hotel in Kobe.

Now, as the lights of Kobe twinkled through the soft purple twilight, I began to realize, for perhaps the first time, the responsibility attached to the assignment. In effect, I had been given a three-year scholarship to learn the intricate spoken and written language of Japan, for eventual service as a naval attaché or in one of the other limited positions for a man with such a specialty.

The 12-hour trip to Tokyo was a kaleidoscope of impressions. Coughing heavy black smoke, the train rolled through the lush green countryside; dodged or tunneled through an endless succession of foothills and mountains, and played tag with a laughing sea, which often seemed within reach. For part of the journey Mt. Fuji dominated the gentle land, with unmistakable possessiveness. It was easy to understand how this giant landmark, drawing the fields and the foothills to its side, was sacred to all Japanese, and to many was the center of the universe.

In noisy Tokyo station I was met by one of the resident language officers, Lieutenant (jg) David Wells Roberts, and my new career began. Roberts, who had been in Japan for about a year, shepherded me through the next few days of formalities, explaining some of the more intricate aspects of embassy life. After reporting to the U.S. naval attaché, my superior, I was no longer required to remain in sultry Tokyo. The language officers were permitted to live wherever they could obtain the services of competent tutors, and some of my alert predecessors had created the custom of spending the summers at mountain or seaside resorts.

Consequently, Wells Roberts and I soon took the train to Karuizawa, a calm little village in the mountains of Nagano prefecture, about a hundred miles northwest of Tokyo. Once a missionary retreat, Karuizawa was developing into a fashionable resort for the foreign diplomatic and business communities and a number of wealthy Japanese. Perched on a 3,300-foot plateau, within an encircling range of mountains, the village was pleasantly cool after Tokyo's moist hot breath.

The next year was a period of intensive but rewarding work and adjustment. In Karuizawa for the remainder of the summer and in Tokyo during the winter, we hammered at the inflexible ramparts of the Japanese language with energy and a modest degree of success. After about eighteen months of daily concentration, through long hours, we were able, in those days, to read a normal newspaper article. After two years it was possible to translate a simple editorial. The average Tokyo newspaper used between 3,000 and 5,000 characters to cover the day's events, each of which was learned by rote.

Tokyo, the capital, with two and a half million people, was the second largest Japanese city at that time, behind the commercial center of Osaka; but it bustled with vibrancy and a sense of purpose. Continuing our studies during the winter, four of us rented a furnished house in Ushigome-ku and our "bachelors' mess" was managed by the mother of Wells Roberts.

During long and untroubled walks through unlighted Tokyo I began to feel the double character of Japan. The capital seemed reasonably adjusted on the surface. Automobiles were scarce, and the narrow, unpaved streets were cluttered with bicycles and hand-drawn carts. Jinrikishas customarily were used for short distances, and the shouts of their pullers contributed to the city's constant undertone of noise. Each day toward sundown Tokyo put on a cloak of pale-blue smoke, as housewives fired charcoal stoves in their tiny back yards to begin the tedious process of preparing simple dinners. Yet Tokyo bore a measure of serenity, and the Japanese had time to demonstrate a great amount of courtesy and friendliness.

A new American ambassador, Charles MacVeagh, took over his post in 1926 with a blast of publicity which illustrated the rather easygoing state of United States and Japanese relations. Shortly after his arrival, this crusty old gentleman was besieged in the Imperial Hotel by a horde of Japanese cameramen, who demanded photographs with quarrelsome persistence. The Japanese were still using old-fashioned cameras and in the dimly lit hotel were obliged to use flash powder. This process was rather like dynamiting a dam. Lighted with a match, the powder flashed with a roar and intense amounts of thick, billowing smoke. At the explosion, the angered ambassador chased the cameramen out of the hotel with his walking stick. He was attacked vigorously in the press for this act, but the Tokyo government, less sensitive than later, ignored the incident. The ambassador simply forgot it.

When he formally presented his credentials to the throne, Ambassador MacVeagh asked the language officers to join other embassy officials for the occasion. It was somewhat like a coronation in miniature. We rode to the palace in gleaming carriages, with prancing horses and brightly uniformed coachmen and footmen. A detachment of imperial cavalry escorted us past curious crowds and into the huge grounds of the palace, in central Tokyo. As we crossed the wide moat surrounding the grounds we slipped into another world. The gardens, behind ponderous walls, were actually a vast hand-clipped cluster of trees and shrubbery, faithfully groomed through the voluntary labor of large numbers of loyal subjects, who considered this work the climax of otherwise unrewarding lives. The palace buildings themselves were deep within the grounds, their gracefully curved roofs invisible from the city. Here, the incomparable skill of Japanese landscape gardeners had created a haven of adroitly managed natural beauty so remote that the clashing emotions of ordinary men could not reach it.

We were ushered into an enormous Western-style reception room in the old Meiji Palace, with a vaulted roof and the uncluttered spaciousness of Japanese architecture. There were several breath-taking golden screens against the walls of the room. Lined up in order of precedence, we proceeded in single file to the adjoining throne room.

Hirohito, who became the wartime Emperor, received us in his capacity as prince regent, acting for his ailing father, the Emperor Taisho. He stood silent and unsmiling during the ceremony, except for an occasional nod of acknowledgment. A young man, scholarly and bespectacled, the Prince Regent appeared gravely aware of his responsibilities.

The summer of 1926 descended quickly upon Tokyo with a blanket of humid heat. We departed at once for Karuizawa—and my life changed again. Soon I was introduced to Edith Frances de Becker, who later became my wife. My knowledge of Japanese did not proceed on schedule during that summer, but I learned a good deal more about a young man's heart than I had known before.

Joseph Ernest de Becker, Edith's father, was an Englishman who had settled in Japan before the turn of the century. He became one of the now vanishing species of foreigners who dedicated his productive life to Japan and, with the added perspective of his background, acquired a deep understanding of Japan and the Japanese. He was an authority on Japanese law, a translator of the Japanese legal codes, and the author of several books on the country. A six-footer, courtly and confident, he spoke the language fluently and had an encyclopedic knowledge of his adopted country.

Mrs. de Becker was a gifted painter and a widely known hostess in Kamakura, the seaside resort near Tokyo, where the family lived. In the 1923 earthquake, however, the house had been demolished. The de Beckers and their two daughters—the two sons were in England at school—moved to Kobe, as did many others who had been caught in the disaster, and their comfortable Kamakura life ended. Mrs. de Becker, who had been seriously injured during the temblor, died in the spring of 1926. As a result, Edith was sent to Karuizawa for the summer to visit friends.

With the usual mobility of my assignment, I received permission to continue my studies in Kobe the next winter. Comfortably established in a house six blocks from the de Becker home, I was able to add another dimension to my background, working with Dr. de Becker almost nightly on a new legal translation. This was an invaluable introduction to the complexities of Japanese law.

On May 14, 1927, Edith and I were married in All Saints Church on Tor Road, Kobe. The ceremony, which attracted numerous Japanese friends, was the first traditional United States Navy wedding in this port city. Wells Roberts, my best man, died heroically in the Pacific War as executive officer of the U.S.S. *Houston.* Among other American naval officers who attended were Lieutenant Commander John M. Creighton, the assistant naval attaché, and Lieutenant (jg) Henri H. Smith-Hutton, who later became my immediate "boss" when I joined COMINCH.

The next year was carefree for Edith and me, in the backwater of Kobe. But dark clouds were beginning to gather over Japan. I was able to read the Japanese newspapers, and the sense of impending tragedy was inescapable. The hypnosis of supernationalism already was being spread across the country by the militarists and their civilian supporters, although opposition was surprisingly strong. Jingoism had gripped the nation briefly after World War I, but had disappeared in the public reaction against the assassination of a prime minister in 1921.

The Japanese Army began the first of its independent maneuvers on the continent which eventually dragged Japan into its almost fatal war. During 1927 and 1928 Japanese troops were shuttled frequently across Central and Northern China. The ostensible reason was to protect Japanese civilians during the civil war exploded by Generalissimo Chiang Kai-shek's military campaigns for control of the country. The real reason, it appeared clearly, was to place Japan in the best possible position to profit from the turmoil.

As my facility in Japanese increased I accompanied the U.S. naval attaché, Commander George McC. Courts, on inspection trips throughout the country. The Japanese authorities showed us only what they wanted us to see, and only in strict exchange for the same privileges extended to Japanese attachés in the United

States. Nevertheless, we were able to acquire a considerable amount of circumstantial evidence which convinced us that the Japanese navy, even then, was violating the strict limitations on naval tonnage imposed by the Washington Treaty of 1922.

From this point onward the Japanese militarists pursued a slow but relentless campaign to extinguish all opposition to their expansionist ambitions. At home, they cowed political leaders with increasingly bold intimidation and, eventually, open assassination. The people remained unchanged, but slowly and almost imperceptibly they were caught in a net of propaganda and surveillance. Abroad, the army conducted military and diplomatic operations with the arrogant independence of a separate government, which in fact it became upon occasion.

This process had just begun when my tour of duty ended in 1928. Regretfully, Edith and I left Japan for reassignment in the United States. For the next five years, through the conquest of Manchuria and the first bold bites at China, I watched the fateful drama from a distance.

During 1929, one of the last ostentatious expressions of Japanese-American friendship struck a note of curious irony. A Japanese naval squadron visited the United States, to a friendly reception. I was detached from duty aboard the battleship U.S.S. *Oklahoma* to serve as personal aide to the commander of the visiting squadron—the late Vice Admiral Kichisaburo Nomura, who, at the time of the Pearl Harbor attack, was the Japanese ambassador to Washington. Nomura, unusually tall for a Japanese, was a robust extravert with an infectious laugh and a keen sense of humor. I found him well-informed on a number of subjects and a sincere admirer of the United States.

When President Hoover received Nomura and reviewed the Japanese midshipmen, many on both sides of the Pacific began to hope for the restoration of full confidence and amity between the two nations. Relations had been troubled by sharp disagreements over disarmament, by a strong Japanese reaction to the immigration limitations imposed by the United States Exclusion Act, and by Washington's growing apprehension over Japanese imperialist ambitions. Nevertheless, the squadron's visit created sufficient warmth so that the late Katsuji Debuchi, then the Japanese ambassador to Washington, told me in a private conversation that American-Japanese relations had never been better.

After these experiences the routine of naval shipboard life began to pall and I became restive over the necessary long absences from home. Furthermore, Dr. de Becker, my father-in-law, had died in early 1929, and his extensive Kobe law practice was proving irksome for his twenty-four-year old son, Eric. I was offered a partnership in the firm. It was a tantalizing proposal, although I knew little about law. Nevertheless, after some soul-searching, I finally resigned from the Navy in 1930 and entered the School of Law at the University of Maryland. Three years later, after graduation and my admission to the Maryland bar, Edith and I returned to Kobe.

IT WAS A DIFFERENT CITY and a different country in 1933. The worldwide depression had struck Japan, spreading unemployment and unrest. Nationalistic fervor had grown, with the consolidation of the army's hold on Manchuria and with fresh military campaigns to capture Inner Mongolia and slices of Northern China. Japan had received universal condemnation for the Manchurian adventure and had expressed its defiance by resigning from the League of Nations, thus beginning the downfall of both Japan and the League. At home, the Japanese extremists turned with suspicion upon the foreigners among them. This feeling was particularly strong in ports like Kobe, where the sizable foreign community was regarded by the jingoists as a spy center. The Japanese people were further troubled and fearful after a series of assassinations in 1932, which irretrievably ended constitutional government.

Nevertheless, I plunged deeply into work, anxious to learn this new profession and to understand Japanese law. The practice itself was interesting, although foreigners were barred from trial work, which was handled by Japanese assistants. In my spare time I turned to translating the Japanese Civil Code, which was basic to most other laws. During my six years' practice in Japan I managed to translate and to publish three codes and numerous laws of great importance to business enterprises dealing with Japan. To some extent this was a thankless task, but it was an excellent way to learn Japanese law and to increase my knowledge of the language.

In the mid-thirties one of my more interesting cases required three trips to Harbin, Manchuria. On one occasion, as the train lurched across the flat prairies of southern Manchuria, I opened the door to the rear observation coach and started to enter. A guard immediately and roughly ordered me to leave. At once, to my surprise, a senior Japanese army officer, whom I did not recognize, countermanded the order and invited me to join him. The coach fell silent, as I made my way toward the rear of the car. Several high-ranking officers watched me coldly.

I landed near my benefactor, a dark, vivacious man, with the elongated nose of the Japanese aristocracy. We talked at length, while the train roared across Japan's new colony. With what appeared to be genuine interest the stranger asked numerous questions about my background. At length, with a polite farewell, he rose and left the train upon its arrival in Hsinking, the capital of Manchoukuo, the new name for Manchuria. I continued to occupy the seat for the remainder of the long journey, and the other officers accepted me, if somewhat ungraciously. The train crew became bowingly respectful. My host, I later learned, was Prince Takamatsu, brother of the Emperor of Japan.

On the snowy dawn of February 26, 1936, a garrison of some 1,500 troops revolted in Tokyo under the leadership of so-called "younger officers," the field grade ranks who had become increasingly clamorous for military conquest. The rebels killed several government leaders and held the heart of the city for three days before order was restored.

The incident deeply shocked the nation and produced a flurry of open criticism against the army for failing to maintain discipline. Criticism of this sort had become rare and, as it turned out, this was the country's last chance to express it. Thereafter Japan was governed by a series of cabinets which remained under complete military control. "Thought police" tightened their censorship over the people, the press and the politicians.

The army then turned to the next phase of its campaign, the systematic detachment of China's five northern provinces. Although the aggressive nature of these campaigns was clear to most of the outside world, the Japanese people were completely misled about their purpose. They were told, among other things, that Japan was forced to defend the Asiatic mainland against two types of communism: the latent threat of Soviet arms in Siberia and the active threat of a Communist victory in China. It was upon this premise that Japan began its fateful alliance with Germany and Italy by concluding the Anti-Comintern Pact in November, 1936.

During this period Edith and I were able to build our own house on the heights overlooking Akashi Strait at Tarumi, west of Kobe, despite the increased difficulty of obtaining proper materials. The view was spectacular. Isolated from immediate neighbors, we looked across terraced farmlands to Akashi Strait and the foliaged beauty of Awaji Island, the eastern boundary of the Inland Sea. The sea below us changed with the seasons and with the clouds, from brilliant blue to angry gray. Most of the marine traffic between Asia and central Japan traveled past our picture windows, the ships cutting white wrinkles in the water. It was a delightful spot for beauty and for quiet study.

But soon it became a melancholy observation post. The Japanese Army launched major hostilities against China in 1937. The militarists had expected a campaign of easy conquest, but instead they committed the country to a long, frustrating and costly war. And so the waters below us churned more furiously. Larger and larger convoys of black ships carried troops and supplies to the mainland; the ships returned with little white urns containing ashes of the war dead.

The next two years were filled with stress and suspicion. The antipathy of the officials toward foreigners increased in direct proportion to the frustration in the China campaign. The pressures around me intensified during 1938, and there was no doubt that, like many others, I had become unwelcome. Each week, uniformed members of the kempeitai, whose presence was enough to terrorize the average Japanese, stalked into my office, their long swords clanking at their sides. Arrogantly they demanded detailed reports of my activities from the Japanese staff. A parade of plainclothes detectives cornered me for long, inquisitorial conversations. They particularly wanted to know my views on the China conflict. The evident purpose was to trap me into the serious mistake of saying that the war was wrong or that Japan was losing.

Finally, there came the expected but chilling summons to visit the procurator, the all-powerful equivalent of a district attorney. As I arrived in my office at about 9 A.M. on a bitterly cold and blustery day in January, 1939, Eiji Nagahara, my principal Japanese assistant, nervously told me that I had been ordered to report to the procurator's office at my earliest convenience. This was a Japanese euphemism which, under the circumstances, meant immediately.

Taking along old Nagahara as a witness, I hailed a taxi and went to the court building. Like all Japanese public buildings, it was unheated, and an icy wind swept through broken windows and open entrance doors. For the next hour, we sat in frozen neglect on a hard bench. A clerk eventually admitted us to the procurator's office. While also unheated, it was luxurious enough to be without a direct draft. The clerk told me to take a seat, but left Nagahara to stand.

As I straightened up I faced the procurator, who was seated at the desk, warming his hands over a hibachi, a charcoal brazier. For a moment we stared silently at each other. Then the procurator began questioning me, in coarse language and with a drill sergeant's tone. Answers to the usual questions about my name, address and business were checked against a report on his desk. Then, abruptly, he asked whether it was true that I had engaged in espionage.

"That is not true," I replied. "The Japanese government is well aware of my naval background, and I have made no secret—"

"You are here," he bellowed, "to answer questions, not to comment on them. Remember that!"

The questioning continued for several shouting, snarling hours. Finally, after signing a statement certifying my answers, I was told to leave.

Although no charges were filed against me and I did not hear again from the procurator's office, the warning was clear. Accordingly, I wound up my business affairs and Edith and I left our first home. We boarded the *President Cleveland* in June, 1939, for the return to the United States. For us, as for many other foreigners at that time, departure was a moment of sorrow for the friends left behind and regret for the sudden ending of a successful career. Yet I felt as if I had been freed from long imprisonment when we finally stepped aboard the American ship and left the dock at Kobe.

From Washington, Japan's inexorable march toward Pearl Harbor was clearly visible. As militarist control tightened over the Japanese Empire, the need for a "face-saving" escape from the hopeless conflict in China became greater, but apparently impossible to achieve. Nevertheless, or perhaps because of this dilemma, after the outbreak of war in Europe Japanese leaders made little secret of their desire to control the Far Eastern colonies of France, Great Britain, and the Netherlands which the metropolitan powers were ill-prepared to defend. Additionally, trade restrictions by the United States and, in 1941, a freeze on Japanese assets in the United States, increased the difficulty of obtaining oil and other essential raw materials so vital for the Japanese war machine.

To the Japanese militarists, therefore, the solution lay in only one direction: a drive southward to the rich spoils of the European colonial empires. But the most vital step was to be the immobilization of the American Pacific Fleet at Pearl Harbor, an operation scheduled to take place simultaneously with attacks elsewhere.

Throughout the long, difficult and often agonizing years between 1939 and 1945 the fate I least anticipated was a return to Japan as an American official.

3

The New Japan

THE TRIP BACK TO JAPAN, in January, 1946, required less than four days, instead of nearly three weeks. Leaving Edith in Washington, I traveled by air across the once-forbidding Pacific, using the island-hopping avenue opened by the war. This speed showed how completely Japan's isolation and remoteness had been abolished. And the circumstances of the flight underlined the new status of the proud island nation, which had surrendered in flames. The only way to reach Japan by air was by military aircraft on an American military airline which operated much as if hostilities were still under way.

When the plane dropped from a cloudless sky over the emerald line of the Japanese islands, Mt. Fuji to my left raised an imperious head, white-haired with snow. The sacred peak still dominated a landscape of neatly terraced farms and shaggily bearded mountains; but it was no longer a sacred land, as the people had believed. The plane leveled off over Atsugi Airfield, twenty-three miles southwest of Tokyo, and I saw the Stars and Stripes floating above a rusty hangar.

Atsugi, carved from farmlands, had served as a strip for training kamikaze suicide pilots. Now it was the principal airport for Allied military air traffic in the Tokyo area. We bumped to a landing and marched quickly through the clean brisk air to the terminal building.

Hundreds of Japanese workmen were scattered around the field, hacking at the ground in small groups, under the supervision of American soldiers. The Japanese wore patched and frayed clothing of all types, including, for the majority, the army uniforms and peaked caps which had been so familiar and so dreaded throughout Asia. They seemed to work willingly enough, if often at a pace too slow to suit their American supervisors, for the cry of "hubba hubba" was frequent. And no resentment whatsoever in this relationship was detectable. For all their traditional impassivity, the Japanese in groups usually betray their mood, to those attuned to them, by generating a sort of unmistakable emotional electricity.

After perfunctory arrival formalities in the Atsugi terminal, my bags were snatched by a crew of ragged Japanese porters and tossed unceremoniously, upside down, into a U.S. army bus. Although the bus was scarred by peeling paint, cracked windows and creaking seats, its motor purred smoothly without missing a beat as we bounced along a dusty, potted and narrow unpaved road which wound through numerous farmland villages on the way to Yokohama. The once remote highway was alive with American army trucks, jeeps, and cars. Dust from the traffic swirled through the air and coated the thatched roofs.

The Japanese people shocked me most. I was surprised by their smallness and lethargy, alongside the tall, well-fed, and vigorous Americans. They were, unmistakably, a beaten people, momentarily despairing and hopeless. Gone were the exuberance and animation of the Japanese crowd—clean and without smell, as Lafcadio Hearn once described it, in the distant past. Instead, on that ride to Yokohama, I saw the sad degeneration of humbled pride. Men and women, who once had preserved the appearance of neatness as a matter of honor, were slovenly, often dirty, mostly ill-dressed. The men no longer cared to hide their worry, their bewilderment, their depression. The women, less visibly concerned, were shapeless and characterless in their baggy wartime costumes, the practical but uninviting mompei, padded trousers. The fields were ragged, the picturesque thatched roofs, upon closer inspection, needed repairs, and the houses sagged.

Only the children were unchanged. They were the same fun-loving, irrepressible, uninhibited youngsters that I had known long before. Standing along the road, in round-faced wonderment, they shouted at the passing cars and waved and saluted, ending each performance with a fractured fragment of the limited, but practical, English vocabulary they had acquired. "Chokuretsu!" "Gummu!" And laughing GIs, in those early days, scattered chocolate and gum across the Japanese countryside by the ton.

The road slipped into the plain containing Yokohama and Tokyo—and we entered the blackened domain of war. I remembered the 15-mile stretch between these two major cities as a tightly packed sweep of houses, factories, and public bathhouses, with scarcely a scrap of empty land. Now it was all a wilderness of rubble. The factories were marked by the locked hands of twisted steel girders. Tall, gaunt chimneys peered over emptiness. Of the wood and paper houses which had distinguished this predominantly middle-class area, only powdered ash remained. For miles there was no sign of habitation and no sign of life. The fire bombs had scoured the land.

Tokyo itself began with row upon row of tiny shacks, put together from the strips of metal and stones which had survived the raging fires. The shanties stretched endlessly across the flatlands, and tens of thousands of people lived in them. They were crude and dismal, but they provided shelter for homeless families, who were unable to obtain assistance from a helpless and befuddled government. Here and there the irrepressible Japanese had planted shrubs and flowers around their rubble homes; and an occasional housewife had hung curtains on tiny windows. From a distance this vast shantytown made it appear as if half of Tokyo had rusted.

In the heart of the city, however, the business buildings and the hotels and most of the mansions were untouched, although often surrounded by ruins. This evidently was due to the practical selectivity of an Allied force which based its military plans upon the expectation that Japan would have to be occupied. The Imperial Palace had been accidentally burned down, although most of its outbuildings remained untouched.

With a sigh the old bus ultimately deposited us at the Dai Ichi Hotel, the newest and most puzzling hotel in Tokyo. Meaning "number one" it had been designed to house visitors for the 1940 Olympic Games, an event for which Japan was vigorously preparing when it turned toward war. It was never clear what type of visitors or athletes the architects had in mind, but possibly a team from Lilliput was expected. The rooms seemed too small for even the Japanese, and the average American sat in the bathtub with his knees around his ears. This was, nevertheless, the billet for Occupation officials who ranked just below the level of general officers, and I was assigned there, along with a number of other innocents.

As I wandered around Tokyo during the next few days, with never an insult or an incident, the validity of the bromidic truism, never lose a modern war, became increasingly apparent. The city was overcrowded, dirty, and incredibly decrepit. Rubble lay in huge piles nearly everywhere, except in the undamaged downtown commercial section. For the Japanese, daily living became a constant battle of overcrowded streetcars, long food queues, unheated homes and offices, and growing shortages of every essential from water to food. Streets were untended and full of potholes, office buildings were grimy and odorous, and stores were empty. A capital once too proud to permit beggars on its streets, now Tokyo was filled with the homeless and the ragged.

But perhaps most striking was the comparative silence, particularly at night, when the city lay in darkness, because electricity was scarce. Always noisy and vigorous, Tokyo had its own particular range of sounds. They had been dominated, in prewar times, by the frog croaking of automobile horns, the sound per-

mitted by authorities seeking to reduce noise. Now there were
virtually no automobiles, and those still operating crept sound-
lessly through the night.

Food was the constant worry of all urbanites during that
troubled period. Wartime rationing remained in effect, but even
so available rations were insufficient for minimum requirements.
The black market flourished, but its astronomical prices were beyond the range of all except the wealthy. Instead, thousands of
city dwellers jammed the trains each weekend with bundles of
possessions to visit the nearby countryside and bargain for food
with farmers and fishermen. This barter system, which sooner or
later involved most of Tokyo's population, was known as an
"onion economy," the peeling off of personal possessions piece by
piece for sustenance. It was illegal to buy rice in this manner, but
hunger knows no law.

This was the country to which I had returned, in what presumably would be a relatively minor and temporary position
under the Occupation.

GENERAL MACARTHUR'S HEADQUARTERS already had become large
and bustling. The Japanese, as well as the Americans, quickly
learned the alphabetization that distinguishes the American
bureaucracy; consequently the Headquarters, as well as the General himself, were known as SCAP. Located in the Dai Ichi Insurance Company building alongside the outer moat of the Imperial Palace, GHQ had become a pervading influence in the lives of
millions of Japanese, reaching out, even at this early date, to
remote rural areas, through the operations of military government
teams.

The initial guidelines of Occupation policy were loose and
unclear. They were summarized in a key sentence of Washington's Initial Post-Surrender Directive:

Disarmament and demilitarization are the primary tasks of the Military
Occupation and shall be carried out promptly and with determination.

Under that broad authority SCAP had initiated a number of sweeping programs between the time of its establishment, on August 30, 1945, and my arrival in early January, 1946. Physical demobilization of the vast Japanese Army was well under way and the destruction of arms and military installations was proceeding. The second general Occupation task was to establish the basis for a democratic government, primarily as a means of preventing revived imperialism. This had produced a flood of directives from Headquarters, demanding fundamental changes in nearly every aspect of traditional Japanese life. Military men were in charge of every important section of SCAP, and often they issued orders with customary bluntness. Under them, a civilian bureaucracy was growing rapidly.

Although the State Department had participated in preliminary planning, its role in Tokyo at this period of the Occupation was limited and only vaguely defined. Our office was known as the Acting United States Political Adviser to SCAP, shortened to POLAD. Headed by the late George Atcheson, Jr., with the personal rank of minister, it operated in many ways like an embassy accredited to the Occupation. This was consistent with the legal concept of General MacArthur as supernational representative of an Allied occupation. But, in fact, the Occupation never became an international enterprise, despite the involvement of all eleven wartime associates. Instead, SCAP was predominantly American in operation, as well as in personnel, to the discomfiture of several Allied governments. The position of POLAD, therefore, was in the beginning curiously half in and half outside the mainstream of Occupation affairs.

I was introduced to this anomaly on my first day in the office of POLAD. George Atcheson greeted me warmly and welcomed me to what he called his shorthanded staff. Although I had been hired as an expert on Japanese law, he said he had no immediate assignment. Instead, he urged me to learn as much as possible about the political situation in Japan.

In explaining this rather curious vagueness, George A., as we called him, said the situation in the Occupation was still confused and many officials had not settled into their jobs. The relationship between POLAD and the military headquarters evidently was not clear, even to him, and he said it was sometimes difficult to determine precisely what functions POLAD was expected to fulfill. George A. said his personal relations with General MacArthur were good, although not as intimate or understanding as he would have liked.

George Atcheson, then forty-five, was an experienced and extremely able professional diplomat, but his background had been almost entirely in China. A former language officer, who spoke Mandarin fluently, he had served exclusively in Chinese affairs between 1920 and 1945, in various posts in China and Washington.

Inevitably, George A. carried his China background and sympathies into the Occupation. Although he was quick to size up factual situations and usually was correct in his analyses, he represented at that time the "old China hand" belief in a tough policy for Occupied Japan. Another official sharing this viewpoint, John Stewart Service, was executive officer of the mission. Born in China, thirty-six years earlier, Jack Service also spoke Chinese fluently and had served most of his career in that country. During the war he was political officer on the staff of General Joseph W. ("Vinegar Joe") Stilwell. Service was a man of quick perception and prodigious output.

At the other extreme, Max Waldo Bishop represented the so-called pro-Japanese viewpoint. A former Japanese language officer, with prewar experience in Japan, Max felt that much misunderstanding was being created among the Japanese by Occupation officials who knew little or nothing about the Japanese people and their problems.

After several conversations with Max, it was clear that the senior officers of our mission were hopelessly divided on how to approach the difficult political questions then arising in Japan. The basic differences were over the degree of severity with which to treat the Japanese. The mission also was divided over such questions as the extent and speed of political and economic reform. These same problems also sharply split SCAP Headquarters and the government departments in Washington, and on many occasions separated the United States from its allies.

At first this situation concerned me greatly. But with more experience I came to understand that there are no clear-cut or easy answers when political considerations and national interests are involved in an experiment as gigantic as the Occupation. I had my opinions on these various problems, of course, but my position was too minor at that time to be influential.

SCAP Headquarters did not often solicit the views of the Japanese in the momentous early days of the Occupation. Nor was there any evidence that opinions volunteered by high-ranking Japanese during frequent visits to Headquarters were incorporated into policy. Instead, SCAP orders usually were issued with a military imperiousness which the Japanese found offensive. Too often the decrees presented for implementation by the Japanese government were conspicuously geared to American, rather than Japanese, psychology. Most of the American authorities, it seemed, regarded Japan as a defeated nation, to be reformed in the shortest possible time. This was an understandable attitude, so soon after the surrender.

A sudden staff change resulted in my early promotion to the position of political reporter, an assignment which required me to observe closely all the crosscurrents in Japan's complex political situation and to report the trends periodically to Washington. This was an exacting task but it enabled me to meet and to know all the major Japanese political leaders and others of influence in industry and similar fields.

It soon became clear that Japanese of this class were dominantly concerned by the possibility the Communists would win political power or that they might even take over the government. This theme runs through the day-to-day diary I kept faithfully at that time, recording conversations with Japanese of all political beliefs. It can be argued that the cold war did not become a universally recognized international issue until a year later, when, in 1947, President Truman initiated countermeasures against Soviet-encouraged subversion in Turkey and guerrilla war in Greece. For large numbers of Japanese, however, the cold war immediately superseded the hot war, without a pause.

Japan certainly was vulnerable to Communist attack, for war and defeat had created a vast psychological upheaval. Destruction and economic distress had bred widespread restlessness. Japanese government leadership was inept and often paralyzed, partly because officials frequently were unable to understand what the Occupation wanted of them. The nation's uncertainty was intensified by conflicting pressures from the victorious Allies who, at the moment of the surrender, became competitors in pursuit of their own national interests. The question was not whether conditions favored Soviet subversion and pressure but whether Moscow would revive its offensive against the non-Communist world. Although many continued to hope for cooperation and peace with Moscow long after the war, the conviction was strong in Tokyo in 1946 that a major task in Japan would be to halt Communist expansion.

Stalin had indicated his intention of applying maximum pressure on Japan by attempting to move Red Army troops into favorable positions on the main islands. First, he demanded an occupation zone in northern Hokkaido which would have placed the cities of Kushiro and Rumoi and all the territory northward of them under Soviet military control. This proposal, made officially on August 16, 1945, was promptly rejected by President Truman. The President told Stalin, however, that "token" Soviet forces, as well as other Allied troops, might be employed temporarily in Japan to carry out the surrender terms if General MacArthur considered this necessary.[1] The Soviets then approached General MacArthur with an official request for a Hokkaido occupation zone. Although the General was legally as much a representative of Moscow as of Washington, he parried this overture, and the

Soviets lost a chance to use the Red Army as a spearhead of penetration, as they had in Eastern Europe.*

Soviet occupation of any part of Hokkaido undoubtedly would have created the same divisions and ceaseless pressures which have plagued Korea, Viet Nam, and Germany. President Truman so interpreted Stalin's original overtures.[2] Moreover, Hokkaido occupies a significant place in the Japanese economy, as the source of about 30 percent of domestic coal. This point was emphasized by a number of Japanese visitors, particularly the late Admiral Teijiro Toyoda, an economic expert who had been a prewar foreign minister and munitions minister in the final cabinet of the war. Expressing his concern over the limping economy in 1946, Admiral Toyoda said: "Without adequate domestic coal, Japan's railways and other transportation would grind to a halt, bringing the entire economy to a standstill. Conversely, the rebuilding of vital industries depends in part, upon the maintenance of adequate transportation. Further, industrial revival is geared to the production of steel, and Japanese mills require special coking coal which they customarily had obtained from nearby areas, now under Communist domination."

In Admiral Toyoda's view, which presumably represented the consensus of Japanese industrialists, coal was a prime key to recovery. While Hokkaido coal was only one part of this complicated situation, it was sufficiently important so that Soviet control of the northern island would have had a major economic impact on Japan.

Thus, the very early recognition of Soviet designs in Washington and in SCAP Headquarters saved Japan from serious distress. The Communists were by no means discouraged, however, and they turned quickly to other methods in the effort to subvert and

* In an interview the General told me that, as SCAP, he could not flatly reject the Soviet request, but as commander he could assign troops wherever he considered necessary. Pretending to welcome the Soviet offer to "help" in the Occupation, MacArthur suggested an occupation zone in heavily bombed central Honshu, the main Japanese island. This position was deliberately chosen, for it was flanked on both sides by two American divisions and therefore would have been militarily untenable for Russian disruptive purposes. The Soviets quietly dropped the idea.—R.B.

subdue the beaten Japanese. Almost from the outset the Occupation was confronted by ceaseless Communist attempts to win power, sometimes by supporting the Allied program and sometimes by strenuously opposing it.

In 1946 American policies were ambivalent and often contradictory. Despite the fact that General MacArthur and many of his subordinates were fighting their own version of the cold war at this early date, SCAP also was implementing directives from Washington which seemed to profit the Communists. Indeed, one had the impression that the United States was encouraging extreme leftism and communism. Nearly all of my Japanese visitors were deeply concerned by this point. It even became necessary to assure Prince Takamatsu, in an informal conversation, that SCAP did not want communism in Japan any more than did the United States government. The Prince had voiced the prevalent Japanese fear that the Communists would gain tremendous power, or might even capture the government, unless SCAP made it clear that it was anti-Communist.

This feeling sprang, no doubt, from a double effect of SCAP policy. Communist leaders, long imprisoned by the Japanese government, had been freed late in 1945 by Occupation authorities. They were permitted to organize, to publish a newspaper, and to enjoy the new freedoms given to all Japanese, including freedom of speech. With these privileges, they were making an undeniable impact upon the Japanese masses. On the other hand, SCAP had issued stern orders purging from all positions of influence the political, industrial, and economic leaders connected with Japan's wartime career. The purge orders were so extensive that nearly every prominent man in these areas, and such a related field as journalism, was removed from authority.

The Communists quickly created a political organization which, by its ruthless discipline, seemed strong enough, at the time, to make substantial political gains. Otherwise, politics were in chaos, with experienced leaders either purged or too uncertain to exercise strong authority. Four non-Communist parties quickly arose, with unclear platforms and purposes, and some 350 local parties were formed, at least in name, by ambitious men. No politician could be certain what his party stood for or indeed what policy it would be permitted by SCAP to advocate, except possibly the numerous one-man organizations designed solely to advance individual interests. In uncertainty and confusion, the Japanese seemed well on their way toward political fragmentation.

The political purge created strong concern not only among the Japanese conservatives, who were most directly affected, but also among the Socialists. Once vigorously repressed for advocating a Socialist form of government, these men under Occupation protection created a political force of some consequence. Several groups of varied outlook had merged into the newly formed Social Democratic party.

Left-wingers were steadily rising in party influence when the Socialists scored their one triumph at the polls in 1947. By winning 143 seats in the House of Representatives, the Socialists, with the support of the conservative Democratic party under Hitoshi Ashida, were able to form their only cabinet in Japanese history. Left-wing party leaders and the Communists, who also gained an impressive popular vote in the election, had endeavored to create a coalition government by themselves, but failed. The Communist plan was to infiltrate pro-Communists regularly into the government, to isolate those opposing them, and gradually to nibble their way to power. Top leadership of the Socialist party was held by moderates under Tetsu Katayama, however, and these men, in cooperation with Ashida's Democrats, blocked the Communists.

The Japanese also were worried by what they considered to be the uncertain attitude of SCAP authorities. Rumors quickly spread that a number of crypto-Communists and extreme leftists were active in Headquarters and were being protected by the section chiefs, who were all military officers. One particularly persistent story was that the Japanese complained about an alleged notorious leftist in the Government Section, which directed such activities as the political purges and the formulation of a new constitution. The protest was met, so the story went, by the reply of the section head, Brigadier General Courtney A. Whitney, that anyone who was good enough to wear a uniform in defense of the United States was good enough to be in his section. Whether true or not, the tale was not helpful in reassuring the Japanese whom we were trying to guide into a "new order of peace, security and justice." Although a number of SCAP officials were investigated on suspicion of being members of the Communist party, none to my knowledge was dismissed in Tokyo on this ground; some were returned to Washington for further investigation.

The rumors were enough, however, to intensify confusion in the puzzled country, particularly when many Japanese interpreted the more drastic SCAP reforms as being too severe and too precipitate.

Our own POLAD office was affected—unjustly, I believe—by charges against some of the staff by Patrick J. Hurley, who retired in a blaze of invective as President Truman's personal representative in China. In his letter of resignation in 1945 and later in formal hearings by the Senate Foreign Relations Committee, Hurley renewed an attack upon George Atcheson and Jack Service which he had conducted in demanding their recall from China earlier in the year.

At the time the charges appeared to me more sensational than warranted by the details made public. This impression was confirmed by rereading in 1963 the transcript [3] of the Senate hearings. It seemed filled with inaccuracies and irascible and unreasonable statements. Working with Atcheson, as chief of the Tokyo mission, and with Service, as the executive officer, I found no justification whatsoever for the slightest suspicion of their loyalty or sincerity.

Nearly a decade later two of our capable Occupation officers were involved in the hearings conducted by the late Senator

Joseph McCarthy. Jack Service was completely vindicated of charges that he was either a Communist or sympathetic to Communist views. The second man, John K. Emmerson, also was completely exonerated of even more specious charges, that he associated with Communists. This was based largely upon an incident directly involving me, and is cited here primarily to expose its flimsiness. Both men had to endure years of patently unfair and unproductive harassment.

Emmerson, another of the group which had come to Japan from wartime service in China, was political officer of POLAD when I reached Tokyo. He was a brilliant language officer and political analyst. As usual, he reported the situation as he saw it and not always as others wished. Consequently, in my opinion, he set a high standard for the weekly political summaries to Washington and to General MacArthur. Emmerson was transferred to Washington in February, 1946, and I took over his position after the unusually short period of seven weeks in the foreign service.

Shortly before his departure, Emmerson asked me to join him for an interview in his office with Sanzo Nozaka, the titular head of the Japan Communist party and the most controversial political figure in Japan at that time. Although I had seen Nozaka distantly at flag-waving Communist rallies, this was my first chance for a face-to-face meeting, and I welcomed it as a means of broadening my background in Japanese politics. During his service in China, Emmerson had spent some months in Yenan, the headquarters of the Chinese Communists, and had met Nozaka there. Emmerson had invited the Communist leader to his office for one of the farewell interviews he conducted with numerous Japanese politicians.

As Nozaka talked to Emmerson and me, he drew on his considerable experience and extensive education to make his points, with quiet insistence. There was no doubting his determination to win power for the Communists, but he preached a form of "peaceful revolution," which, at that time, could only have reflected Stalin's strategy for Japan. Nozaka said his task was to create the image of a "lovable Communist party," a policy he pursued for years in opposition to more belligerent Japanese comrades, until Moscow itself changed the line.

The details of our one-hour, closed-door meeting with Nozaka reached Washington and became the basis of McCarthy's charges against Emmerson. There was no question in my mind, however, that this interview was normal and necessary to the process of gathering information for the use of SCAP and the State Department.

These were some of the complications surrounding the immense task of the Occupation. The job of demilitarizing Japan and introducing a series of reforms, which originally constituted the SCAP assignment, were great enough without the additional Communist offensive. In the Occupation we had to learn a complete new strategy for a very vicious and dangerous cold war.

At the time there was no warning of the series of events which would involve me deeply in that conflict.

4

Occupation Diplomat

THE OCCUPATION changed swiftly under the pressures of Japan's immense problems and, eventually, the unexpected vigor of the Communist attack. Originally, the Occupation was to be only temporary, as President Truman advised Stalin in 1945, but it lasted nearly seven years.[1] The first limited task of demilitarization and partial reform soon expanded into extensive social renovation, a revolution by decree. The United States had no initial plans for rehabilitating the battered country, but eventually billions of dollars were invested to put the Japanese back on their feet. Finally, American arms were pledged to Japan's defense by General MacArthur, long before Washington appeared ready to accept such a radical shift of policy toward the late enemy.

The character of the rough military Occupation, with its all-male air and battlefield camaraderie, changed almost as quickly. SCAP Headquarters was organized along quasi-civilian lines by early 1946, with complicated political and economic problems superseding military questions. In the summer of that year, dependent wives and children arrived, bringing with them the atmosphere of home and vast quantities of necessities and luxuries, unknown to the Japanese and almost forgotten by the American combat men. At first the Army planned to accommodate the entire Occupation in homes and buildings requisitioned from the Japanese, and no plans were made for new American construction. Accordingly, a large proportion of the homes of upper-class Japanese were taken over, because no others suited American requirements. All the residences needed extensive renovation, at a cost of billions of yen. This helped to create further resentment and uneasiness among the same Japanese who felt that many Occupation reforms were unjustly directed at them. The available accommodations were inadequate, however, for the thousands of Occupationaires—the term manufactured at that time—who arrived in Japan. Large numbers of homes, schools, clubs, and barracks were constructed through Japanese contractors. The Americans worked with amazing speed, in Japanese eyes, and by the fall of 1946 the first new English-language schools were opened in Tokyo. All pretense of a temporary Occupation was gone.

The American community in Tokyo became a city within a city, preserving its own culture and customs. This was duplicated throughout the island nation, even in remote villages where military government teams sometimes became the first resident Occidentals in Japanese history. SCAP also became a government within a government, and all power was concentrated in the neat and prim Dai Ichi building. General MacArthur exercised his authority through the existing Japanese governmental machinery and its various agencies. The United States Initial Post-Surrender Policy directed him to use the Japanese government, including the Emperor, to the extent that this practice furthered United States objectives. Further, the Post-Surrender Directive specified that "The Japanese Government will be permitted . . . to exercise the normal powers of *domestic* administration." * In practice, MacArthur relied almost entirely upon the Japanese authorities to run the country and to carry out American directives, but his authority was always visible.

GENERAL HEADQUARTERS functioned in a dual capacity, as both a military and a political command. For military purposes, Mac-

* Italics added.

Arthur maintained the customary army organization, which also conducted a considerable volume of business concerned with the Occupation. For Occupation purposes, he augmented this structure with a number of additional sections dealing with specialized functions to implement directives sent from Washington. These included such subdivisions as the Government Section, Economic and Scientific Section, Legal Section, Civil Information and Education Section, Natural Resources Section, Public Health and Welfare Section, and the Civil Property Custodian, whose task was to restore Allied assets taken over by the Japanese government during hostilities.

General MacArthur concurrently was commander in chief of the Far East Command (FEC), which gave him authority over all American military forces in the area. Originally, these totaled some 400,000 officers and men. In addition to the job of providing for a force of this size, the FEC, among other tasks, built a number of airfields which were necessary for logistical support at the time. These bases became invaluable during the Korean War.

Despite the complications of this dual task and the large and elaborate organization which SCAP soon became, the Occupation generally was regarded within Japan as General MacArthur's one-man show. His personality dominated nearly everything done by American authorities. His many statements and press releases set the tone of the entire Occupation, and to most Japanese he was the fountainhead of Allied power. This concept was enlarged by MacArthur's policy of remaining aloof from the Japanese, an attitude which gave him the appearance of replacing the hitherto inaccessible Emperor.

The General was governed, however, by basic and detailed directives formulated in Washington during the closing days of the war and sent to him at the start of the Occupation. Eventually, policy was established by the Far Eastern Commission, composed of the eleven Allied belligerents in the Japanese war, which sat in Washington. But the Commission had no direct authority over MacArthur. Instead, its terms of reference specified that the chain of command from the United States Government to the Supreme Commander and the Supreme Commander's command of occupation forces

would be maintained.[2] The Joint Chiefs of Staff acted as the transmitting agency for policy decisions reached by the Far Eastern Commission and subsequently prepared as directives to MacArthur by the United States government. This somewhat cumbersome procedure was established by the Moscow Foreign Ministers' Conference of December, 1945. It occasionally produced dissatisfaction within the Far Eastern Commission over MacArthur's implementation of its policy decisions. Further, in practice, he often anticipated Far Eastern Commission policies. The Commission then would reach a formal decision, sometimes months later, to authorize a policy which already had been carried out.

Under these swift changes, the functions of our Political Adviser's Office also quickly expanded and solidified. On April 15, 1946, George Atcheson assumed a threefold position. The original post of political adviser became the least important of these assignments and was preserved primarily to perpetuate the role of the State Department. George A. also became chief of the Diplomatic Section, a division of SCAP Headquarters created to act as the foreign office for the Occupation, and in practice for the Japanese government. The Initial Post-Surrender Directive was interpreted to eliminate Japanese authority in foreign affairs.

Atcheson's third and most important task was to serve on the Allied Council for Japan. This body, created by the 1945 Moscow Conference, was a four-power advisory group intended primarily to "assist" SCAP. Atcheson was named deputy for the Supreme Commander, chairman of the Council, and its United States member. Other members were Soviet Russia, the British Commonwealth (representing jointly the United Kingdom, Australia, New Zealand, and India), and China. In other words, the Council carried to Japan the concept, so cherished by the wartime leaders, that the Big Four powers could cooperatively maintain the peace at the end of hostilities.

But the advisory body immediately became the focal point, in Japan, for the diplomatic cold war. As George Atcheson's assistant and adviser, I was involved in the Council's affairs almost from the beginning. Meeting biweekly in the paneled conference room of a former Japanese office building, the Council was supposed to discuss major Occupation problems and to relay advice from the member nations. Instead, with full publicity, it became the sounding board for Soviet propaganda and, at times, a debating forum between East and West. Other members, on various occasions, also presented conflicting views, some of them critical of SCAP.

Reports of "clashes" and "heated arguments" in the Council characterized its early worldwide press coverage, and George A. expressed concern over the organization's merits. When he asked my opinion, I advocated a continuation of the Council, but with all possible effort to make it more constructive. The majority of debates had been dominated by criticism and no usable recommendations had been sent to SCAP. Still, I reasoned, the Council had its uses as a forum. When Occupation policies turned more toward rehabilitation, as I felt was necessary, it would be in our interest to have the Soviets indiscriminately criticize them. This would place the Soviets in opposition not only to the Americans but to the Japanese people as well; for, I believed, the country soon would realize that we were attempting to re-establish it as a viable nation. To my mind, this was a gambit which, if used properly, could not lose. George A. was somewhat doubtful, but he conceded the point.

The months rolled along busily, and my desk was cluttered with an increasing number of diversified problems. A few hours of a typical day might produce these questions: the political aspects of taxation of Formosans in Japan; and clearance of Soviet couriers with a planeload of sealed materials. I was also asked to determine whether trade should be allowed between Japan and Italy, a country with which we were not then legally at peace.

What special rations, if any, should be supplied to Austrian nationals? Finally, I was directed to determine the feasibility of permitting two Japanese newspapermen to accompany an impending whaling expedition to Antarctica.

The work was stimulating, and I decided to enter the career Foreign Service, thus completing the cycle which had begun with Bill Turner's telephone call in Washington during the early postwar days. Since my assignment to Japan had been temporary, I was required to take special examinations for appointment as a Foreign Service officer. This process was completed late in 1946, after a quick trip to Washington.

THE ENDLESS AND almost incredible readjustment of two former enemy peoples to each other became more difficult as additional Americans arrived in Tokyo. In the areas they touched the Americans altered almost everything, down to the point of supplying names for Tokyo's streets. The Japanese had left them unnamed for centuries, preferring to specify addresses by a seemingly complicated formula of ward and neighborhood designations. In retrospect, the amazing fact of this period was the disciplined acceptance by the Japanese of SCAP orders which greatly changed their lives. They also accepted the presence of opulent, well-fed Americans with the same impassiveness, despite their own uncertain living conditions. Although petty thievery was commonplace, there was not a single incident against Occupation personnel which might have been construed as politically motivated.

On the other hand, the general behavior of American Occupation troops, especially the combat men who first entered Japan, was particularly impressive. Collectively, they were exceedingly effective as ambassadors of good will. The country was surprised and pleased by the natural manner in which the early Occupation soldiers acted and spoke; by their helpful behavior toward Japanese women and older men, and by the unmistakable pleasure they found in giving presents to the children. These men came close to the Japanese people, and gave them a worthy cross section of America.

Months after reaching Tokyo I was introduced to General MacArthur during the bustle of a reception at the Chinese Mission. Although the General seldom attended the frequent social functions which characterized official life, he was on hand early with Mrs. MacArthur for the Chinese celebration of the traditional Double Ten (October 10) national holiday in 1946. When I arrived, George A. immediately presented me to the General, who was standing momentarily by himself. Tall, austere, and dignified, MacArthur clearly did not enjoy the milling, murmuring throng around him. He greeted me politely, but there was no time for conversation, before someone else demanded his attention. During this moment Mrs. MacArthur joined us and made herself known, with lively informality. She was petite, attractive, gay and friendly, more outgoing than her husband, but she never lost her inherent dignity.

THESE WERE SOME OF THE TRENDS sweeping Tokyo when, in August, 1947, George Atcheson was called to Washington for consultation, and I was designated to assume his triple diplomatic position during his absence. The POLAD staff had been altered considerably by reassignments, and I had become George A.'s deputy. En route to Haneda Airport, on the muggy day of August 17, for his departure we discussed my impending duties with what, afterward, seemed to be prophetic urgency. He gave extremely helpful advice on my new responsibilities as acting chairman of the Allied Council and warned me against becoming involved in what he called the "palace politics" of the enormous SCAP Headquarters.

At the airport George A. invited me aboard the special B-17 plane, a converted wartime bomber, which had been placed at his disposal. It was equipped with leather seats, compartments, a worktable, and other conveniences for the high-ranking officers to whom it was assigned.

When I complimented him on making the journey in such a plush aircraft, George A. replied laconically: "It's not the plane that I would choose for such a long trip." Then, as I turned to go, he said: "Bill, if anything happens to me, will you and Edith please look after Mariquita?" I assured him that we would watch over his wife, even though we were expecting his early return. The stubby ex-bomber, with its four pounding engines, then clawed through the early morning haze and disappeared.

That was the last I saw of George A., a friend, mentor, and teacher. Early the next morning Headquarters called me with word that the plane had crash-landed some seventy miles off Honolulu. Atcheson was missing. His death was confirmed by several survivors.

Deeply saddened by this loss, I went through the motions of conducting business in our humming office. Diplomacy does not pause for the personal problems of those involved in it. My one concern was to handle the position as George A. would have wished, and beyond that I had neither ambition nor expectation.

When I called upon General MacArthur later that day for instructions, Atcheson's death was carved on his face. For all of his long combat record, the General was a deeply sentimental and sensitive man. He did not always attempt to hide his feelings publicly, and he seldom did so in private. As he paced his office in the Dai Ichi building on this occasion, it was obvious that Mac-Arthur had valued George A. as both a friend and one of his principal advisers.

The interview was a fitting epilogue, I thought, to Atcheson's sometimes stormy career during the Occupation. In addition to the numerous problems of his office he had frequently been under fire, as various nations and groups within the United States sharply criticized policies unwelcome to them. At one time Secretary of State James F. Byrnes had been obliged publicly to deny reports of a rift between MacArthur, on the one hand, and Atcheson and Jack Service, on the other. The rumors apparently were prompted by the fact that George A. was preparing for one of his periodic trips to Washington for consultation. They sprang, no doubt, from the continual philosophical clash between the enlarging forces advocating a moderate Occupation and the hard-line "old China hands." At the height of this particular rumored rift, George A. had told me General MacArthur had warmly thanked him for his services and had expressed the hope that he would return quickly to Japan after his consultation in Washington.

At the end of our brief talk I asked the General for instructions concerning the threefold job which George A. had left behind. He answered immediately and crisply: "Carry on business as usual."

A short time later, on September 2, 1947, General MacArthur, through General Order No. 16, appointed me as deputy for SCAP on the Allied Council and, consequently, its chairman and member for the United States. I was also appointed chief of the Diplomatic Section, thus moving officially into two of George A.'s several positions. The title of acting political adviser was withheld by the State Department until January 7, 1949, although I also undertook these duties immediately. The appointment evidently caused considerable eyebrow-raising in Washington. News stories on October 23 reported that a career Foreign Service officer, Maxwell M. Hamilton, was being reassigned to replace Atcheson. The stories quoted a State Department memorandum stating that Hamilton was being recalled from his post as minister to Finland to take over the position in Japan and, concurrently, to serve as deputy to Secretary of State George C. Marshall for peace treaty negotiations. Hamilton was a former chief of the department's Division of Far Eastern Affairs and, incidentally, an "old China hand."

On this same day I was shown a telegram from the Secretary of State to General MacArthur, suggesting Hamilton's appointment as the SCAP political adviser. MacArthur himself allowed me to read his reply, which said, in essence: "Sebald is doing a fine job and I prefer no change in the present situation." That was the end of the matter officially.

In the psychology of the moment, my position was strengthened inadvertently but definitely by Moscow. Toward the end of October, 1947, the Soviet press took out after me with typical intemperance, and I became a member of the select but enlarging group of American officials who could and did say: "At last I've arrived. I've made Moscow's blacklist." Angered by my statements before the Allied Council, the controlled Soviet newspapers began misquoting my remarks as the peg for their own propaganda on the alleged purposes of the Council. The attack was synthesized by this article, distributed by the official news agency Tass under a Moscow date line, October 20, 1947:

Such a man is Mr. Sebald, Chairman of the Allied Council for Japan, and Chief of the Diplomatic Section of General MacArthur's Headquarters. Sebald has long been connected with MacArthur's Headquarters, first as an intelligence officer, then as a diplomat.

The American press speaks of Sebald as an able diplomat and a worthy student of "the school of General MacArthur." Recently exchanging his naval officer's uniform for the diplomatic morning coat, the "student of MacArthur" has become a student of Marshall and is trying to surpass both of his teachers in helping the Japanese reactionaries and in slander against the Soviet Union.

The reason for creating the Allied Council for Japan is known to all. It was created by a decision of the Moscow Conference of foreign ministers of the U.S.S.R., U.S.A. and Britain in December, 1945, *to exercise control over Japan jointly* with the Supreme Commander of Allied Powers and to confer with the latter on questions of occupation policy. *It is included in the mission of the Allied Council to work out, with the Far Eastern Commission, jointly agreed-upon policies concerning conquered Japan.**

However, MacArthur and Sebald accept proposals not from the representatives of the Allied Powers, but from the reactionary circles representing the interests of American monopoly. In helping to revive militaristic Japan, MacArthur and Sebald render poor service to the cause of peace.

This was the cold war in full voice, although at the time few ears in the West appeared attuned to it. Having failed to capture all or part of Hokkaido island through the subterfuge of a

* Italics added.

"temporary" occupation force, Stalin turned next to the attempted subversion of the Allied Council. Success in achieving an equal voice in policy through the Council would have enabled him to disrupt the Occupation by political means almost as thoroughly as would the physical presence of autonomous Red Army troops. The Council thus became the focal point for his diplomatic war against Japan, and he used it ruthlessly.

Consequently, I regarded the chairmanship of the Allied Council as the most important and the most trying of my three overlapping positions. As MacArthur's deputy on this body I had unlimited direct access to him. He made this clear almost immediately after my appointment. "Come and see me at any time," he said, with the intent, steady gaze he used to emphasize a point. "My door is always open." During the next three and one-half years he never refused to see me, even when I requested an interview on extremely short notice. He always made room as quickly as possible on his busy calendar. Invariably, I entered the room with a feeling of welcome, even when the signs portended trouble ahead. Over the years, this close and understanding relationship between MacArthur and myself—a representative of another department of the United States government and at times the bearer of unwelcome news—was of inestimable value in expediting business on a governmental or diplomatic level.

MacArthur made no secret of his dislike for the Allied Council, which he regarded as an unwanted intrusion into the Occupation and an undesirable vehicle for Soviet propaganda. As the Allied body sank into seeming impotence, it came under attack from other quarters, including a large number of political commentators. But I regarded it as a highly important element in the regime of control of Occupied Japan and a useful organization for the United States. I state this conclusion unequivocally in retrospect, despite the preponderance of adverse testimony.

The Council, by its terms of reference, was advisory and consultative except for certain limited control authority which was specified but never exercised. Thus, it had no executive authority.

Nevertheless, it served as a safety valve for the release of pressures created by the aftermath of war. The meetings were followed avidly by the Japanese press. A Japanese government representative attended all sessions, to report them firsthand to the prime minister and the Foreign Office. In many respects, the Council provided the one ray of hope, at that time, for the Japanese people, because it was the only forum in which their problems and their future were discussed openly and freely.

It was evident from the outset that the Soviets intended to use the Council as completely as possible for their purposes. With this reality the basic problem, as I envisioned it, was to turn the Soviets' strategy back against them; not, as was so often done, to bemoan the existence of the Council and to wish it away. Here, in this strange and strained atmosphere, we acquired our first experience and assembled some of the tactics in the long battle against Moscow's persistent effort to subvert and subordinate all international organizations to its purposes. In other words, we conducted the preliminary skirmishing for what became major campaigns in the United Nations. Thus, for me, there were tension and challenge in every Council session, even those which were reduced by circumstances to mere formalities.

Although the creation of the Council during the Moscow Foreign Ministers' Conference in 1945 was regarded as a concession to Stalin, its terms of reference to my mind constituted a masterpiece of diplomatic drafting. By limiting the organization to purely advisory functions, the American Supreme Commander remained supreme. In the terms of reference this was assured, also, by the provision that the chairman (and member for the United States) should be the Supreme Commander (or his deputy). Over the years, the other Council members took an extremely caustic view of the restrictions in the fundamental charter. Even our friendly Allies were restive under this all-American impress of the Occupation and sought to give their nations a more powerful voice, particularly in economic affairs.

A code of relatively simple but extremely important rules of procedure, which I had formulated at the request of George A., had been adopted by the Council at a meeting held on September 4, 1946. Among other points, these rules provided that there was to be no vote on specific issues and no veto, and that the rules could be changed thereafter only by unanimous agreement. No appeals were permitted from any ruling by the chairman, a provision that obviously gave him considerable authority. Finally, the rules provided that each subject to be discussed before the Council had to be placed on the agenda in writing at least five days beforehand. This requirement, in my view, was extremely important. It prevented spontaneous propaganda discussion of events or disturbances which were current and therefore fresh in the mind of the Japanese public. It meant that, on many occasions, the Council met with no business before it. Between each Council meeting, however, a number of SCAP directives almost invariably were issued. By assembling in silence and without business during its often ridiculed, unproductive meetings, the Council actually served to endorse by implication the actions undertaken by SCAP during the previous weeks. Thus, the bulk of SCAP's work was tacitly underwritten by the Council, at least in Japanese eyes. The rules of procedure remained in effect until the council was abolished in April, 1952, when the Japanese peace treaty became effective.

The propaganda conflict between the United States and Soviet Russia was sharp, of course. Each meeting called for special handling and considerable advance preparation, to anticipate the arguments and allegations which might be made. It was clearly apparent from the Council's early days that the Soviet member was under instructions to do everything possible publicly to foster and to encourage the Japan Communist party. He also obviously followed orders to present proposals to obstruct and destroy the economic rehabilitation of the country. At meeting after meeting, we listened to the Communist line condemning plutocracy, capitalism, imperialism, antidemocratic elements, and the rest of communism's tiresome slogans. Whenever violence occurred within the country, such as a mob's forcible entry into the prime minister's official residence, the Soviet member promptly complained of "police brutality." The purpose was to obscure the fact that these violent demonstrations were inspired and led by Communists.

My new position as chief of the Diplomatic Section also required me to spend much time on lesser problems. Many of these appear ludicrous in retrospect, for they involved now faded questions of rank and prerogative, but at the time they were deadly serious. They serve as a reminder that, quite apart from the shock of the cold war, the Allies were rather poorly prepared to conduct even a simple occupation. We all learned as we went along.

In taking on the duties of acting United States political adviser to SCAP, for instance, I was more like a United States ambassador to an American command. I was the representative of the Department of State in Japan, and its eyes, ears, and voice at SCAP Headquarters. Although General MacArthur did not consult me for political advice concerning the Japanese, the State Department expected me to offer counsel on matters in my area of responsibility and in regard to affairs of concern to the department. This was to be done either at Washington's request or on my own responsibility. Further, on paper at least, I was the channel of communication between the Secretary of State and the Supreme Commander.

Unfortunately, there were some handicaps to the smooth operation of this system, and particularly to the channel of communications. It was not uncommon at this time, for example, for telegrams from the Secretary of State, addressed to me, to be acted upon in SCAP Headquarters and replies sent back to Washington without the matter being called to my attention. All telegrams were transmitted through army channels and cryptographic systems and went first to Headquarters. GHQ had become such an enormous, sprawling empire that the failure to deliver my messages was attributable, on occasion, to an understandable lack of coordination. But at other times the messages and the problems they raised were deliberately intercepted and acted upon by the Chief of Staff or by MacArthur himself. The justification seemed to be that the questions asked by the Department of State, to put it bluntly, were none of its business. It took several years of patience, indoctrination, explanation, and occasional serious protests to convince the personnel of GHQ that communications addressed to POLAD were a matter of departmental privilege. *

A second question of concern to me, for the proper representation of the Department of State, was the Occupation attitude toward Japanese nationals. No SCAP directive prohibited entertainment of Japanese by SCAP officials, but the practice was somewhat frowned upon, especially in the early days. This may have stemmed from the fact that, as a matter of principle, General MacArthur did not entertain any Japanese socially. Headquarters usually tried to take its cue from the "old man's" actions. Yet, when I asked him specifically, the General said firmly that the question of whom I entertained was solely my own decision.

Feeling strongly on this point, I exhorted my staff to meet as many Japanese as possible, particularly leaders in government, the professions, and business. Despite the SCAP purges and the attitude of ostracism Headquarters often seemed to apply to purgees, I told my associates to cultivate any of these disbarred men with whom they would associate in normal times. The purpose was to ensure, to the greatest practicable extent, continuity of communication with Japanese leaders in all fields. When the Occupation ended and normal diplomatic relations were re-established, we would need all possible knowledge and contacts in Japan.

Following these precepts I had entertained a number of Japanese, while the political reporter of POLAD, long before it was fashionable even to recognize them. One was Saburo Kurusu, the special envoy to Washington at the time of Pearl Harbor, whose name once had been one of opprobrium in the United States. He

* See pp. 120–121.

had been sent to Washington to assist Ambassador Nomura in conducting diplomatic negotiations while the Japanese assault fleet was en route to Pearl Harbor. Kurusu insisted he knew nothing of the attack plans and was merely carrying out his duty as a diplomat.

Retired during and after the war, Kurusu came to see me in the Imperial Hotel and, since Japanese then were not allowed in the public dining room, we lunched in my quarters. He was an entertaining and witty man, with a sharp mind. After thirty-six years in the foreign service, he called his life "the wasted experience of a diplomat." Half-seriously, he said his career had provided him with material for a book on things not to do as a diplomat; a sort of bible for neophytes in the profession. He dismissed the war with the comment: "No one can tell me anything about the war. I started it!"

The purges left few Japanese leaders of capacity available for top positions, but two outstanding men did arise to give the country the stability it needed at a crucial period. One was the late Kijuro Shidehara, ambassador to the United States in the early twenties and one of the fine, intelligent, and highly courageous Japanese of the old school—the man whom I had seen defy the militarists in the late twenties and a prime minister early in the Occupation. The second was Shigeru Yoshida, whose long career as prime minister became historic in the tumult of Japanese politics. Yoshida had been turned down by the militarists as a nominee for a cabinet position in the thirties and later had been arrested by them on suspicion of plotting to end the war. These patriotic Japanese were among our good friends.

During this period my wife and I were invited to call unofficially upon the Emperor and Empress at the imperial villa in Hayama. I readily obtained General MacArthur's permission to accept the invitation, and at the appointed time we drove to Hayama, a year-round resort about twenty-five miles southwest of Tokyo, on Sagami Bay. As our car drew up at the villa we were met by several court officials, including Matsudaira, Mitani, and

Kuroda. They were dressed in formal morning clothes—striped trousers and morning coats—in contrast with our informal attire.

We were led to a large drawing room where, after a few minutes, the Emperor and the Empress were announced. They warmly shook hands with us, and the Emperor invited me to sit in a chair beside him. The Empress indicated that my wife should sit next to her on a large couch. Hirohito began speaking and expressed the hope that we could carry on our conversation in Japanese. He put me at ease at once by suggesting that I not attempt to converse in the difficult and stilted court language, but rather that I employ the more familiar form of everyday conversational Japanese.

While the Empress spoke to my wife about life at the Hayama palace, as the villa was called, the Emperor told me of his keen interest in some of the problems of the new countries of Asia. He was also deeply concerned with the difficulties being experienced in bringing about the economic rehabilitation of Japan. In response to his questions I was able to explain some of the policies which were then in course of implementation.

Within a short time we both were enjoying ourselves in a relaxed and pleasant and friendly visit. Over cups of tea and modest sandwiches and cakes, we discovered that our hosts were two simple, charming people who had adapted themselves to the new Japan and the complexities brought on by the presence of an Allied military occupation. Edith and I were tremendously impressed by the simplicity and unassuming manner of the royal couple, their interest in and curiosity concerning the everyday occurrences in the so-remote world about them.

Hirohito wore a dark-blue business suit which might have been tailored in London. I was surprised at his apparent youthfulness—we were born in the same year—despite a few gray flecks at his temples. When the audience was about to come to an end, the Emperor, as the courteous host that he was, motioned for us to precede him and the Empress out of the room. We observed court protocol, however, and stood aside as they left the room.

Thus ended a most pleasant and relaxing interlude from the harsher affairs and duties of the Occupation.

From my observations of the Emperor at this and other, later, meetings I was certain that he would never again allow a revival of the old prewar emperor system. It seemed evident that he was aware of the changed Japan, and that by personal example he wanted to exercise a steadying influence on his sometimes turbulent and uncertain people, even though his political power had been so greatly circumscribed.

Although I mingled freely with the Japanese as political reporter and as chief of the mission, the restraints of the SCAP attitude on this type of "fraternization" delayed the normal diplomatic practice of entertaining prime ministers and cabinet members while they were in office. It was not until mid-December, 1948, that I felt free to invite a number of Japanese cabinet ministers and their wives, together with chiefs of several foreign missions, to a buffet dinner. The party showed that SCAP did not object to such functions, and the immediate result was that most of the diplomatic missions began to entertain the Japanese. In retrospect, I feel certain that this trend was salutary, as peace will never be on a solid footing until the peoples of the world understand each other. Further, I believe that the activities of the POLAD staff in mingling with the Japanese, when they were being ignored by the Occupation, helped to cultivate many of the friends the United States now has in that highly important country.

Then, there was the battle of protocol.

It has been said that protocol marched into Tokyo ahead of the troops, and I am prepared to believe it. In Occupied Japan protocol could be defined as the social code to protect the privileges of rank. Rank determined the priority and quality of housing accommodations, the assignment of automobiles, recreational facilities, and other privileges. Although my American army friends often denied the existence of such a system, I can vouch for the fact that protocol was an important and unbeatable part of life during the Occupation. This was particularly true when the arrival of foreign diplomatic missions—the equivalent of embassies—created the constant round of receptions and formal functions which came to be known as the "diplomatic circuit."

In fact, the only official establishment under the Occupation in which there was *almost* no protocol, to my knowledge, was the American Embassy residence during its occupancy by General and Mrs. MacArthur. They confined their entertainment largely to informal luncheons, regardless of the guests' importance. The General and his wife seated themselves at opposite ends of a long table, with the guest of honor usually at Mrs. MacArthur's right. Stag luncheons, at which Mrs. MacArthur was almost always present as hostess, were frequent. Invariably, those present were allowed to choose their own places, except for the guest of honor, and the usual result was polite jockeying for position near the hosts.

Other households, even on private occasions, generally allocated seats by protocol, and the first never—or almost never— came last. In this military Occupation, army and navy and air force officers invariably took precedence over the civilian, regardless of his position. This was undoubtedly one of the reasons why the majority of Allied diplomatic missions were headed by high-ranking generals rather than diplomats.

The campaign for diplomatic equality consumed considerable time and energy in the Headquarters. To my complaints on this problem, MacArthur replied, with drawling humor: "It never bothers me where I sit. The problem is to be invited." In long sessions with his chief of staff at that time, Major General Edward M. Almond, I bargained over a complicated system of assimilated military ranks for my staff, by which I hoped to make my three counselors of mission senior to the rank of brigadier general, with other staff members given corresponding status. Almond firmly held his position, contending that two "generals" were sufficient for my command, myself and my deputy, the senior counselor. As usual, we compromised on General Almond's terms. The Department of State did not bother to answer my requests for help.

As life in Tokyo grew more complicated, the position of chief of the Diplomatic Section assumed the multifaceted aspect of any foreign minister. I was obliged to be alert to both the trivial and the significant involving sensitive diplomats from many diverse countries. Whereas once my job had involved listening to the woes of the Japanese, now my time was devoted increasingly to the complaints of my diplomatic colleagues. They protested the housing accommodations allotted to them by SCAP and complained of discrimination or Japanese police "brutality" against their nationals. They came to me to demand the arrest of certain Japanese who had escaped indictment as "war criminals." Our office also provided all types of domestic services for the diplomatic corps, from housing to ration cards. On more than one occasion I had to listen patiently while an aroused diplomat complained that he had been "forced" to display his identification card in order to ride free on a Japanese train. There were dozens of similar problems in this capital of raw sensitivities, particularly among those Asians who still smarted from the indignities inflicted on their countries during the Japanese occupation.

In this atmosphere formal visits to Occupied Japan required unusual preparation and vigilance. One of the most ticklish was the 24-hour state visit of President Syngman Rhee of Korea and his devoted, Austrian-born wife in October, 1947. Arriving to full honors as the guest of SCAP, Rhee undoubtedly was conscious of the irony: the former "revolutionary" and leader of anti-Japanese forces in Korea was elaborately received in Japan, once the hated master of his people. Then seventy-three, the white-haired Rhee resembled a friendly, wrinkled old patriarch, but he participated in numerous social engagements with surprising vigor and enthusiasm.

There were some 600,000 Koreans in Japan, many of whom were Communists and bitterly anti-Rhee. Although we had no fears of incidents by Japanese, extensive security precautions were necessary to protect the president from his own divided countrymen. Wherever he went Rhee was surrounded unobtrusively by police and detectives, some of whom even served as waiters, as part of a security network arranged by Major General Charles A. Willoughby, the SCAP intelligence chief. During a small "family" dinner, which we gave at our residence near the American Embassy for the Rhees, special agents surrounded the house and lurked in the garden. Despite stern orders which I had given to our household staff to remain indoors throughout the dinner, a handyman attempted to slip out. He was brought down immediately by four burly Japanese police and only by a miracle escaped being shot.

On another level, a second visit at this time was highly productive. John M. Cabot, the United States consul general in Shanghai during this critical period, and his wife arrived for what turned out to be a working vacation. There had been a rather sharp misunderstanding between SCAP and our whole China establishment, based largely, I believed, on the inability of the two sides to understand each other's problems. In Shanghai, SCAP appeared arbitrary and short-tempered. This attitude was exacerbated by the vicious, anti-SCAP Chinese press which, possibly, was attempting to protect itself in advance of the imminent Communist capture of the port city. SCAP Headquarters, on the other hand, felt that Cabot's reports were critical and lacked understanding of the true situation in Japan. We occasionally received these reports for informational purposes. Cabot's visit provided a means of easing the tensions through personal contact between the men chiefly involved.

A little-known wartime tragedy required my constant attention for an entire year in 1948–49, with unexpectedly significant results. During the final months of the war the Japanese government had agreed to deliver Red Cross parcels to American prisoners held in camps throughout Asia, and Washington in turn had guaranteed safe-conduct for the vessel involved. The Japanese ship *Awa Maru,* under this protection, safely completed a voyage from Tokyo to Singapore, carrying 800 tons of parcels for prisoners in Southeast Asia.

On the return voyage to Japan, in April, 1945, the vessel, still under safe-conduct, carried a total of 2,004 Japanese, including a crew of 148. While cruising in a heavy fog off Okinawa, however, she was torpedoed and sunk by an American patrol submarine. Only one Japanese survived and was picked up by the submarine, the U.S.S. *Queenfish.* The *Awa Maru* was fully lighted, as the safe-conduct provided, but she was about eight miles off the prescribed course and roughly thirty-two miles ahead of her predicted position.

As the good faith of the American government was involved, Tokyo was informed through Swiss authorities that the United States accepted liability for the sinking, settlement to be made after the conclusion of hostilities. Four days before their surrender, the Japanese officially submitted an indemnity claim for 220 million yen, about $55 million at the prevailing rate of exchange, and demanded immediate payment. Although Washington felt that the claim was highly inflated, liability was not denied. The settlement, naturally, was postponed by the more pressing requirements of surrender and occupation.

In April, 1948, I was instructed by the State Department to discuss the claim informally with the Japanese Foreign Office in an attempt to reach a more equitable figure for eventual negotiation and settlement. Before doing so, I took up the matter with General MacArthur, whose blessing would be necessary before the Japanese authorities could make any settlement whatsoever.

MacArthur's reaction reflected his capacity to reach the heart of any complicated problem quickly. The claim, he said, technically could be considered as abrogated when Japan surrendered unconditionally and, by clear implication, assumed responsibility for obligations resulting from all types of military action, including the accidental torpedoing of the *Awa Maru*. Furthermore, he pointed out that the United States had given the Japanese people many hundreds of millions of dollars in food and other commodities since the start of the Occupation. He suggested that the Japanese government forget the claim as a token of appreciation for this United States assistance. Having proposed these ideas, the General authorized me to proceed with the negotiations.

Hitoshi Ashida, then the prime minister, and his successor, Prime Minister Yoshida, accepted this suggested settlement without hesitation when I outlined MacArthur's thesis to them. Various delays, however, took place in our negotiations and the matter was not finally approved by the Japanese Diet until April 6, 1949. On April 14, Yoshida and I signed the completed agreement, and MacArthur attested to it as SCAP.*

The *Awa Mura* settlement became important because, in an accompanying agreement, the Japanese government recognized for the first time that it was legally responsible for repaying the costs of the Occupation and the United States economic assistance during that period.† The understanding of Japan's legal responsibility served as a precedent in later Japanese-American negotiations to settle Japan's indebtedness for the so-called GARIOA (Government and Relief in Occupied Areas) funds which it received during the Occupation. A figure of $1.8 billion was finally established for the GARIOA debt and, after prolonged negotiations, the Japanese government agreed to pay the principal sum of $490 million over a period of fifteen years. The agreement was signed on January 9, 1962, and entered into force on September 11, 1962.

IN CARRYING OUT THE variegated functions of my SCAP office I often felt as if I were trying to ride a herd of horses simultaneously. The situation would have been complicated enough if all the Allies and all agencies of the United States government had been in agreement on our Japan policies. Instead, widely different suggestions, criticisms, comments, and orders came from the Far Eastern Commission, the Departments of State and Army, the

* See Appendix A for the resolution adopted by the Diet authorizing negotiation of an agreement of settlement.

† See Appendix B.

Joint Chiefs of Staff, the Congress, and all the Allied capitals. Within Japan these were further augmented by the directives of SCAP, which often anticipated and occasionally conflicted with those of the Far Eastern Commission, and by the public and private comments of members of the Allied Council and the various diplomatic missions. Japanese officials made their own comments, but these were voiced mostly in private and were seldom influential during the first few years of the Occupation.

This fantastic tugging and pulling went on incessantly beneath a barrage of international press coverage. This continued at a high pitch because the experiment in Japan was sufficiently unusual to constitute news for an extraordinary length of time. The Communist press, of course, attacked us in full voice. The Allied press often was critical of SCAP, partly in a reflection of national frustration within Japan and, perhaps, in reaction to postwar conditions in Europe. The press of Asian nations cried out repeatedly, in memory of Japanese conquest, for harsher measures than SCAP was willing to employ.

The American press fully reflected the divisions within the United States government and Congress over the Japanese experiment. In time it also gave full weight to the dissenting comments of special American groups, particularly business men who opposed the measures being taken by SCAP against Japanese industrialists. The American news agencies had quickly begun distributing their worldwide reports in Occupied Japan, and the conflicts of policy were widely known among Japanese newsmen, although they did not always publish them.

As POLAD my chief worry was to avoid conflict between SCAP and the Department of State, while still performing my job in the best interests of the United States. On one side of this triangle, I was a senior member of SCAP's staff and a section chief on a level with men whom I saw constantly and whose judgment and knowledge became familiar. Moreover, as SCAP's political adviser I was directly under General MacArthur.

Simultaneously, I was the representative in Japan of the Secretary of State, who was the President's chief adviser on foreign affairs. As an American, I wanted to contribute what I could to the immediate and future position of the United States in this part of the world.

The problem of sorting out these mixed allegiances arose primarily in regard to the reports that our office supplied to the Department of State. Then, as now, government offices in Washington were insatiable in their demands for information from the field, to form the foundation for policy. We supplied the regular political and economic reports normally prepared by an embassy abroad, numerous special reports, and answered innumerable inquiries from the Department of State. The question was whether to trust the judgment of SCAP officials in regard to the Occupation or to report the situation in Japan as we saw it, even if our views diverged from those of Headquarters. I had always believed that Washington and the President could be guided effectively only by receiving completely candid views from field representatives, uninhibited by local loyalties to another government agency or by the prospect of some future Congressional inquiry. It was upon this basis that we prepared our reports of Occupied Japan. Although this was a delicate matter, I found no instance of paralysis through conflicting loyalties, despite my occasional worries. In instances where our reports were of direct concern to SCAP, I used my own discretion in showing them to General MacArthur beforehand.*

* Through the years I was able to build up a staff of loyal, intelligent, and hard-working officers. I was proud of them and their accomplishments. From the outset of the assignment, I received invaluable assistance from U. Alexis Johnson, then in charge of the Consulate General in Yokohama. A complete list of the men who served so ably during this important period would be too lengthy. But I might mention, among the senior officers, Cloyce K. Huston, Niles W. Bond, Cabot Coville, C. Nelson Spinks, John M. Steeves, James Byrd Pilcher, Carl H. Boehringer, Saxton Bradford, Frank A. Waring, and William A. Diehl. Among the younger officers were such outstanding men as Richard B. Finn, David M. Bane, William H. Sullivan, James V. Martin, Robert W. Adams, Franklin Hawley, David Osborn, Edward Seidensticker, Stanley S. Carpenter, and Richard A. Ericson.

5

The United States Job

THE AWESOME WORDS of the Potsdam Declaration * of July 26, 1945, outlining minimum Allied terms for Japan's surrender, warned the Japanese that their society would be altered drastically. Subsequent instructions from Washington, furthermore, gave General MacArthur ample authority and extensive guidance for the wholesale reforms carried out by his headquarters. But the Japanese clearly were unprepared for the far-reaching revolution imposed upon them, and it is doubtful whether many Americans anticipated its thoroughness. The complications of such a vast social experiment in the postwar environment of Japan were equally unexpected by all involved, and as a result the Occupation followed a somewhat erratic and controversial course until mid-1949, when the pressure of events changed it from reform to rehabilitation.

The formal instrument of surrender, dated September 2, solidified what was, in effect, the unconditional surrender of Japan. It incorporated the provisions of the Potsdam Declaration. It also stated that the "authority of the Emperor and the Japanese Government to rule the state shall be subject to the Supreme Commander for the Allied Powers."

On August 29, 1945, the substance of the "United States Ini-

* See Appendix C for text.

tial Post-Surrender Policy for Japan" had been transmitted by radio to General MacArthur. This document was approved by President Truman on September 6, and thus became the official policy of the United States government. It provided broad guidance for SCAP and, in essence, was an enlargement of the Potsdam Declaration.

The primary outlines of Occupation policy were laid out in considerable detail in this document. They were elaborated later in the "Basic Initial Post-Surrender Policy," a 10,000-word directive to SCAP, dated November 1, 1945. Defining SCAP's authority and providing guidance for the initial post-surrender period in great detail, the directive was dispatched to General MacArthur by the Joint Chiefs of Staff on November 8, 1945.

Although Allied disputes and divergences of viewpoint were frequent, the consensus was that Japanese society constituted a self-perpetuating instrument of imperialism. Therefore the framework of society had to be destroyed to prevent a revival of imperialism; this belief automatically meant that reform must be as thorough as possible, regardless of other consequences. But the validity of the assumption was questionable at the time and certainly has become more questionable with the passage of the years. It was based more on a Western view of the situation than on informed analyses of Japanese character and history.

When I reached Tokyo in early 1946 it appeared that policy already had become an end in itself for the bureaucrats in SCAP Headquarters and that paper work was the means to that end. The flood of directives to the Japanese had become so immense that I doubt if anyone could have kept track of all of them. This may have been due in part to the scarcity of qualified personnel for the task the Allies set out for themselves. A concerted drive had been made by Washington to recruit the many hundreds of necessary officials, technicians, and advisers. Many of ability were found, and others of competence came from military government teams or from special wartime training schools. But the required numbers of qualified personnel never arrived.

Consequently, SCAP had to depend heavily upon military men who had little or no experience in the problems of government with which they were to be faced during the next half decade. All SCAP sections, except my own, were headed by officers, and the majority of policy-making officials came from the U.S. Army. Japanese implementation of SCAP directives was checked by other military men in the Military Government teams, under the Eighth Army, which were scattered throughout the country. They, too, added a certain amount of inexperience and incompetency to a confused system. There was no adequate precedent in the history of the United States or, indeed, in the recent history of man for the Occupation. But this did not prevent the Americans from embarking with uninhibited enthusiasm upon the task of altering the entire Japanese structure—political, economic, and social—seemingly regardless of the consequences.

The fundamental Occupation task, demobilization and demilitarization, became SCAP's easiest and most thorough accomplishment, despite prior forebodings by a number of Allied military officers. The United States policy, which the Allies endorsed, was clear and explicit on this point. The Japanese military establishment of several million armed men, stationed in Japan proper, was to be disbanded, with officers and men sent home. All arms, ammunition, and other war equipment were to be scrapped and Japan was "not to have an army, navy, air force, secret police organization, or any civil aviation."

Japanese government agencies substantially completed disarmament and demobilization by December 1, 1945—less than three and one-half months after the surrender—without a single untoward incident. One of the world's great armies and the remnants of one of the great fleets disappeared. The men drifted to their homes and melted into society, despite dire predictions that they might re-emerge as disruptive units. Naval vessels were dismantled and cut into scrap; live shells and ammunition of all sorts were dumped into the sea; guns were melted down, and side arms of every style were confiscated. Even samurai swords, many of

79

them family heirlooms, and hunting pieces were declared illegal.

The success of this operation immediately raised a grave and perplexing question. How was demilitarized Japan to be defended, in the immediate present and in the future? The islands were almost surrounded by Soviet might, stretching from the Kuriles through Siberia to North Korea, but the problem of Japan's security was completely ignored in official Allied statements. Although the presence of General MacArthur's large combat army implied protection for the Japanese, there was no official assurance that it would be used to defend their homeland. Nor was there any guarantee as to how long American troops would remain in Japan. Instead, most if not all the Allies clearly demonstrated that the concept of defending the late enemy was anathema to them in the postwar mood. Washington gave no public indication that it was concerned over the absence of security for Japan, despite its strategic importance on the flank of Asia.

As far as the Japanese could see, Allied policy on this question was embodied principally in MacArthur's public promise to turn Japan into the "Switzerland of Asia." The slogan was readily accepted by large numbers of Japanese, but most government officials, and many others, were deeply concerned by the Soviet threat. While carrying out demobilization, the Japanese government sought also to obtain assurance that Japan would not be abandoned in a predatory world. But this became an extraordinarily difficult project.

The nearest approach to a defense pledge was a statement issued by General MacArthur in May, 1947, denying press speculation that he had told Emperor Hirohito the United States would defend Japan. But he said the nation's security was "entrusted" to the Occupation forces until a peace treaty was signed.

This was the situation in February, 1949, when Kenneth C. Royall, then Secretary of the Army, arrived in Tokyo for one of the most controversial visits of the Occupation. With a large official party, Secretary Royall inspected United States military units in Japan as part of an intended routine journey. Before leaving the country to inspect other units in the Western Pacific, Royall invited ten American correspondents to the American Embassy for cocktails. The ensuing frank and open conversation with the newsmen was designated as a background news conference, "not for attribution"; meaning, according to well-established practice, that the secretary's comments could be reported without identifying him as the source. Royall also specified that nothing could be published about the meeting until five days after his departure from Tokyo.

On February 12, two days after this deadline, the Japanese press broke out with a rash of stories which rocked the country. Some of the stories, which were supplied by American news agencies to their subscribing Japanese papers, said bluntly that the United States probably intended to abandon Japan as a liability in the event of a major war with Soviet Russia. They quoted an unnamed high United States official as saying: "I don't know what our troops could do in Japan in the event of war. I am not certain we could hold Japan, nor am I certain it would be worthwhile as long as we have Okinawa and the Philippines." The official was further quoted as saying: "America is not obliged to stay in Japan. We don't owe the Japanese anything, not even a moral obligation. We had the right—and the duty—to disarm them after the war, even though someone else may later cut their throats." When asked whether the United States should not defend Japan if only as a matter of prestige, the official reportedly said: "If it is just a question of prestige, let's get our troops out now." [1]

Friends in the American press corps told me that the Japanese press knew about Royall's meeting with the American newsmen and was aware that he was the source of the stories. This gave them greater credence in the Japanese circles most concerned. The controversial statements were reported primarily by the United Press. I noted in my diary at the time that balance and carefulness were shown by such correspondent friends as Russell

Brines and Tom Lambert of the Associated Press and Howard Handelman of International News Service. On February 16 a UP dispatch from San Francisco quoted Royall as saying: "I held no off-the-record press conference in Tokyo of any kind whatsoever. A few reporters who had covered my trip expressed a desire to give me their views and I said I would be glad to receive them but would not make any statements. I made no statements to them at that time as to Japan or any plans relating to Japan." This was followed, however, by an "I was there" story by-lined by Peter Kalischer, a UP reporter in Tokyo, purporting to give the full details of the meeting and identifying Royall as the source.*

All this was temporarily disastrous to our policies, not only in Japan but in the entire Far East. General MacArthur later told me that the incident had deteriorated into a "liar-calling contest" which, he said, was a body blow to United States prestige throughout Asia. At least, the United States had been penalized again for the national custom of airing our disagreements in public. To many Japanese, Soviet power immediately became far more formidable.

The significance of the question raised by the Royall interview, both within Japan and internationally, perhaps was illustrated by the general reaction to one of my speeches. The "Royall incident" was very much alive when I fulfilled a prior engagement to deliver the commencement address at St. Paul's University, in March, 1949.

Referring to communism, on that occasion, the key sentence of my speech was: "The United States does not intend to allow

* As one of the correspondents who attended the session with Royall, I can affirm that afterward there was no agreement among the newsmen present on the Secretary's precise statements, and apparently no notes were taken. The UP version was the most dogmatic to be published throughout the incident. I reported, contrarily, that Royall had made it clear the United States had made no policy decision to abandon Japan. He did say that Japan's strategic importance and the obligation to defend it were being questioned by some officers; a fact known to most correspondents in Japan. It was possible to interpret Royall's remarks as supporting those urging abandonment of Japan, but this was far different from the implication that the Secretary of the Army was enunciating policy or reporting unanimous opinion. My

Japan to become victim to that type of insidious, concealed aggression and infiltration which thrives on chaos and fear." The reaction was instantaneous. Local newscasts referred to my statement as a reaffirmation of a strong United States policy. The Japanese press reported the speech prominently and made my remarks into a flat United States commitment to defend Japan.

Then I began worrying that Washington might turn on me for exceeding the position it wanted to take on this question, for the statement had been made without prior consultation. No reaction arrived. Possibly I was saved by the attention given to Secretary Acheson's important speech at the same time, announcing the formulation of the Atlantic Pact. Later, checking the statements of guidance which are sent periodically to all posts to acquaint them with Washington policy, I found the same sentiments outlined clearly for the information of American Officials.

SCAP was almost as thorough in eliminating Japan's wartime leaders as in demobilizing its military establishment. The Potsdam Declaration laid the foundation for a purge of leadership without specifying the extent. The initial United States policy directive carried this concept further by sketching three broad areas for change. The first attacked the actual military hierarchy, to which there was no important opposition, not even in Japan. Officers were stripped of rank and authority and, among other measures, hundreds of jingoistic secret societies were disbanded. More controversially, the directive specified that important exponents of militarism and aggression were to be arrested for fu-

version was published in the *New York Times,* among other papers, but naturally received less attention than the more equivocal UP stories. Actually, the incident assumed greater significance than appeared to be warranted at the time and certainly more than was justified by subsequent United States policies. Neither Royall's frankness nor his "background" meeting with the correspondents was unusual. These sessions are held frequently by Washington officials. In this case, Royall may also have intended to float a trial balloon in advance of a military economy program, undertaken later that year. The fact that his remarks acquired unusual durability seems to illustrate the extent of Japanese nervousness over the security issue and the distrust that existed during that period between SCAP Headquarters and Washington.—R.B.

ture disposition and those charged with being war criminals were to be tried.

In the second category, SCAP was directed to encourage a desire for individual liberties and democratic processes. He was to use, not support, the existing governmental machinery, and the directive specifically prohibited upholding the Emperor in opposition to evolutionary changes. The people were to be given an opportunity "to become familiar with the history, institutions, culture and the accomplishments of the United States and the other democracies." The directive also provided that "Democratic political parties . . . shall be encouraged. . . . Persons unjustly confined by Japanese authority on political grounds shall be released . . ." There was no direct mention of purging leaders who might stand in the way of these approved trends. Yet the men accused in the Potsdam Declaration of deceiving and misleading the Japanese people also were, in general, those who had imposed and maintained a military dictatorship for nearly fifteen years.

In the detailed policy directive of November 8, 1945, the "Basic Initial Post-Surrender Policy," the Joint Chiefs of Staff directed SCAP:

. . . in no circumstances will persons be allowed to hold public or any other positions of responsibility or influence in public or important private enterprise who have been active exponents of militant nationalism and aggression, who have been influential members of any Japanese ultra-nationalistic, terroristic or secret patriotic society, its agencies or affiliates . . . or who manifest hostility to the objectives of the military occupation.

Additional provisions named specific organizations and certain classes of individuals against which retributive action was authorized, including disbarment from public office or, in certain categories, arrest and detention as suspected war criminals.

The scope of this broad guidance is suggested by the political and social history of Japan during the militarist period, between 1937 and 1945. Although I am convinced the majority of the people did not want war and conquest, there was no public protest during this period and no organized opposition to the war effort. This was due partly to the constant threat of the police, partly to the general Japanese desire to conform to the prevailing opinion, and very largely, to deep veneration for the Throne by virtually every Japanese. To oppose war, particularly after Pearl Harbor, was, in the popular mind, to commit the unpardonable sin of opposing the Emperor's wishes; for the militarists had obtained his command to open hostilities. In this atmosphere every public official and every man of prestige, throughout these eight years, if not longer, was committed to the war effort and supported it, albeit with varying degrees of enthusiasm. Only those who were in a position to retire, voluntarily or otherwise, could avoid involvement during the militarist period.

SCAP plans and orders to implement the Washington directive were prepared by the Government Section of General Headquarters, under Brigadier General Courtney Whitney. After initial staff work, two directives were issued to the Japanese government on January 4, 1946, under the customary abbreviation of SCAPIN (SCAP instruction). The first, No. 548, ordered the dissolution of ultra-nationalistic and secret societies which, sprouting by the hundreds during the militarist period, claimed hundreds of thousands of members. The second, SCAPIN 550, directed the Japanese government to remove from public office all officials of sonin rank, the third highest level of officialdom, or higher. The order also eliminated a large number of officials in particular categories, such as war criminals, career and special service military personnel, and many others. Specifications were laid down for the general guidance of the Japanese government, which was charged with implementation of the order.

The purge struck violently. Of the Shidehara cabinet, then in power, only three members were clearly exempt from removal, although the cabinet held office until the April 10 elections. Shidehara's Progressive party, which held a majority of 257 seats in the House of Representatives, was practically decimated. Despite its name, the party was strongly conservative. In fact, the nature of the political purge meant that it fell almost entirely on right of center factions, for very few leftists held any position of influence during the militarist period. The Communists, then emerging as a disciplined political party, were not affected at all, because they had been underground or jailed since the early thirties.

The Japanese government estimated that, if the purge were carried out by categories, some 200,000 persons would be affected. It therefore proposed a somewhat different procedure, designed to lessen the impact. General Whitney informed Prime Minister Shidehara, however, that the purpose of the directive was to cleanse the government of elements which by their acts or associations had participated in Japanese expansion.[2]

The directive was implemented with considerable dispatch. Although the political parties experienced a period of shock, confusion, and reorientation, the administration of government, according to the Government Section, was not seriously disrupted. On November 8, 1946, the purge was extended to local levels.

The Government Section reported that a total of 717,415 persons in all categories were screened by March, 1948. Of these, 201,815 persons were purged, including 115,416 career military officers.[3] Many prominent Japanese industrialists, bankers, diplomats, labor leaders, lawyers, clergymen, and professors spent an enormous number of man-hours in reviewing and assessing the careers of those involved.

The purge unquestionably was political and therefore of prime interest to the Department of State. But I do not recall that our office or section was ever consulted in connection with it, except possibly in the most cursory fashion; nor was our advice solicited on the possible future foreign policy implications. We were not kept informed, on a continuing basis, of the implementation of the directive. On the contrary, a staff memorandum within GHQ charged the Government Section with responsibility for all matters relating to the purges, including the removal and exclusion of Japanese from national and local posts, interpretations, opinions, and instructions, and supervision of the Japanese government's administration of the order.

One year later, on January 4, 1947, the purge was extended to all economic organizations, and to newspapers, radio, and other information media. The economic purge, as it was called, forbade any relative of a purgee within the third degree by blood, marriage, or adoption from succeeding to the appointive office from which the purgee had been removed.

Prime Minister Yoshida particularly questioned this guilt by relationship concept in a letter to General MacArthur on December 21, 1946. "I remember reading," the prime minister wrote, "something about a law or practice in China centuries ago that when a man was found to have committed a grave offense, all his relatives used to be sentenced accordingly. But I think the modern conception of justice let go completely free all relatives of even a murderer." Yoshida then proposed alternative language for Article X of the purge order, the section dealing with relatives of purgees, which he said would accomplish the same end.

MacArthur replied by letter dated December 26, 1946, rationalizing the reason and the need for Article X. The General emphasized the concern of the Allied Powers over the problem of providing an untainted leadership in Japanese political and economic life.[4]

The removal of economic and public information leaders resulted in the disbarment of several thousand men, actually a relatively small number of executives. But the effect on the Japanese business world was the same as if, in the United States, the top management and directorships of the five hundred largest American banks, corporations, and similar enterprises suddenly were fired, all at once, in disgrace. Such a move might not wreck the American economy, but it certainly would jolt it heavily. In Japan, economic conditions were so fragile that maximum skill and experience, particularly in management, were vital. Moreover, the Japanese industrial and banking complexes were tightly integrated under the control of eleven principal business empires.

87

These were the so-called zaibatsu, the family enterprises which had maintained strong cartels, some for generations. Under this system, a relatively small number of the top executives had far more power and greater responsibility than most of their American counterparts.

The economic purge in all of its ramifications created widespread criticism, particularly in the United States, and became far more controversial than that involving political figures. To most thinking people, the economic directive made little sense. But, in both Washington and Tokyo, the principle of reform for reform's sake seemed to dominate.

Quickly, the economic assault developed into full-scale trust busting as part of a concerted attempt completely to change the country's economic structure. In addition to their purge from active business, members of the eleven families designated as zaibatsu were required to sell their industrial securities for nonnegotiable government bonds, the value of which was reduced by confiscatory taxes. They were also forced to liquidate most of their other assets, thus carrying out the unwise business operation of turning solid assets into currency at the height of severe inflation. Further, holding companies were dissolved, trading combines labeled as "monopolistic" were disbanded, and hundreds of new companies were organized to replace the former giants.

The authority for all this was stated bluntly in Washington's Initial Post-Surrender Policy. "The existing economic basis of Japanese military strength must be destroyed and not be permitted to revive," the document said. The theory was that a small number of zaibatsu controlled the total industry so tightly that it could, and did, deliver it wholesale to the support of military conquest. This was a doubtful premise and was never proved. The extent of voluntary cooperation by Japanese industrialists with the war effort was difficult for any foreigner to ascertain in the months immediately preceding Pearl Harbor. It was significant, however, that the militarist-dominated government in late 1940 put into effect an extensive new economic organization

which government spokesmen said would secure more war production, "by force, if necessary." [5] Nevertheless, the SCAP theory
was that a more competitive "free enterprise" economic system
would prevent future Japanese militarists from dominating the
industries which were necessary for conquest.

Despite the official explanation for these economic policies,
they impressed me as being vindictive, destructive, and futile.
Significantly, they were spurred by pressures not only from
Washington but from the Soviets. Moscow's representatives on
the Far Eastern Commission and the Allied Council constantly
sought to increase the pace and severity of economic "reform."
The purpose was obvious. It was true that Japanese industry was
closely integrated and far more tightly controlled during the war
than in the United States. But in many conversations with SCAP
officials I insisted that the reforms were self-defeating. In the end
it took the realities of hard cash and tremendous United States
expenditures to convince the trust busters and reformers.

In addition to the widespread physical destruction left by the
war, which included the obliteration of many prime industrial
plants, Japan completely lacked the essentials for a viable
economy. There were insufficient fuel, power, raw materials, oil,
and transportation. Most of all, there was no will to resume production. MacArthur on several occasions referred to Japanese industrial activity and output at the beginning of the Occupation as
"zero." This was literally true, and the situation had only slightly
improved when the economic purge raised new complications in
1947. The Japanese economy was too complex to respond to a
simple military order to "get going."

Economically, Japan faced an entirely new situation when the
war ended. There were no neighboring sources of food or industrial raw materials, and Japan had been shorn of its empire. The
vast merchant fleet was gone. In time, six million Japanese were
brought home from all parts of Asia, adding more mouths to a
population that was increasing naturally by about 1.5 million
annually. Eighty percent of cotton textile productive capacity

had been scrapped during the war. Hostilities had completely destroyed 25 percent of total industrial capacity, with a further one third materially damaged. The displacement of silk by synthetic fibers had almost eliminated a primary source of dollar earnings for Japan. The dollar shortage became increasingly critical as the necessity grew to import food and raw materials from the United States, with no meaningful exports to pay for them. Japan had not been self-sufficient in foodstuffs since about 1912 and had depended upon foreign trade for survival. But trade patterns were shattered and, even if Japanese industries could produce, the possibility of restoring vital markets in the Far East and South Asia was dimmed by political unrest and continuing anti-Japanism in those areas. The specter of starvation literally hung over Japan.[6]

Despite these seemingly insurmountable problems, SCAP's initial economic objective was merely to prevent disease and unrest in accordance with the responsibilities of an occupying power under the Geneva Convention and pursuant to its directives from Washington. The Initial Post-Surrender Directive had specified that Japan was expected to provide goods and services to meet the needs of the occupying forces without causing starvation, widespread disease, or acute physical distress within the country. The Japanese further were to meet the requirements for reparations, while satisfying what the directive termed reasonable peaceful requirements of the population.

Heavy inflation was another factor causing enormous difficulties during the period between 1945 and 1949. The note issue stood at 15 billion yen in March, 1946, after currency conversion reduced it from 62 billion yen. By the end of 1948 the total issue was 368 billion. The rate of increase was 135 percent during 1947 and 65 percent during 1948. Heavy taxation and a balanced budget for the following fiscal year produced a degree of stabilization at around 300 billion yen.

This fiscal situation was threatening, until the United States took vigorous countermeasures early in 1949. SCAP received an interim directive from Washington to proceed toward economic stabilization. Joseph M. Dodge, a Detroit banker, arrived to take charge of the program and assumed tight control, with Mac-Arthur's full backing. During most of the next three years Dodge worked closely with Hayato Ikeda, the minister of finance who became prime minister in 1960. Dodge's stern measures, designed to bring order into the realm of Japanese governmental finance, emphasized balanced budgets, reduction of the note issue, payment of outstanding governmental debts, and generally tight money policies. They were not popular with the Japanese, but they were based upon sound and orthodox economic principles.

As the months passed, the expert handling of the monetary problem, sharp credit management, and general easing of the previously harsh and repressive SCAP economic measures produced vast improvement in the economy. While much remained to be done, there was a revival of confidence in the Japanese business world. The wheels of commerce and industry began to hum, and unemployment decreased markedly. This was fortunate for, upon the outbreak of the Korean War in June, 1950, Japan became an important supplier for the United Nations military forces in Korea.

SCAP undertook the most stringent of these economic measures only after previous efforts to persuade Japanese authorities to tackle inflation and fiscal imbalance appeared fruitless. Originally these steps represented a huge gamble, in many ways. In addition to the opposition of Japanese financial interests, tight money policies were harsh measures for a people who had already reached an extremely low level of existence. It is no exaggeration to say that failure on the part of the people to respond might well have made the entire United States position in Japan untenable. The great bulk of the Japanese, normally a thrifty and conservative people, did respond, however, and eventually so did the great majority of Japanese businessmen. As a result, Japan was saved from economic, and perhaps political, disaster. The significance of this was underlined in later years by the fact that

Joseph Dodge, so severely criticized early in his tenure in Japan, was decorated for his services by the Japanese government in 1962.

Yet the government and SCAP were heckled continually by a series of "quickie" strikes of government workers, most of them Communist-led, in such services as the post office, tax collecting, telephones, telegraphs, and railways. Deeply concerned by these labor upheavals and particularly by the extent of Communist influence behind them, I voiced my feelings strongly to General MacArthur during a well-remembered conversation in his office in April, 1948.

The General disagreed and said his analysis indicated that domestic political considerations—principally the attempt to overthrow the Ashida government—were the chief factor in the demonstrations. He stated that he was convinced Communist influence was declining in Japan, adding that there were fewer Communists among labor leaders than ever before. How firmly he believed this assessment at the time was never completely clear, for MacArthur often used visitors as a sounding board to test new ideas of his own, which might later be abandoned, or to seek a reaction to reports given him by his staff. In any case, I replied that the facts did not support this conclusion. Perhaps my judgment was influenced by a huge demonstration which was taking place, while we talked, in the Imperial Plaza, directly across from the Dai Ichi Headquarters. The demonstration was dominated by numerous red flags and banners, the usual identifications for the most leftist unions, as well as the Japan Communist party.

MacArthur's analysis of the situation seemed to agree with that of his Labor Division chief, James S. Killen. An enthusiastic and dedicated American labor official, Killen had set out vigorously to create a strong labor movement in Occupied Japan. In several conversations with me Killen emphasized his belief that the most effective defense against communism in Japan was a healthy labor union movement. "Labor in Japan," he said one day, "must probably learn the hard way by participation in strikes, unrest, and for a time, false leadership. When the laboring man has been sufficiently fooled by his Communist leaders, he will throw them out. Communism cannot be fought with a gun or club—it must be defeated by democracy standing on its own feet."

Deeply involved in this battle against enormous day-to-day problems, I was unprepared for the shock of Washington's view of the same struggle. It was a distorted view, I found on a combined consultation-vacation trip in May, 1949. In a few days of roaming through the bureaucratic forest I could see clearly why Washington and Tokyo differed so often over policy and over the methods of implementing policy in Occupied Japan.

Washington itself can be frustrating for a Foreign Service officer who is called back on consultation. Everyone is so busy and so preoccupied with his own problems and pressures that the visitor inevitably feels himself to be a nuisance and a needless distraction. What appear to be weighty problems and challenging situations in the field lose their sense of urgency and importance in the capital, with its worldwide perspective and greater sense of proportion. I rationalized this explanation while knocking on doors and seeking appointments with the men who supposedly wanted to consult me. Far from soliciting Tokyo views of the Occupation, the Washington officials involved with the problems of that experiment seemed disinterested. Washington, the capital of the postwar world, seemed far removed from the realities of what actually was the American occupation of Japan.

At the top, the Washington view appeared somewhat clearer than at the operating levels. For instance, Dean Rusk displayed a surprising knowledge of the Far East and Japan, which were distant fields from his current area of responsibility. He had just been appointed deputy undersecretary of state, a position requiring extensive concentration upon the broader aspects of foreign policy. Rusk had a restrained, intelligently relevant, and down-to-earth manner of speaking. His subtle sense of humor was refreshing. These qualities proved invaluable when, less than a year later, he became assistant secretary of state for Far Eastern Affairs.

Secretary of State Dean Acheson stood out most clearly among the many and diverse personalities then in the State Department. Tall, urbane, and always outwardly poised, Secretary Acheson had a sharp penetrating wit and the capacity to probe quickly to the essentials of every problem. He had just returned from meetings of the Council of Foreign Ministers in Europe. The Council was designed to perpetuate the wartime cooperation of the major Allies, including Soviet Russia, by drawing the foreign policy chiefs closer together. Acheson described it, however, as "the most impossible institution ever invented by man." It was, he said, "a body which is unable to function and which has no right to exist." Daily meetings lasted eight hours, he added, "accomplishing fifteen minutes' work, the Council by its very nature being unable to agree." As he talked, I recalled that the foreign ministers of the United Kingdom, United States, and Soviet Russia, with the concurrence of China, had been responsible for creating the Allied Council for Japan.

Discussing the Occupation itself, Acheson raised a point which had been troubling many of us. He expressed hope that a serious effort could be made to reduce the enormous number of American and other officials who had swollen the SCAP bureaucracy. Since 1948, I had felt that Headquarters had become too gigantic and too meddlesome. The Secretary also expressed belief that the Occupation should be placed on an advisory and policy level, instead of continuing as an operating organization with deep involvement in virtually all Japanese affairs. Admittedly, he said, such a shift would create problems of assembling men with the proper qualifications to handle delicate questions which arise under such a system.

When I returned to Tokyo, in late July, 1949, I had an immediate opportunity to present this idea, and many others then held in Washington, to MacArthur. The General greeted me warmly; then, as was his custom, began probing for my impressions of the sentiment in Washington. We discussed at length the views of various Washington officials that the impact of the United States military upon the Japanese people should be eased, that the extent of the purges should be curtailed, and particularly that the number of personnel in SCAP should be drastically reduced. Some Washington officials specifically had contended that the entire Occupation could be carried out, on a guidance and policy level, by two hundred carefully selected people, instead of the thousands then employed.

"It can't be done, Bill," MacArthur said, "for the very simple reason that two hundred people of the kind envisioned are not available and could not be recruited and trained in the foreseeable future." Pacing the floor and frequently lighting his pipe, the General was equally adamant on the question of reducing the extent of the purge. "This," he said bluntly, "would be premature." Nevertheless, he added that policies to lessen the impact of the Occupation already were prepared and were being implemented. The General said he had anticipated this trend by inserting a particular phrase in his public message issued the previous May 3. On that day, commemorating the anniversary of Japan's new SCAP-directed constitution, the General had told the Japanese he would continue the transition of the Occupation "from the stern rigidity of a military operation to the friendly guidance of a protective force."

On the fourth anniversary of Japan's formal surrender, September 2, 1949, MacArthur inserted a challenging sentence in his customary statement to the Japanese people. He said bluntly that communism as a major issue in Japanese life was past. I was not so sure that this expressed an accurate evaluation of the Japanese situation at that time and felt in any case that the assertion was too categorical. It was not clear, however, whether the statement represented the General's own conviction or whether, as often happened, he was trying to reduce Japanese fears.

Many influential Japanese had become increasingly worried by the ruthless and expanding activities of the Japan Communist party. Among them the late Hidenari ("Terry") Terasaki, a court official, discussed the question at length during our frequent conversations. Terry had attended Brown University and spoke English fluently. After his death in 1950, his devoted American-born widow, Gwen, told his story in the poignant book *Bridge to the Sun*.

Terry was adviser and liaison officer for the Emperor with SCAP (goyogakari) and was, therefore, in constant touch with the intimate details of the political situation. Probably the frankest Japanese I have known, Terry was exceedingly helpful in explaining the reactions of his people to the sometimes quixotic actions of the Occupation. Moreover, as an adviser to the Emperor, he was able to convey some of my views and explanations of American policy to court circles and, indeed, to the Emperor himself.

Time and again Terry expressed his concern that nothing apparently was being done to counteract the rapid growth of the Communist party in the fertile field of postwar Japan. Although a man of great discernment and understanding of democratic methods, he emphasized his belief that SCAP was creating a great danger by showing too much leniency toward the Japanese Communists. The old-time Japanese party leaders, who had been released from imprisonment in late 1945, quickly had formed a new party under their control. It was allowed to become a legal political entity and to operate openly and with complete freedom. Simultaneously, Terry pointed out, the Communists were permitted to infiltrate key labor unions and to win control in many of them. Since newsprint was extremely scarce and valuable, it was tightly rationed and controlled through import licenses. Terry blamed SCAP, however, for tolerating the manipulation of licenses within the Japanese government which permitted the Communist party organ, *Akahata* (Red Flag), and hundreds of other Communist publications to obtain adequate newsprint. All of them constantly castigated the Japanese government and, often, SCAP as well.

Privately I had to agree with these views. The original release of the Communist leaders appeared necessary under SCAP's directives and the campaign to spread democracy. But it should have been obvious to the responsible American officials that Japan's democracy was too new to withstand the assault of such an experienced and disciplined enemy.

On the other hand, the man who emerged from this period as "Mr. Conservative" in Japanese history, former Prime Minister Shigeru Yoshida, maintained strong confidence in the stabilizing influence of MacArthur and in democratic procedures. A dyed-in-the-wool conservative and ardent anti-Communist, an autocrat in handling subordinates, Yoshida nevertheless understood and practiced democracy in its broad sense. During the six-year period from 1946 to 1952 he was prime minister five times, the longest record in Japanese parliamentary history. This was an extraordinarily difficult period for a Japanese political leader, because he had to sponsor most of the SCAP reforms which the Japanese disliked, while also meeting the challenge of the opposition parties, including the Japan Communist party at the height of its political influence.

Yoshida, a former diplomat, entered politics at the age of seventy under the Occupation. He came with clean hands, so to speak, for he had been in retirement throughout the war. Fortunately for him, the Japanese Army vetoed his selection as foreign minister in 1936, when the government of Koki Hirota was formed. Instead, Yoshida was sent to London as ambassador, a post he held until retiring from the foreign service in March, 1939. During the spring of 1945 he was imprisoned for forty days on suspicion of plotting to end the war. He emerged as foreign minister in the cabinet of Prince Naruhiko Higashikuni, which was formed just before the Occupation began.

Independent, strong-willed, blunt, brusque, and arrogant at times, Yoshida nevertheless had the facility of cooperating with the Occupation authorities without compromising his principles. There were occasions when, as prime minister, he was charged with carrying out what appeared to him to be unreasonable instructions. He did so and still managed to escape the onus of failure which he had predicted for himself on several occasions. Although he was embroiled frequently with SCAP's Government Section, and particularly its chief, Brigadier General Courtney Whitney, Yoshida maintained implicit faith in the justice and fairness of General MacArthur, whom he respected and admired.

In dealing with underlings Yoshida often was autocratic, especially when the image of Japan was at stake. Once he gave a dinner in honor of my wife and me. Among the guests were a Japanese foreign service officer and his wife who were to leave shortly for the United States on a very desirable assignment. This couple lived in the suburbs and had to catch the late train home or spend the night in the city. So they excused themselves and departed before the rest of us. Several days later I learned that Yoshida had canceled the assignment on the ground that the Japanese couple should have known better than to leave before the guests of honor.

Yet Yoshida also had a puckish sense of humor and was an affable, thoughtful host, in the old Japanese tradition. A short, stocky man, he peered at everyone, it seemed, with quizzical appraisal through rimless pince-nez. Once called a Japanese Churchill, Yoshida promptly replied: "Yes, but made in Japan." On one occasion he asked me if I could arrange to have his house returned to him, since SCAP had requisitioned it for the use of the Soviet Mission. "You see," he explained, "I am anti-Communist, and I don't like to have Bolsheviks in my home." We managed to oblige him.

There was, too, a pronounced element of thoughtful loyalty beneath the armor which Yoshida habitually wore in public. He once told me how Baron Kijuro Shidehara was selected as prime minister in 1946, when the Higashikuni cabinet resigned. Yoshida said he recommended Shidehara, the old-line antimilitarist to MacArthur, and the General's first question was "Does he speak

English?" When Yoshida said Shidehara prided himself on his English, the next question was "How old is he?" The answer, that Shidehara was in his seventies, seemed to clinch the choice. Yoshida laughingly added that he never had nerve enough to tell Shidehara the criteria for his selection.[7]

In my view, Yoshida was the outstanding Japanese statesman of the Occupation period, a reputation which possibly, for the present, is denied him in Japan, but a distinction history no doubt will accord him. Perhaps his steadfast belief in democracy, which was far stronger than his periodic demonstrations of personal autocracy, provided a lesson for all of us. Yoshida led his conservative party to increasingly greater strength at the polls during Japan's most troubled period. The Japan Communist party reached the height of electoral strength in the election of January 23, 1949, when economic distress mingled with the uncertainties of the Occupation to create great popular restlessness. The Communists polled almost three million votes and won thirty-five seats in the Diet. Yoshida's Democratic-Liberal party obtained an absolute majority, however, and thereafter the Communists dwindled to an insignificant political element. The wily old prime minister successfully waited out his enemies.

It is remarkable, in retrospect, that the Japanese people did not break totally under the stresses and strains of those early, confused Occupation years. If they had done so, the entire society might have been thrust into chaos. This, of course, was the central Communist purpose; and it might be said that the superimposition of harsh Allied reforms upon the battered and bewildered Japanese people gave them their greatest opportunity to infiltrate an industrial nation. Their failure is attributable to many factors, including a number of American contributions which were more beneficial than those discussed at this point.

One of the most important elements in this situation was the discipline—perhaps social consciousness would be a better term —of the Japanese themselves. This Japanese contribution was acknowledged by General MacArthur in his statement on the fourth anniversary of the Japanese surrender, when he said:

Of the Japanese people I can pay no higher tribute than to repeat that they have fully and faithfully fulfilled their surrender commitments and have well earned the freedom and dignity and opportunity which alone can come with the restoration of a formal Peace.

6

Working with MacArthur

No ONE KNEW the private feelings of General MacArthur when he bounded from his personal plane, the *Bataan,* at Atsugi Airfield on August 30, 1945, and stood, at last, on Japanese soil. It would have been surprising and out of character, however, if he had not thought back over the long road from Brisbane, Australia; the dirty, muddy, bloody journey across New Guinea and the Philippines and intervening islands. The end, this end, had never been in doubt for the proud, elderly General with the inflexible will.

Now the man of destiny had arrived in the land of his destiny, unarmed, confident, and in command of the situation. He was, as always, impatient and restless, for there was work to do, after the formal Japanese surrender. The surrender ceremony itself had been delayed for two days, until September 2, because the islands had been lashed by a typhoon, a development symptomatic of events that were about to break over Japan. MacArthur and most of the Allied representatives on this solemn occasion appeared in plain uniforms, without neckties. The Japanese observed strict formality. Foreign Minister Mamoru Shigemitsu and his civilian colleagues wore top hats and morning clothes, a reminder that, after all, this was the Orient.

The surrender ceremony culminated an effort of such unity and well-coordinated skill that the component elements of the war are sometimes forgotten. With Allied support, United States power reached Tokyo through New Guinea, the Solomons, the Gilberts and Marshalls, Saipan, Tinian, the Philippines, Iwo Jima, and Okinawa. It was in all aspects a war involving all forms of military arms and services—land, sea, and air. Although Soviet Russia's one-week campaign across Manchuria was a strategic and political element in the final Japanese decision to surrender, it was significant that no Allied combat man considered this drive as a tactical contribution to final victory. The route to Tokyo was, indeed, across the Pacific.

For days before the surrender ceremony, Washington had worked feverishly to establish some sort of control group to handle the occupation of Japan. A body known as the Far Eastern Advisory Commission had been organized in late August. But the Russians, for reasons of their own, refused to sit on it, and the Commission withered on the vine. Yet the Occupation had to proceed. So the United States radioed the outlines of its initial policy to MacArthur the day before he landed at Atsugi, and followed with further directives and guidance.

This meant that, from the Allied viewpoint, the Supreme Commander's authority rested upon a patchwork of informal arrangements of various kinds. In reality, it was based mostly upon MacArthur's prompt and thorough assumption of the authority given him and the swift implementation of directives as he thought they should be carried out. This was, at best, peculiar machinery for such an enterprise; so peculiar, in fact, that in retrospect it is amazing that it worked at all.

It was not until the Moscow Conference of December 27, 1945, that these matters, and particularly the regime of control, were tidied up and regularized. The Conference established the Far Eastern Commission[1] of all eleven Allied belligerents with the premise that it would formulate basic policies for the Occupation and would review interim actions which SCAP had taken without its prior authorization. This system never quite worked in practice. I know of no instance when the Commission even attempted to reverse or to veto action taken by MacArthur, or was able to impress its views on MacArthur against his wishes.

In establishing the Allied Council for Japan, the Moscow meeting had in mind the maintenance of an on-the-spot advisory group which, however, lacked any direct authority over the Supreme Commander. Instead, he was identified as "the sole executive authority for the Allied Powers in Japan." While he was expected to consult beforehand, whenever possible, with the Allied Council, the agreement specified that his decisions were controlling.

Thus, as far as Allied controls were concerned, MacArthur literally was on his own for the first four months of the Occupation; thereafter he conducted a successful rearguard action against any dilution of this autonomy. Although Washington's directives were detailed during this period, the General had great latitude in interpreting and implementing them. On political matters he was not under specific day-to-day control from Washington.

This was heady authority. Never before in the history of the United States had such enormous and absolute power been placed in the hands of a single individual. The regime of control, now complete and immutable, had to be made to work if the sacrifices of the American people and of their allies were not to be wasted. The way it worked depended primarily upon MacArthur. At this period, the coupling of MacArthur to great power and authority seemed entirely natural. In an over-all sense, the Occupation operated well. That it did may be attributed to the personality, experience, assurance, image, and—for lack of a better word—the wizardry of MacArthur.

It was with this man of almost limitless authority, the proconsul of a troubled nation, the benign conqueror, that I worked in a strange dual capacity: as his subordinate and, simultaneously, as the representative of the Department of State, an entity which often he seemed to regard as foreign and hostile. From countless visits his plain office became almost as familiar to me as my own, more comfortable establishment a mile away. With perhaps typical perversity, the General had selected a small, inside room in the Dai Ichi building which the Japanese insurance executives had used for storage. While his aide, Colonel Laurence ("Larry") E. Bunker, commanded a striking view of the Imperial Palace moat from an adjacent outer office, MacArthur's single window looked out only on a blank wall. The General worked in a room of polished neatness; no visitor ever saw papers on his unadorned desk. It was an office made friendly by crumpled, leather-covered, and overstuffed furniture. Its aloofness was underlined by the absence of telephones or typewriters; the General wrote his pronouncements in cramped longhand.

There was always a touch of drama in the General's greeting: the quick bounding from his leather desk chair; the strong handclasp; the hearty words of welcome, always personal and warming; the penetrating eyes. Almost invariably, he seated the visitor on the worn leather divan, then lunged into a nearby chair. Soon he was on his feet again, propelled by the intensity or the challenge of his words. He paced the narrow runway of his office, in cadence with his thoughts; restless and eager. For this field commander, who liked to probe the most distant front lines, to the despair of his staff, confinement in a shoe-box office seemed to be extraordinary self-discipline.

During many interviews, MacArthur discussed just about every facet of the Occupation and its many problems with me. He liked to "think out loud," using the visitor as a sounding board. Often I would read in published announcements some of the ideas that had been previously expressed. Others, of course, never appeared publicly.

From his odd ivory tower MacArthur had a phenomenal grasp of the situation within his area of responsibility. He never traveled within Japan and left Tokyo only for infrequent appearances at nearby Haneda Airport for the visits of high-ranking persons. Until the Korean War, his journeys outside the country were limited to quick flights to Manila in 1946 and to Seoul in

1948 for the independence ceremonies of these two nations. In each case he returned to Tokyo immediately after the ceremony. Instead of personal observation, MacArthur familiarized himself with his command through voracious reading and close, shrewd questioning of innumerable visitors.

The perennial Occupation question was how this man of action, who passed his seventieth birthday in harness, renewed himself for the enormous energy he used in his job. Most of his subordinates had to leave crowded and clamorous Tokyo periodically for a change of air and relaxation from the murderous pace which MacArthur set for his staff. The Occupation quickly rehabilitated Japanese recreational facilities, from golf links to ski lodges, and they were well patronized. But MacArthur and a few of his key officers plodded ahead, month after month, on a seven-day week and, often, a ten- or twelve-hour day. The General himself usually reached his office at around 11 A.M. for two or three hours' work before luncheon at his residence. After a regular hour's nap, he was back in the office at 5 P.M., leaving usually after 8 P.M. He had no hobbies, except his reading, and few diversions, except movies at his embassy home. Yet the General, an ardent sports fan, kept abreast of baseball and football results and standings in the United States.

Although I attempted to maintain the relatively normal working hours of an embassy, from 8:30 A.M. to 5:30 P.M., it was not unusual to be summoned to the Dai Ichi building to see MacArthur at 7 P.M. or later for a conference of unspecified duration. Nor was it extraordinary to be called by MacArthur personally on the telephone in the early morning to discuss matters requiring immediate attention. The General used the telephone in his residence extensively before going to his office.

With this schedule, it was not surprising to hear MacArthur's explanation for refusing an offer of one million dollars to write his memoirs while still acting as SCAP. He said he turned down the proposal because he would have to pay most of it in taxes anyway, and he did not think he could work any harder for the

United States government than he already was doing.

His refusal to alter or lessen his personal schedule was, of course, a prime conversational topic in the Occupation, particularly among those who felt themselves chained to the General's dedication. Few realized, perhaps, the personal factors involved in at least one of the several occasions when he declined invitations to visit the United States. During the presidential election year of 1948, MacArthur's immediate staff encouraged the use of his name as a potential Republican candidate for the presidency. In fact, some were riding the political horse so vigorously that they already had jobs picked out for themselves in case of victory. At the time I did not realize that MacArthur himself was politicking, so low key was the question kept within Japan, but I learned later that he actually had sought the nomination. The first test was the Wisconsin primary on April 7, 1948. Despite advance optimism in Headquarters, the results were disastrous. The next day I called at the Dai Ichi building for a regular conference. But the Chief of Staff, Major General Paul J. Mueller, who had kept himself strictly aloof from politics, held up a warning hand. "The General is as low as a rug and very disappointed," Mueller said. I decided to delay my visit until a more propitious time. At our next meeting, however, there was nothing downhearted about the General.

Nevertheless, it was generally recognized that MacArthur's political chances could only be saved by a timely visit to the United States. Possibly that was one reason why, in early May, 1948, the Senate Appropriations Committee asked MacArthur to testify personally in Washington. After a one-day silence, while political speculation gained momentum, the General turned down the invitation. In a lengthy statement he said he had no wish to return to Washington, as his purposes in doing so would be misinterpreted as politically motivated. He had just lost out in the Nebraska primary, placing fifth, and the refusal to leave Japan seemed to end all chances of re-establishing himself as a serious contender. Irrespective of the motives underlying the General's refusal, I am inclined to believe that he was sincere in his repeated statements that he would make no overt move toward seeking the nomination. The thought occurred to me at the time that, despite his ambitions, MacArthur perhaps was not really interested enough in domestic politics to act like a politician instead of a general.

He was a general in every action, of course, with the naturalness of a lifetime in positions of command. Curiously, this was particularly noticeable in the ostentatious social life spawned by the Occupation. Aside from the usual diplomacy of a world capital, Tokyo in these years attracted a large number of world leaders and many cabinet ministers, legislators, and distinguished men and women in other fields. Yet, in my experience, MacArthur was the only man who served as a "head of government," as in fact he was, without feeling obliged to entertain every politically powerful visitor to his domain. It became standard procedure for MacArthur to look to my wife and me for assistance in handling distinguished visitors whom the General may or may not also have invited to embassy luncheons. We took up this additional burden as a matter of routine.

MacArthur also entertained on his own terms. In addition to avoiding formal dinners and other evening events, so beloved on the social circuit, he established a peculiar routine. Guests, assembling for luncheon, would be greeted in the huge embassy drawing room by Mrs. MacArthur, a slight, sparkling, and poised woman, known widely by her first name, Jean. Often she would be the only woman present, but with Southern charm and a soft Tennessee accent, she invariably kept the conversation lively and made everyone, from prime ministers to generals, feel at home.

"The General," as Mrs. MacArthur invariably called her husband, whether speaking of him or to him, usually appeared in the drawing room after all guests had arrived. He always walked first through the silent and sometimes skeptical guests, to Mrs. MacArthur. "Hello, my dear!" he would say, kissing her. Then, and only then, he turned to his visitors, welcoming each with a warm handshake and a personalized greeting. Often the General startled his guests by recounting minute details of a previous meeting in the distant past, a memory feat in which he delighted.

The greetings over, MacArthur would take the guest of honor by the arm, announcing that everyone must be hungry, and would lead the way into the dining room. The absence of protocol often created unusual circumstances, and once six foreign ambassadors found themselves in the junior positions at the middle of the long table. No one seemed to mind this oddity, although necks arched vigorously whenever, as customary, MacArthur began discussing state affairs. When the coffee had been served, the General and Mrs. MacArthur, without further ado, would proceed to the hall and bid good-by to their guests. The party was over.

On one of these occasions I found myself with a group of senators and congressmen, who belonged to two of the many Congressional committees and subcommittees which regularly "investigated" the Occupation. After being told firmly by one of the visitors that we Occupationaires were living in a self-created dream world, I drifted over to join Senator Homer Ferguson, who was standing alone by a fireplace in the drawing room. At this time, in 1949, the senator was a powerful senior Republican in the Senate and a man who looked the part, with his shock of white hair and what struck me as a fierce countenance. He was inspecting the fireplace with a critical eye, then slowly he glanced at the ornate walls, the crystal chandeliers, and the huge windows in the reception room.

"Who," he asked me abruptly, "owns this magnificent palace?" The implication was quite clear that the Occupation probably was needlessly spending the American taxpayer's money to maintain the place.

"This is the American Embassy, Senator," I replied. "It was built during President Hoover's administration and for a time was known as 'Hoover's folly.' Now it is worth probably ten times its original cost." Then I explained that it was being used only temporarily as the residence of General and Mrs. MacArthur and, in time, would again become the American Embassy.

"Humph! I see," the senator said. I thought there was a note of disappointment in his voice.

Congressmen were among the most articulate commentators on the Occupation, but they were by no means the most caustic or the most powerful forces with which MacArthur felt he had to deal. He often differed with the Far Eastern Commission, and fought various departments of the United States government, both publicly and privately, in order to run SCAP as he thought best. Less widely known is the fact that he sometimes protected his rear, like a good tactician.

One of the undramatic but complex problems with which I wrestled in mid-1948, for instance, resulted in this MacArthur tactic. The problem concerned a Japanese request for permission to send a whaling expedition to Antarctica. Among other reasons, the Japanese needed the fats and proteins from a good catch. After considerable communication with Washington, we finally were told to go ahead with the expedition. At this point, I was informed that MacArthur had asked the Joint Chiefs of Staff to obtain for him an official interim United States directive authorizing the project, the Joint Chiefs being the channel of communication for governmental instructions. Puzzled by what seemed to be an unnecessary request for authority, I asked the General why he did not simply go ahead on his own responsibility. "Once the directive is received," the General replied, "they can fight it out in the Far Eastern Commission while we go about our business."

Events proved that MacArthur had correctly estimated the situation. A number of countries were interested in expanding their own activities in Antarctica, and the Japanese project was strongly opposed in the Far Eastern Commission and elsewhere. Armed with special authority, SCAP paid no attention to this opposition. Japan thereby began what has become a rather substantial postwar whaling industry.

Perhaps the General's apparent change of heart—for he ordinarily was not so reluctant to take the initiative—was the result of an earlier diplomatic embarrassment. This involved the rather ticklish affair of the United Nations Temporary Commission on Korea (UNTCOK). The Commission grew out of the efforts of the United States to meet its obligations under the Moscow Agreement of December, 1945, which provided for the eventual independence of Korea. Faced by the continued Soviet refusal to cooperate in this project or to permit access to Sovietized North Korea, the United States raised the matter in the United Nations General Assembly. As a result, the Assembly established UNTCOK in 1947 to visit Korea and to observe the election of Korean representatives with whom the Commission could consult on measures to establish a unified government for all of Korea.

The nine-nation Commission failed to obtain Soviet permission to cross the 38th parallel into North Korea. Deciding that its work was finished, it voted to come to Japan from Seoul to write its report. When the administrative officer, R. S. Hausner, arrived at Haneda Airport to make arrangements for the visit on May 4, 1948, SCAP had received no word of the Commission's intentions. The Chief of Staff, therefore, questioned Hausner's presence, since entry into Japan was limited to those with special permission. Furthermore, SCAP took the position—rightfully, in my view—that it should not become entangled in the Korean impasse by admitting to Japan a commission accountable only to the United Nations General Assembly. Several days later a mild furor arose when it became publicly known that SCAP had refused permission for the international group to enter Japan as a body.

MacArthur reversed himself on May 13 and issued a press release, saying that UNTCOK could enter the country, if it desired. Meanwhile, the Commission itself had decided to go to Shanghai, and the report was written there. MacArthur's reversal, I later learned, was the result of Washington pressure which he attributed to the State Department. Subsequently he told me with considerable vehemence and strong language that this decision by Washington resulted in a needless and callous public humiliation for him. And so it seemed at the time. One result evidently was his later caution in the matter of the Antarctic whaling expedition.

MacArthur's sensitivity to any criticism was well-advertised during this period, and his reaction to press attacks was painful to watch. In the continual press attention paid to the Occupation, MacArthur, as an American, and being MacArthur, was a natural lightning rod for criticism. A less sensitive person or a more practiced politician most probably would have ignored the whole business as an occupational hazard. The hypersensitive General, however, often replied to the attacks on him, either directly or through personal spokesmen, thus furnishing the press with more copy and adding fuel to the controversy of the moment. Neither MacArthur nor his advisers seemed to understand how often this tactic helped to enlarge and prolong issues that otherwise might have died from undernourishment.

Within Headquarters it was universally recognized that anyone who contributed to a bad press for the Occupation was on dangerous ground. This was particularly true for the meetings of the Allied Council which often produced international headlines. Whenever I called on MacArthur to report on one of the more dramatic sessions, he usually asked: "Were many of the press present?" If the Council session went well from our viewpoint, and was fully reported, the atmosphere in MacArthur's office immediately relaxed; otherwise, it was strained.

In addition to frequent and ill-advised attempts to refute published stories in the world's newspapers, the General and likeminded aides often lashed at State Department representatives for merely reporting what was being printed. During the obviously pro-Communist attack on SCAP by Shanghai newspapers in 1948, for instance, MacArthur personally ordered me to draft a lengthy press release of rebuttal, based upon the accounts of the press campaign transmitted to Tokyo in routine State Department telegrams. This was done, although I felt that little could be accomplished against this propaganda except to provide factual information to our Embassy in Nanking and the Shanghai Consulate General. My press release eventually was made public in Shanghai, but only after it had been modified to eliminate the name-calling which had been inserted by some of SCAP's staff officers.

As the routine State Department telegrams of information reaching Tokyo continued to report anti-SCAP press stories from various parts of the world, I tried to convince MacArthur that this was normal procedure. By relaying word of published criticism, embassy officials merely were carrying out their duty of summarizing the foreign press, without in any way taking sides. My orders from MacArthur, nevertheless, were: "Have the State Department stop this criticism of the Occupation and SCAP!"

One particularly delicate incident of this type resulted from a conventional telegram, known as the weekly press report, which, under unified communications procedure, was filed by the military attaché in Bangkok to Washington, with an information copy for Tokyo. Summarizing the Thai press, the attaché relayed a story that "MacArthur is blocking the return of Siamese gold in Japan, according to a report to the Siamese government from Washington." This was dynamite at SCAP Headquarters, because it was true and because it was based upon a principle which MacArthur felt very strongly. The gold in question allegedly had been deposited in Japan by the wartime Siamese government, an ally of Japan. The successor government in Bangkok now wanted it back. MacArthur was not satisfied with the evidence that had been presented. Further, he felt that existing directives did not authorize him to return the gold merely upon the unilateral demand of the Siamese government.

In any event, MacArthur again sternly instructed me to stop this type of State Department criticism. I pointed out vainly that the telegram was intended only to keep us informed of published press comments. The matter drifted on interminably, until, fourteen months later, SCAP was directed by the United States government to turn over the gold to the Siamese. The huge load of precious metal, valued at more than $43 million, was flown to New York City for deposit.

MacArthur's public quarrels with individual news correspondents became celebrated, during the period when the Occupation commanded headlines. More surprisingly, they never ceased, although this was one battle the General never could win; for the newsmen invariably had the last word in print.*

MacArthur's trait of sentimentality was particularly apparent each January 26, his birthday. Although he worked as usual, his office was open to all who wanted to congratulate him on his birthday—SCAP officials, newsmen, and visitors who knew of the custom. The General obviously relished these visits. He sometimes used them to plant new ideas with his callers, and frequently slipped into a moment of self-revelation during the social occasion. On this day, his always neat desk usually held a single gift, a handmade pipe rack or similar present given to him by his son, Arthur, then a youngster. MacArthur, extremely proud of the boy, sought to give him a normal life by preventing any extraordinary publicity about him. But the birthday gifts could be photographed and described in detail.

During my birthday call in 1949 the General and I talked Japanese politics at some length. General elections had been held three days earlier, and Prime Minister Yoshida's Democratic Liberal party had won. "The elections," said MacArthur, "were a great victory for the conservatives and will stabilize Japanese politics for four years." When he had finished this summation, I said: "General, I would like to quote a Japanese proverb which

---

* In most cases, these press skirmishes were magnified out of all proportion. A few of the resident press corps continually attacked MacArthur, not always accurately or justifiably, and some in turn were criticized publicly by SCAP spokesmen. MacArthur privately accused most of these controversial newsmen of ultraleftist sympathies, naming also a couple of alleged ultrarightists. These labels were largely justified. In the early Occupation years, the press corps itself was so divided ideologically that the majority seldom spoke to a closely linked leftist minority. Some of this dissident group wrote obviously distorted copy, and a few appeared to involve themselves directly in Japanese political affairs. The majority of the press corps, however, was

says, 'In victory, tighten your helmet strings.' " * I explained that the history of Japanese politics demonstrates that no party in power remains stable, adding that any weakening of the ruling party, at that time, could only benefit the Communists. "I therefore hope," I said, "that we will not pull the rug out from under the government."

I think the General was rather annoyed by this remark. His voice dropped and he obviously held himself in check as he said: "I will, of course, support the government as may be appropriate."

The exchange was part of our frequent differences of opinion over the strength of communism within Japan. In addition to his comment to me that the Communist influence in Japanese labor was overrated, MacArthur had expressed belief that the Soviet Mission was "incompetent and lazy." To this I could not agree, and I said so. In the Allied Council, we bore the brunt of the cold war attacks planned and organized by the 400-odd Russians working in the Soviet Mission at that time.

Despite these privately expressed views of MacArthur, he engineered the most stinging rebuke to the Soviets that I have seen in a diplomatic document. One day I was summoned to see the General in the Dai Ichi building, "at once." MacArthur already was in consultation with staff officers when I arrived, discussing the reply to an official protest by the Soviet member of the Allied Council over the maintenance and strengthening of American bases in Japan and Okinawa. The Soviet letter of com-

---

conscientious and honest, and covered the Occupation fairly and thoroughly. Although I wrote many factual stories contradicting SCAP communiqués, MacArthur never refused to see me and never mentioned my copy. Covering Headquarters was far more difficult than covering Washington, and "freedom of the press" often was curtailed. I believe this was due less to MacArthur's policies than to the fact the Occupation was conducted by military men. They preserved their customary military sense of supersecrecy and doubtless would have done so under any circumstances. This assessment, of course, does not nullify the fact that SCAP was hypersensitive and that many official statements were grossly inaccurate and misleading. But a conscientious reporter usually could dig out the facts.—R.B.

  * *Katte kabuto no o wo shimeyo!*—a phrase attributed to Ieyasu, founder of the Tokugawa Shogunate.

plaint, furthermore, had been given to the press before delivery to Headquarters, a flagrant discourtesy which made MacArthur furiously angry. The draft reply was a scorcher. I said so, and made several suggestions for deletions, which were accepted. Even so, the SCAP reply ended on the note that the Soviet member's letter was a "provocative impertinence."

When I called on the General on his seventieth birthday, in 1950, he was in fine form; witty, and happy to see his callers. Upon leaving I congratulated him on his good health and appearance and expressed the hope that I might be as vigorous if I reached the same age. "Bill," he said, "I feel like a one-horse shay. I am the only one on active service from the Military Academy prior to the class of 1909." His class, incidentally, was 1903. "General," I said, "you can't have it both ways; experience is garnered only over the years, and age and experience therefore usually go together." Later, as I thought over this remark, I felt that I had been somewhat presumptuous, especially as MacArthur successively had been the youngest in these positions: division commander in France during World War I, active major general, superintendent of West Point, chief of staff of the Army, and full general. However, he did not seem to mind.

It was ironic that six months to the day from that comment, the Korean War involved MacArthur in one of the most frustrating military operations any American commander has faced. The "one-horse shay" was obliged, of course, to continue his multitudinous duties as SCAP while directing the campaign in Korea, an added element which drew deeply on his reserves of age and experience.

Of all his nonmilitary skirmishes, MacArthur's relations with the State Department probably have been reported in the fullest detail. These relations generally have been described as universally bad. This is not correct. On the whole, they were excellent at the top level. They became increasingly worse, however, at the lower levels of SCAP and State Department. But this was not necessarily all one-sided; that is, it did not result entirely from

SCAP's attitude toward State. Symptomatic of MacArthur's distrust of the State Department lower echelons were his warnings to me, on at least two occasions, that "the bureaucrats" were after my job and would be happy to have it occupied by someone with career ambassadorial rank.

At the start of the Occupation, MacArthur told me, the State Department lacked understanding of the proper functions of a political adviser to SCAP. The result was that George Atcheson's office was treated, by both State and SCAP, as a separate and independent organization. "It was only when the Diplomatic Section was organized at my suggestion," the General said, "that a closely coordinated and integrated American effort became possible." He made these comments while reminiscing about the early period of SCAP, before my arrival in January, 1946. The pertinency of his remarks was emphasized, however, by George Atcheson's statement in 1946, that relations between his office and SCAP were correct but neither warm nor close.

It should have been quite obvious that two separate American organizations during the Occupation would cause a conflict of policy and would not work. The system of accrediting the State Department representative to SCAP and simultaneously making him head of a SCAP section, under which I operated, seemed to be the only method by which an integrated American effort could be made to function. There were problems of authority and loyalty, but they were less repressive than the original plan of maintaining two competitive branches of the American government.

MacArthur had an unusually broad view of foreign affairs, for a military man, and this characteristic, no doubt, prevented many problems that otherwise might have arisen. By contrast, the Chief of Staff during the latter years of MacArthur's service, Major General Ned Almond, looked upon diplomatic affairs as an unholy nuisance. In his view foreign diplomats as such had no standing whatsoever in a military occupation. They were just there. As for the State Department, he simply did not like it and flatly told me so. But Almond's blind spot, as I regarded it, did not make life any smoother for the chief of the Diplomatic Section, whose job, among other things, required obtaining SCAP-controlled housing and rations on behalf of sensitive and temperamental foreign diplomats.

During much of 1949 there were recurrent rumors out of Washington that the State Department was about to take over control of the Occupation. I had no information on this point and was unable to understand any reason for the speculation. If the report had been true, I would have opposed the change on the ground that the State Department was not an operating agency. It could not properly undertake such a gigantic operation, and to do so would weaken the department's main function of advising the President on foreign relations. The Army, to my mind, of all United States government departments, was best able to conduct the job.

Nevertheless, the speculation continued, largely through press reports, and MacArthur became increasingly irritated and annoyed. The implication, of course, was that the General was not doing his job properly and that the State Department could do it better. Moreover, such a change would have meant that MacArthur, for the first time, would leave an unfinished assignment. He asked me one day whether these rumors were being fed to the press by interested parties in the State Department. If so, he demanded to know the names of those responsible. I replied that, in my opinion, the stories were generated by the newsmen themselves. We never discussed this topic again.

Whatever latent suspicions MacArthur might have retained, he was always courteous and cooperative during the frequent visits of senior Foreign Service officers. It was my custom, when one of these officials arrived, to seek an interview for him with SCAP. Not one of these requests was turned down, and the General always was gracious and gave generously of his time. One of these occasions arose when Everett F. Drumright arrived in Tokyo to become my counselor. During our interview MacArthur amazed both of us with his detailed knowledge of the China of his day, Drumright being an old China hand. We got on to the subject of economics, and MacArthur expressed his basic philosophy. He deprecated the general leveling down of wealth and its corollary, the lack of incentive created by the ease with which lower economic groups benefited from this process. The General also advocated basing a nation's currency on a stable supply of gold as the only method of maintaining confidence, a subject of great significance at the time in inflationary Japan.

The mood was different in advance of a scheduled visit by W. Walton Butterworth, Assistant Secretary of State for Far Eastern Affairs, in February, 1950. To my surprise, the atmosphere around Headquarters was somewhat frigid, although normally staff officers hospitably received top-ranking Department of State officials. When I asked MacArthur the reasons for this atmosphere, he told me, quite frankly, that Butterworth had the reputation of being "anti-Occupation" and "anti-MacArthur." I had found no evidence to support this supposition during an earlier trip to Washington and doubted the report. The General said that, whatever the truth, he wanted Butterworth treated with full dignity. Later MacArthur had a lengthy interview with Butterworth and invited him to luncheon, with no sign that any suspicions had been voiced.

Although the outbreak of the Korean War transformed Tokyo into a military command post, the parade of foreign visitors continued and the complex problems of the Occupation grew more numerous. The demands upon MacArthur's time were incredible. Nevertheless, he was the head of our temporary government and was expected to fulfill that role, regardless of his other commitments. This circumstance involved me in another thankless and unpleasant wrangle during the early war period.

Sir Alvary Gascoigne, the widely traveled and normally mildmannered head of the United Kingdom Liaison Mission, had sought to call upon MacArthur for several weeks, without success. This was due partly to MacArthur's increased burdens. It seemed that the British diplomat had complained to his Foreign

Office about being kept in purdah. London, in turn, had instructed its Washington Embassy to take up the matter informally with the State Department. One of our officers then wrote to me, asking that I speak to the General. As the letter contained a reasonable request and in no way attempted any derogation of authority, I allowed the General to read it.

The reaction was immediate. MacArthur burst into a long tirade, charging that a State Department clique was attempting to undermine his position. I strongly disagreed and said that the writer of the letter had acted in a perfectly straightforward manner. He replied that he had not meant to imply that the letter had not been written in good faith. When I then suggested that it might be useful were he to meet occasionally with various chiefs of diplomatic missions in Tokyo to give them a firsthand rundown on Korea, he promptly said that this would serve no useful purpose; moreover, they had no responsibility for Korea. "And why," he added, "as a sovereign, should I? President Truman doesn't do so, nor does the King of England or any other head of state. However, I will see any chief of mission who has legitimate business to transact."

This brief skirmish was followed by a pillorying of the State Department which, he said, he would one of these days "blast wide open." From all this I gained the impression that someone in Washington was feeding highly distorted information to MacArthur and that the motives of the rank and file of the department were suspected by him. I did not feel that the General's outbursts were directed against me. On the contrary, with me the General was consistently courteous and friendly. But on occasions such as this, I figuratively dug in my heels and refused either to budge or to become angry, despite the outbursts against "Washington interference, headed by the State Department crowd." I knew that, once I allowed my inner feelings to show, my usefulness in every sense would be gone.

Procedurally, the relations between my POLAD office and SCAP Headquarters remained complicated. One aspect of this conflict was MacArthur's disposition to conduct, on his own, business which the State Department considered within its province. This point was never adequately settled, although the General often was very polite about his interference. Once, in March, 1950, when I was instructed by Washington "to consult" the General about a proposed policy matter, he blandly told me he already had taken action and I should not bother about the question. Pointing out that I had been instructed to pursue the problem and to report back to my superiors in the department, I argued that I should be allowed, at least, to carry out my orders. The General expressed regret about the whole affair; but I felt, accurately, that it would happen again.

The second aspect of this controversy was the long attempt to obtain use of my own and separate codes for purely State Department business. This issue had become rather symbolic of the department's effort to maintain some form of separate identity in Occupied Japan. After lengthy negotiations, the Army and State Departments reached an agreement in Washington, the gist of which was telegraphed to me. It provided, in essence, that POLAD could have his own codes "for use at his discretion" to transmit official communications to Washington, without routing them through SCAP Headquarters for clearance. When I produced the telegram, however, MacArthur said he preferred retaining the current system of integrating the State Department mission within his Headquarters. He insisted he could not allow one of his subordinate commands to communicate with Washington without his knowledge. In that case, he said, the United States would have to establish a separate mission for the State Department, with the same status and relative inaccessibility of other diplomatic missions. And, finally, he would appoint one of his own officers as chairman of the Allied Council, because he contended it would be improper to have the head of the United States Mission in that position.

These conditions, in my view, would divide the United States effort in Japan too much, and the result would not warrant pressing the issue, merely to obtain the convenience of my own codes. Accordingly, I told the General I would prefer leaving the situation unchanged. He agreed. But a week later, when I showed him a copy of the Army-State agreement, he said, surprisingly, there was no objection to the use of State Department codes on business which was purely that of State, in which he did not have a primary interest! After some further discussion I was ordered finally in May, 1950, to place our own codes into immediate effect. This accomplishment had taken four years and nine months.

Perhaps the most serious single issue between MacArthur and State Department officials in Washington was over the status and future of Formosa. As early as 1949 this question blew into public controversy. Late in that year the contents of a department guidance paper on Formosa became known to the press, producing headlines in many parts of the world. In essence, the paper cautioned State and USIA officials to prepare the groundwork in their areas for the possible loss of Formosa to the Chinese Communists. It did not, as generally supposed, advocate abandoning the island to the Peking regime, but it outlined a number of arguments minimizing its importance in case the Communists took it over.

I was queried by urgent telegram on the news stories, the inference being that either SCAP or the Diplomatic Section had deliberately leaked the story to the press. MacArthur told me he knew nothing about the incident. Apparently assuming that I had inadvertently disclosed the paper, he offered, however, to help me get out of the difficulty. I said that no one in my section, including myself, had even seen the document, hence we could not be involved in making it public. After considerable telegraphing back and forth, it was discovered that several copies of the guidance had been mailed to the SCAP information officer in an unsealed envelope. The corporal on duty, thinking it was a press release, had given it to a correspondent who happened to be talking to him at the time.

This incident was typical of the kind of minutiae with which

121

the Supreme Commander frequently was needled by Washington. Perhaps this is inevitable when a huge bureaucracy is involved. But it was also illustrative of the lack of trust and understanding between Washington and Tokyo which appeared from time to time.

It was public knowledge, however, that MacArthur frequently told visitors Formosa should be saved at all costs, if only for its strategic position, while some Washington officials seemed reconciled to its probable loss. Almost as quickly as they established control over the mainland, the Chinese Communists made the capture of Formosa a major goal. MacArthur's attitude on this point was well-expressed during a talk with Karl L. Rankin, who visited Tokyo in July, 1950. The former consul general in Hong Kong, Rankin had just been appointed chargé d'affaires and minister in Taipei, the capital of Formosa, and later would be named ambassador to the Republic of China, headed by Generalissimo Chiang Kai-shek. Speaking of Chiang, MacArthur told Rankin: "If he has horns and a tail, so long as he is anti-Communist, we should help him. Rather than make things difficult, the State Department should assist him in his fight against the Communists— we can try to reform him later!"

A little more than a month after the Korean War erupted, MacArthur and some of his top military staff made a quick visit to Formosa, to confer with Chiang and his generals. This trip, which was never adequately explained, became a significant factor in President Truman's decision to remove General MacArthur from his commands.* It also added further tensions and controversy to SCAP-State relations.

Two days before his departure on July 31, 1950, MacArthur told me of his intention to make the journey. He asked me to send an alerting telegram to our chargé d'affaires, Robert C. Strong, who was in charge of the Embassy until the impending arrival of Rankin. I notified Strong that the SCAP party of sixteen officers would arrive in two C-54 planes; and later I briefly informed

* See pp. 225ff.

Dean Rusk, Assistant Secretary of State for Far Eastern Affairs, when the group left Japan. Otherwise I expected to play no role in the affair.

On August 3, however, the Secretary of State instructed me to ask the General for further information on the Formosa visit. I had seen MacArthur once after his return from the two-day visit to Taipei, but he had appeared tired and promised to tell me about the trip later. When I relayed Secretary Acheson's request for information, MacArthur made it clear that he had no intention of providing details. He replied, in effect, that the talks were purely military in nature, that they were limited to matters of military coordination between the Chinese government and himself as theater commander, and hence what was said and done was his sole responsibility and not that of the State Department. But, I insisted, military agreements of this type could eventually have a direct bearing upon the formulation of foreign policy. The General irritably replied: "Bill, I don't know what you are talking about. The Formosa policy already had been established by President Truman's order of June 28, directing the Seventh Fleet to prevent any Communist attack on the island or any assault from Formosa against the mainland."

The General emphasized, however, as he had once before, that Chinese government officials in Taipei believed the State Department was hostile to them. He evidently accepted this Chinese assessment, and felt that it had a bearing on his responsibility to defend Formosa. Referring to my instructions from Washington, MacArthur said the SCAP reply to State would have been most peremptory if I were not in the middle of this disagreement.

During this interview, as always, MacArthur treated me courteously, despite his deep feelings over the principles involved. But the episode was distasteful to me, for I sensed a growing rift between the American authorities in Tokyo and Washington which, if not corrected, could only lead to disaster.

As a direct result of MacArthur's visit to Formosa, President

Truman sent his roving envoy, W. Averell Harriman, to Tokyo for the announced purpose of briefing MacArthur on American policy. Harriman, all business and bustle behind a friendly manner, accomplished his unusual mission in two days, but no details of his talks with MacArthur were made known, not even to SCAP officials. In fact, the underlying purpose of Harriman's visit never was entirely clear to us in POLAD, although we had a definite stake in it. We could only guess, as did many others, that the President was seeking to reinforce his strict policy that Formosa should not be used as a base of operations against Mainland China.

The Harriman visit did provide a peg for another of the interminable and unfortunate press controversies which helped to exacerbate Tokyo-Washington relations. On the day after Harriman's departure from Tokyo, MacArthur showed me a UP dispatch from Washington which quoted the State Department spokesman as saying, in response to a question, that the department did not know why MacArthur failed to take his political adviser on the visit to Taipei. Nor did he know, the spokesman added, whether the General had given me a report of his conversations with Chinese officials. My comment was that, if I had gone along without permission, I would have had my throat cut. "Not," said MacArthur, "before they had boiled you in oil."

More seriously, I was inclined to ignore the Washington story as a transitory episode in the relentless campaign of the press to generate news whenever possible. I had given no indication, and intended none, that I thought MacArthur should have taken me along with his military staff, in my capacity as his political adviser and State Department representative. On the contrary, I accepted MacArthur's decision on the composition of his staff as one of the peculiarities of my job. The General had not asked me to accompany him to Manila or to Seoul for independence ceremonies, nor had he invited me on his various trips to the Korean War fronts. That simply was MacArthur's way of operating.

It was also his way to attack these press criticisms instead of shrugging them off. In response to this particular story, he inserted a specific answer in a press release of August 10 explaining the journey to Taipei. The visit, he said, "dealt solely with the problem of preventing military violence to Formosa as directed by the President—the implementation of which directive is my responsibility. It had no connection with political affairs, and, therefore, no suggestion or thought was ever made from any source whatsoever that a political representative accompany me."

My personal reaction to this newspaper skirmish was deep distress that MacArthur should lend himself to protesting too much about small matters, in this case his failure to invite me; an aspect of the episode which Washington quickly indicated was not an issue. I was concerned that these public statements, far from convincing the world that the United States meant business in Asia, gave aid and comfort to the enemy by demonstrating divisions in our leadership and weaknesses in our national purpose.

This, in outline, was the rough-hewn character of the man who represented the victorious Alliance in defeated Japan. But the Alliance itself became the second front in MacArthur's constant skirmishing with the outside world.

7

Allied Council for Japan

IF MACARTHUR'S INTRACTABILITY and sensitivity sometimes were galling to Washington, they were even less welcome to most of the Allies. Foreign press criticism attacked virtually every aspect of the General's manner and his method of operation. In particular, he was accused of turning the Occupation into an all-American show, thus personally depriving the wartime Allies of a "just" voice in the administration of defeated Japan. From the Allied viewpoint, there was some validity in the charge.

At the outset it was obvious that Washington officials were prepared to accept considerable Allied military and political participation in the Occupation. American dominance was made clear in the Initial United States Post-Surrender Directive. This document also provided that American views would govern in case of a dispute. But the establishment of the Far Eastern Commission and the Allied Council for Japan actually were concessions to Allied demands for a political voice. And President Truman, among others, seemed to expect that a token Soviet occupation force of troops would be stationed in Japan, at least temporarily.[1]

MacArthur, no doubt, would have been justified by his instructions in permitting the Far Eastern Commission to exercise greater influence and authority, and in allowing Soviet armed forces within Japan. Instead, he imperiously froze out all mean-

126

ingful foreign interference. A less resolute commander doubtless would have succumbed to the constant pressures against him. If this had happened, the Occupation itself might well have been a complete fiasco.

Nowhere was this point more clearly illustrated than in the record of the Allied Council for Japan. This organization of the four principal Allied Powers was, as we have seen, created in late 1945 largely as an advisory body for SCAP. Its limited control authority was sharply circumscribed by clear diplomatic language and was never used. Nevertheless, the effort to circumvent these restrictions was continual, and the Council itself quickly became the eye of the cold war hurricane in Japan. The Council's alternate impotency and quarrelsomeness revealed clearly, to my mind, how ineffective any truly international control agency would have been.

MacArthur's battle with the Council began at its opening session, on April 5, 1946. The organization met in the paneled second-floor board room of a building, owned by the Meiji Insurance Company of Tokyo, a short distance from SCAP Headquarters. The building itself had been requisitioned as headquarters for the Far East Air Forces. It swarmed on this occasion with officers, newspapermen, and the curious. There was an air of interest and anticipation in Tokyo, particularly among Japanese who hoped that, somehow, the Council would give them their first voice in Occupation affairs.

But military police guarded all entrances, carefully scrutinizing the special credentials required for attendance at the meeting. Theoretically, Japanese nationals were permitted to attend Council sessions, but they found the MP scrutiny so devastating that all but a hardy few preferred to stay away. In any event, the Japanese were required to enter the building by a back door, a condition which apparently rankled deeply, for years later this practice was mentioned tartly in the memoirs of former Prime Minister Yoshida.

The rather small board room was crowded for the inaugural

session, as it was during all subsequent meetings of importance. Bright camera lights splashed across the polished mahogany table and bored into the eyes of the four Council members and their assembled staffs. Newsmen fought for chairs, and ordinary spectators were packed into every available corner.

The Soviet representative, Lieutenant General Kuzma N. Derevyanko, was a bull-necked man who appeared to have been poured into his tight uniform, with its mortarboard shoulder insignia. He slouched in his chair, smoking a pipe incessantly, and constantly regarding the room with suspicious eyes. Derevyanko spoke only Russian, which was translated, often jerkily, by a frightened covey of interpreters. The Soviet General, who had signed the Japanese surrender as his country's representative, was capable, however, of robust backslapping when the occasion permitted. He became a friendly extravert at frequent diplomatic parties.

In contrast, the British Commonwealth was represented initially by a quick-witted Australian professor, W. Macmahon Ball. He was an M.A. from the University of Melbourne who had studied political science at the University of London and had traveled widely in Europe. Ball's analytical mind and his polished debating ability easily made him the most articulate of the Council members. He used sharp wit on occasion to enliven otherwise austere and serious discussions. Besides reflecting British frustration over many SCAP policies, Ball carried into the meeting room the distrust and bitterness which many Australians held toward the Japanese at that time. With these qualities, the Commonwealth representative often spoke with asperity against SCAP policies. MacArthur regarded him as "something of a gadfly."

Lieutenant General Chu Shih-ming, the Chinese representative, was an erect and proper professional military man. Although the only non-American member on whom SCAP could count at that time for support, he also had moments of protest. General Chu usually remained quiet and impassive during fiery debate, regarding the proceedings with an air of detached boredom. Yet he was quickly conscious of prerogative, and his smooth, rather youngish face did not always hide the disdain he appeared to harbor for the diplomatic spectacle he was obliged to witness.

MacArthur made his one and only appearance before this group, on opening day, in the plain khaki uniform, without decorations, which he had worn since the surrender ceremony. As he opened the session he glanced carefully and searchingly around the table, while the crowded room quieted and motion-picture cameras whirred softly. Speaking in his customary high-pitched voice and reading his own rolling words, the General attempted to hobble the Council tightly in the second sentence of his fifteen minute address.

"As the functions of the Council will be advisory and consultative," he said pointedly, "it will not divide the heavy administrative responsibility of the Supreme Commander as the sole executive authority for the Allied Powers in Japan."

In other words, the bluff Derevyanko, the impatient Macmahon Ball, and the impassive Chu—and the sensitive countries they represented—were dismissed with the blunt, though entirely proper, injunction to avoid interfering in SCAP's administrative business. From that point onward, much drama was provided by SCAP's methods of enforcing this edict and the endeavors of other members to evade it.

MacArthur did commit SCAP to help the Council in its work by providing copies of all directives as they were issued to the Japanese government. Matters of substance, he said, normally would be laid before the Council prior to action. He promised that any advice from the whole Council or any individual member would be welcomed and would be given "most thorough consideration." Finally, he told the Council, there was "nothing in its deliberations to conceal even from the eyes and ears of our fallen adversary." Therefore, "to promote full public confidence in its aims and purposes, it is advisable that all formal sessions be open to such of the public and press as existing facilities will accommodate." The Council was thus, at its inception, sentenced to the full glare of public scrutiny in every act and deed. From the viewpoint of international relations, this procedure had both advantages and disadvantages.

The General also summarized the rather substantial achievements of the Occupation during the little more than seven months that it had been in operation. He spoke strongly against critics "who . . . would exploit as slaves a thoroughly defeated nation and people." He pointed out that the lack of any successful precedent for a military occupation had made it necessary "to devise new guiding principles and new methods." Then he expressed hope that each Council member would exert his best effort to support the "far-reaching policy formulated at Potsdam."

When he came to a discussion of the then impending new Japanese constitution, to be submitted to the next session of the Diet, MacArthur dealt at length with the article outlawing war and formal Japanese military forces. His voice became clouded with emotion and, with obvious sincerity, he made an elaborate appeal for a continued evolutionary march by mankind toward a higher law of international social and political morality, heralded by Japan's renunciation of war. His closing words made clear that this principle was uppermost in his mind:

We sit here in council representatives of the military might and moral strength of the modern world. . . . May we further universal adherence to that higher law in the preservation of peace which finds full and unqualified approval in the enlightened conscience of all of the people[s] of the earth.

MacArthur had made a similar appeal in the hush of the surrender ceremony aboard the U.S.S. *Missouri*. He had repeated it in statements to the Japanese people, and they, at least, had begun to respond with gratitude. Now the words were addressed to a formal body, representing the most powerful military alliance in history. Outside, the unrepaired rubble of war cluttered the streets a few blocks away and the long queues of hungry Japanese continued to march to the countryside for food. The first confrontations of the cold war, in Manchuria and Iran, were dimly distant.

MacArthur's voice faded away into silence. There was a rustle of papers, someone cleared his throat, and the General quickly departed, with his immediate staff. Admonished, placated, and challenged, the Council settled back to its work. MacArthur had yielded the chairmanship to one of his closest combat friends, the late Major General William F. Marquat. An easygoing, affable antiaircraft officer, Marquat looked and often talked like a football coach.

Now, in his first plunge into diplomacy, he settled himself into the chairman's chair and opened the meeting to the business of adopting rules of procedure. A stocky man of action, the chairman made every effort to be informal, reasonable, and amenable to compromise. But wholehearted, unanimous agreement quickly became impossible, as each member advanced his own, predetermined ideas of how to proceed. Derevyanko quickly demanded the elimination of all newspaper representatives. General Chu quietly but firmly requested "a little more comfortable way" of meeting by extinguishing the glaring photographers' lights. Macmahon Ball suggested that the Council meet formally in public and informally without press coverage, a motion that was adopted.

Eventually, a loose set of rules was agreed upon, only to be broken immediately by the Soviet representative. Speaking rapid, guttural Russian, General Derevyanko made a request which struck me, seated with the SCAP advisers, as a tip-off on what to expect from the Soviets for the remainder of the Occupation. He attacked the "increasing activity of the reactionary forces during the election campaign" which was under way in Japan. The Soviet member then demanded that SCAP warn the country that all elected members of the Diet would be checked, and if the majority proved "unsuitable," new elections would be ordered. This may have been only propaganda, but it followed the typical self-serving Communist line.

Marquat, attempting to be agreeable, noted that the meeting was designed only to adopt rules of procedure, but he accepted comments from the members to forward to SCAP. Derevyanko thereupon read into the record a request for numerous documents of various types, retroactive to the beginning of the Occupation, and on a continuing basis. More bluntly, he sought to make the Council into a restraining influence on SCAP, despite MacArthur's warning, by demanding copies of all draft orders to the Japanese at least seven days before issuance. The result obviously would have been to delay and further complicate the already complex operations of Headquarters. Nevertheless, Macmahon Ball supported the Soviet's requests in part and did so with considerable persuasiveness. For different purposes, both men, it appeared, were attempting to endow the Council with more authority than its terms of reference justified.

With this beginning, the second session of the Council, two weeks later, became unique, to say the least, in the annals of such international organizations. MacArthur's closest adviser, Brigadier General Courtney Whitney, appeared in person to answer a formal request by the Soviet representative for a progress report on the implementation of the political purge. Derevyanko had made the mistake of asking for an appropriate SCAP official to inform the Council on this question "as fully as possible." Whitney obliged, by reading a three-hour report, with a one-hour break for lunch. As head of SCAP's Government Section, Whitney was, of course, the suitable official for this task. Moreover, he was a lawyer well-accustomed to verbal rough-and-tumble tactics. Behind a rather mild face and a soft voice, he hid a caustic wit and fierce dedication to MacArthur.

Whitney's address and an additional hour of procedural wrangling stretched this marathon second meeting across eighty-three pages of minutes. Nothing was accomplished, and the session was resumed two days later. Whitney appeared again and the following exchanges took place:

BRIG. GEN. WHITNEY: . . . The Supreme Commander will reserve the right at any time to send representatives before this Council. . . . The Council is here for the purpose of constructive assistance only . . .

MR. BALL: On a point of order, Mr. Chairman, may I interrupt please? Mr. Chairman, didn't I understand that we are going to confine ourselves to procedural questions this morning?

BRIG. GEN. WHITNEY: This is a procedural question. I am not in agreement that matters in answer to propositions placed in the agenda be submitted in written form. I say that the Supreme Commander, at any time that a criticism is publicly leveled at his administration, is entitled to come himself or to send representatives before this Council and just as publicly give the answer.

LT. GEN. DEREVYANKO: I am interested to ask what is the reason for a belief that the Council Members intended to criticize the Supreme Commander? What is the reason for such a speech?

MR. BALL: Now, do I understand General Whitney to indicate that it is for SCAP and not the Council in certain circumstances to determine how we shall conduct our business? I am not sure how General Whitney is speaking this morning—as a member of SCAP, as a member for the United States, or in what capacity.

THE CHAIRMAN (*Maj. Gen. Marquat*): Well, I invited General Whitney to speak for me in this instance.[2]

Thus, the pattern for public and widely covered meetings was established early. MacArthur did not attempt again to talk the Council to death, but he was unyielding against attempts to dilute his authority. A three-cornered fight soon emerged: the overriding East-West conflict; a controversy between SCAP and the Council, collectively anxious for more stature; and finally, numerous publicly voiced divergences of opinion over the philosophy of the Occupation. These ranged from differences between the United States and its allies over the severity with which to treat the Japanese to specific criticisms that SCAP was both too "liberal" and too "conservative" in its policies.

Marquat gratefully relinquished the chairmanship after refereeing the second meeting, and George Atcheson took over the position. During the first year, until his death in mid-August, 1947, sixty-four subjects were placed on the Council's agenda, covering almost every major problem of the Occupation. The growing importance of the United States–Soviet clash dominated nearly every session. This was reflected by the fact that, of the agenda items, thirty-three were proposed by the Soviet representative and twenty-eight by the United States member. Macmahon Ball introduced two topics, and General Chu one. On the whole, the meetings were orderly and decorous, but the atmosphere frequently became tense.

In general, the SCAP subjects on the agenda were designed to explain publicly and constructively certain policies which were being implemented or to provide progress reports on long-range reforms. In this respect, the Council served as a sounding board to inform the Japanese on such vital subjects as educational changes, improvements in public health, and encouragement to labor unions. It served also as an arena to seek Allied support, if only by indirection, for SCAP policies.

It was not surprising, therefore, that the Soviet member failed to offer a constructive topic throughout the life of the Council. Invariably his items for the agenda were designed solely to forward Soviet aims, in three main categories, and this purpose was pursued with increasing sharpness. First, the Soviets attempted to embarrass SCAP in the eyes of the Japanese masses, hoping thereby to reduce the immense prestige of the United States. Secondly, Moscow sought to make maximum use of the Council to support the Communist party of Japan. Finally, the Council became a weapon to forward the strategic plans of the Soviet Union in Japan and Northeast Asia.

Derevyanko and his alternates carried out these objectives with single-minded intensity, considerable ruthlessness, and thorough unscrupulousness. They were, in effect, high-level propagandists, and nearly every sentence they uttered in public sessions appeared to have been carefully weighed for its propaganda effect, both in Japan and elsewhere. In particular, the opening Soviet statement at each important session was calculated to create a specific issue capable of catching world headlines. It apparently made no difference to the Soviet member whether his statements were true or false; or whether, as often happened, they were based merely upon wild rumors planted by Communist agents in some docile and obscure newspaper in the free world. The Soviets knew the advantage of taking the initiative, through criticism or by making harsh charges. They knew, too, that sensational remarks became news and, in most cases, would win prominence in the well-represented "capitalist" press. The American member, backed into denial and explanation, seldom could overcome the original charge, because world interest quickly shifted. Worse, he was often forced by his denials into lending authenticity to the most implausible charges which the world otherwise might have ignored.

But the Soviets were not always clever or successful. Time and again the Russian representatives on the Council proved that they were more familiar with bombast, distortion, and propaganda than with substantive and procedural debate.

Derevyanko's apparent inability to foresee his adversary's reaction had permitted General Whitney's "filibustering" speech. And the Soviet member made a similar mistake during an evident attempt to embarrass me when I conducted my first business meeting as chairman, after George Atcheson's death in 1947. I was aware that the Soviets usually seek to test and to dominate any new Western official facing them for the first time in a responsible position. With ammunition at hand, I opened the Council meeting prepared to move into any opening that the Soviet member might give. The chance came during a discussion of some leftover business from Atcheson's tenure. He had informed the members that SCAP no longer would compile detailed information in special form for the Council, "except in appropriate need."

When I raised the question again, Derevyanko protested against what he called this "change of procedure." Diplomacy being what it is, that was all the opening I needed. Promptly I launched into a lengthy recapitulation of the Council's status, as SCAP saw it. My purpose was to capture the initiative and to prove that I would not allow myself to be needled through the device of a procedural attack, and I felt that both objectives had been achieved. For some time I had believed that we had lost the initiative, and I was determined not to allow this again. As Mac-Arthur once said to me on this highly important technique: "Bill, spit in his eye first. That gives you the initiative and puts him on the defensive." This may have been inappropriate advice for diplomacy, but I never forgot it.

Furthermore, the Soviets were incredibly clumsy and inept whenever the debate left their favorite battleground of emotion and vituperation and entered areas where their callous thrust for power could be countered by facts, figures, and dates. An opportunity to do this arose during the Occupation, most notably, on the sad and vital question of the repatriation of Japanese prisoners of war. With many lapses, this problem dominated the Council for more than three years. Accordingly, it will be discussed at some length here, both as one of the major stories of the Occupation and as a further illustration of the Council's role in the East-West conflict.

At the end of the war more than six million Japanese civilians and soldiers remained in the overseas empire which Japan had carved out for itself. Under the Potsdam Declaration, they were to be repatriated to their homeland. Moreover, reverse repatriation was available for more than one million Koreans, Chinese, and Ryukyuans who were in Japan largely against their will, having served for the most part as forced laborers during the war. SCAP made this a top priority project. Amid the momentous problems of the early Occupation days, considerable attention was given to the interchange of these men, women, and children cast in the backwater of war.

In June, 1946, George Atcheson first raised before the Council the failure of Soviet Russia to participate in this program. Since the previous October, Atcheson reported, the repatriation of Japanese from United States-controlled areas had been 93 percent completed. The total was 94 percent from Chinese-controlled regions, less Manchuria, and 68 percent from regions under the British. No Japanese had been returned from the territory conquered by the Red Army during its brief war. The exact number of Japanese captured by the Soviets during that thrust and their "whereabouts are unknown to General Headquarters," Atcheson reported. A year later the total of Japanese remaining in Soviet hands was estimated to be 761,000, but Soviet intransigence prevented Allied and Japanese authorities from obtaining any precise figure.

Great pressures had been rising for the return of the Japanese prisoners of the Soviets, and SCAP had been applying a considerable amount of backstage persuasion on the Russians to release them. Involved was virtually the entire Kwantung Army, including thousands of young conscripts. Large numbers of Japanese civilian men, women, and children also had been caught by the swift Red Army drive. The Japanese government, in addition to anxious relatives, had been demanding word of the prisoners with increasing concern.

Yet, the first Soviet response to Atcheson's oblique attack in the Allied Council was a feeble and fruitless effort to contend that the status of the prisoners was none of the Council's business. The weakness of the Soviet case gave SCAP a modest though hollow victory. Nevertheless, for some unaccountable reason, the repatriation question did not reappear on the agenda for more than another year. SCAP continued to prod the Soviets through normal nonpublicized diplomatic channels. As one result, Moscow changed its position and authorized Derevyanko to sign a formal agreement for limited repatriation. This arrangement, concluded on December 19, 1946, provided for the return of 50,000 Japanese prisoners monthly.

As chairman I again placed the matter before the Allied Council on October 29, 1947. I contended, quite accurately, that the Soviets were sabotaging the effort to complete repatriation. It was then that I revealed the estimate of 761,000 prisoners still in Soviet hands. By contrast, I pointed out that a total of 5,765,244 had been repatriated from other areas by October 23. Excluding about 67,000 who had been captured in Manchuria, only about 10,000 remained to be brought back from China proper and Southeast Asian areas. In addition, an aggregate of 1,170,000 Chinese, Koreans, and Ryukyuans had been sent to their home-lands from Japan.

The Soviets had begun repatriation under the agreement with SCAP, and the estimate which I gave the Council represented those still remaining in Red Army prison camps. Moscow, as usual, had interpreted the accord its own way, as meaning an *average* of 50,000 monthly, instead of setting this figure as the *minimum,* which SCAP envisioned. Accordingly, the Soviets maintained an average of 49,454 returnees monthly. This figure was made possible by a relatively large number of releases from the Dairen area at the outset of repatriation. The monthly totals dropped during the four months beginning in June, 1947, as Moscow began to weed out the prisoners who had been captured farther north.

The crowded Council chamber was silent, except for the flutter of cameras, as I made these points, slowly and deliberately. The Soviet member was seated almost opposite me, and I spoke directly to him. General Derevyanko had been recalled tempo-rarily to Moscow and, on this occasion, his place was taken by Major General A. P. Kislenko, a dour man who merely glanced at an empty pad in front of him while I talked.

"If you accept," I said directly to Kislenko, "SCAP is prepared to assure you, within forty-eight hours, that there will be enough shipping to return 131,500 repatriates in one month. In thirty days, we can step up this rate of flow to 160,000 per month."

Kislenko remained sullenly silent. One of the half dozen ad-visers behind him blinked. The tension in the room grew stronger.

"Within five months," I added, "SCAP is prepared to return to Japan every Japanese now in Soviet-controlled areas."

A soft murmur floated through the Council chamber. No one

spoke, but the rustle of paper in the press section became a dialogue of headlines.

The Soviet authorities, I pointed out, had failed to provide any information on their prison camps, and the resultant concern within Japan had bred numerous rumors, including the widely believed estimate that the death rate was between 20 and 30 percent. Of the many thousands of officers in the Kwantung Army, only 2,005 had been returned. Although hundreds of generals and admirals were known to have been captured, only one former rear admiral and one ex-lieutenant general had reached Japan.

"We have substantial evidence to show," I continued, "that the Soviet authorities are carrying out intense efforts to indoctrinate selected prisoners in anti-American and anti-Occupation feelings."

Kislenko had not moved, and he did not react visibly as I continued to voice a number of other arguments. When I had finished, Kislenko began to reply in the robot fashion to which we had become accustomed, as if hundreds of thousands of prisoners, the fears of an anxious nation, or even the mounting emotion within the Council chamber could be ignored, on Moscow's command.

". . . the discussion and solution of the problem of the repatriation of the Japanese from Soviet territory," he said in a flat, dry voice, reading from a paper before him, "is not within the purview of the Allied Council for Japan."

Kislenko followed the traditional Communist pattern during the remainder of his long, rambling presentation. He made little attempt to refute my arguments or to meet them on their merits. Instead, he confined his reply to an exaggerated attack upon the unemployment of repatriates within Japan and the alleged lack of assistance to these unfortunates by the Japanese government and SCAP. Although I had specifically discussed the elaborate organization which existed to give the returnees financial and physical help, Kislenko attempted to bolster his charges with a number of rather flimsy Japanese newspaper articles. Finally, he complained bitterly about "propaganda hostile to the Soviet Union with regard to repatriation."

The Soviets were completely isolated on this issue. The British Commonwealth and Chinese members fully supported SCAP during the Council meeting. The Japanese and foreign press, as might be imagined, gave wide play to the session, bulwarking the SCAP position. Although the Japanese press was prohibited from criticizing any of the Allied Powers, a steady stream of editorials and comments made it clear that repatriation was demanded. Many Japanese friends called to thank me for bringing up the issue, and I received hundreds of letters and telegrams of appreciation from individuals throughout Japan.

MacArthur, who had seen the wire stories, seemed pleased with the session and complimented me on the way I had handled this difficult subject. He said, however, that he felt we should give the Soviet member an opportunity to show what could be done to improve the rate of repatriation. During succeeding weeks the Soviets made no move, of course, to step up the return of prisoners or to accept the offer I had made before the Council. There the matter rested. On several occasions I recommended to MacArthur that we reinstate the repatriation issue in the Council. But he had decided to let the Allied body wither into uselessness, and I could not change his mind. As month followed month, I informed the General that a number of Japanese friends had relayed to me the great disappointment felt by relatives of the prisoners that SCAP was doing nothing to hasten their return. The question was not returned to the agenda, however, for another twenty-six months.

Despite the constructive effect of the repatriation issue, the general performance of the Council had been discouraging from SCAP's viewpoint. A large number of important questions had been placed on the agenda, but it soon became evident that the members seemed more prone to criticize SCAP actions and policies than to support them publicly. It was rare, indeed, for even the British and Chinese representatives to voice spontaneous satisfaction or gratification over what had been accomplished. Macmahon Ball had resigned and returned to Australia, so his particular brand of criticism was removed. His successor, Patrick Shaw, was a pleasant and cooperative man. I often frankly discussed some of my problems with him and always felt free to do so.

As for the Soviet member, his contributions usually were carping, critical, and damaging to the best interests of the United States.

These circumstances, and the resultant "bad press," irritated MacArthur. The General felt that he was carrying out the intentions of the Moscow Agreement, at the cost of considerable time and effort, by providing special reports to the Council. The returns, as he saw it, were not worth the effort. Accordingly, MacArthur decided to allow the Council to drift, to avoid any effort to keep it alive, and above all, to prevent SCAP from again becoming the target for what he believed was ill-informed and unfair criticism.

As a result, the Council did, indeed, languish during the full years of 1948 and 1949. Out of fifty-three meetings, there were no agenda items for forty-seven, and they followed a swift adjournment procedure that usually lasted less than a minute. During these two years the Soviet member placed four subjects on the agenda, the Commonwealth representative one, and, at the last meeting of 1949, SCAP provided one item.

The SCAP question again was repatriation, a subject for which I had received MacArthur's concurrence for rather unusual reasons. During the long silence on this topic, pressures within Japan had risen alarmingly. There was a distinct possibility, for one thing, that they would result in violent demonstrations against the Soviet Mission, a development which, under the circumstances of the Occupation, SCAP was obliged to prevent. I had received an avalanche of postcards and letters urging SCAP action from relatives and friends of the imprisoned Japanese; a flood that, quite literally, totaled perhaps one million communications.

Citing these points to MacArthur on December 14, 1949, I renewed my request for another Council session on the question. To my great satisfaction, MacArthur agreed to revive the issue before the Council. He said he rarely struck until he was ready but, when he did, he used every force at his disposal. This was a matter of timing, he added, and now the timing was right. "Go ahead," the General told me, "and pull no punches." The subject, therefore, was announced for the 102nd meeting of the Council, on December 21, 1949, with the requisite five days' notice.

The Council chamber was crowded when I arrived ten minutes before the 10 A.M. meeting, with my counselor, Cloyce Huston, and C. Nelson Spinks, head of the political section. Promptly at 9:59 we entered the floodlighted chamber. The other three members were already seated, their staffs clustered around them. General Derevyanko had returned from Moscow and occupied the Soviet chair opposite me. He shook off my greeting, his blunt face stony and unsmiling.

As soon as the session had been opened and the minutes of the previous meeting approved, General Derevyanko raised a procedural question. The complaint was quickly buried, and I announced that consideration of the repatriation issue would begin.

Derevyanko again interrupted and, obviously under Moscow instructions, read a brief formal statement. "I do not deem it possible," he said, "for me to take part in the discussion at this meeting of the question which is not within the scope of the Allied Council and I reserve the right to return to these questions." He then picked up his papers and, followed by his advisers, stalked out of the room. This act scarcely produced a ripple among the spectators.

Ignoring the walkout, I proceeded with the SCAP presentation. My statement was a 5,000-word recapitulation of the status of Soviet-held Japanese prisoners, based upon the calculation that

376,000 were still missing. This figure was distilled from the interrogation of hundreds of thousands of returned Japanese soldiers and civilians, carefully cross-checked and rechecked. Working with the Japanese government and with the office of Major General Charles A. Willoughby, MacArthur's chief of intelligence, we had assembled an impressive array of dramatic, but saddening, information about this army of missing men. In numerous conferences during the week before the Council session, we hammered down facts and figures until I was completely satisfied that every aspect of my official presentation was based upon credible evidence.

Our information was gathered, then, while the Soviets were trying to kill this vital issue with silence. In order to forestall a possible effort to plead again that the question did not concern the Occupation or the Council, I had brought four huge bales of letters and postcards to the table. Another 102 bales of similar size were in an outer office. They contained the estimated more than one million communications on repatriation which had been received from interested Japanese during the preceding month.

As I proceeded with the carefully documented indictment, which my formal statement became, the Soviet prison camps and their ragged, neglected inmates became real in the Council chamber; and perhaps it was no wonder Derevyanko did not want to be present.[3] I demonstrated, for example, that in the first sixteen months probably 51,332 out of 209,300 prisoners in certain camps had died of malnutrition and disease. This was a calculation based upon the interrogation of returnees, and it covered the period from the end of the war to 1946, admittedly the worst months, when the Soviet authorities were ill-prepared for their hordes of prisoners. We found, also, that the percentage of deaths decreased with time, presumably because the weakest had died early and camp conditions became more stabilized.

This abnormally high early death rate of perhaps 25 percent was due, we discovered, to disease, exposure, insufficient clothing, malnutrition, fatigue, forced marches in bitterly cold weather, inhuman working conditions, and sheer neglect by the Soviet authorities.

By reconstructing the available evidence we computed the probable death toll at 374,041 for the period through 1948. This was strikingly close to the figure of 376,000 which the Japanese government insisted were missing.

My statement also concentrated upon a second problem of increasing concern to the Japanese and to the Headquarters, the political indoctrination of prisoners into communism. This effort had intensified with time, and those willing to accept Communist tutelage were given preferred status. As I pointed out, "with the candidates in a state bordering on complete prostration, psychologically upset through sudden and final defeat, weakened by gruelling work and with subsistence on semi-starvation-level rations, resistance became understandably low. Their one lifeline was hope of early repatriation." The promising "students" of communism among the prisoners were given further training at special schools, including a "finishing" school. At the port of embarkation, for the return to Japan, usually Nahodka, Siberia, final Communist party rallies were held as the prisoners prepared to board ship. Pledges to join the Japan Communist party were demanded and given.

The results were indicated by the fact that thousands of thoroughly indoctrinated repatriates had arrived in Japan wearing red armbands and carrying red banners. They resisted those who attempted to help them at the Japanese repatriation centers and went their own way. They quickly made contact with local Communist party members, received instructions, then disappeared to help spread the virus of communism throughout the country.

The Soviets attempted their usual counterattack, designed to divert attention from the main issue. Derevyanko immediately fired a somewhat intemperate letter to General MacArthur, castigating the Japanese government for alleged antidemocratic measures concerning trade unions. He also attacked the "Occupation

authorities" for tolerance and indulgence "toward the antidemocratic actions of the Japanese government, the policy which . . .
creates a real menace of the revival of the old fascist order in
Japan." The lengthy letter further listed a number of asserted
"antidemocratic actions" against certain "progressive elements,"
most of which were known to be Communist-dominated organizations.

With their customary tactics in such circumstances, the
Soviets released the letter to the press before MacArthur had
received the original. This was a familiar tip-off that they were
interested primarily in publicity. When I called on the General
later in the day, he handed me Derevyanko's letter, adding a few
unprintable epithets, which he was fully capable of voicing on
appropriate occasions.

"Look at this, Bill," he said, obviously angry. "This is sheer
Communist poppycock."

"Why not ignore it, General?" I commented after reading the
letter. "There is no point in playing it up and giving Derevyanko
the added opportunity of publishing his reply. You might comment on it through the press—and if asked, I could do the same."

"Fine," the General said. "But if you do comment, make it
strong."

MacArthur issued a press release the next day. The General
mentioned the Soviet member's reluctance "to listen to so grue-
some and savage a story in all its harrowing barbarity. It could
well chill and sicken even a hardened soldier." Referring to
Derevyanko's letter, MacArthur said its "moth-eaten charges"
normally could be ignored. "But when . . . they . . . are
freshly dusted off to act as a smokescreen to distract attention
from the investigation of the dreadful fate of hundreds of thousands of Japanese prisoners probably dead on Soviet soil, they
represent a callousness of hypocrisy I cannot fail to denounce."

In my statement, issued several hours later, I referred to the
fact that MacArthur had first read the Soviet letter in the press, "a
rather unusual method for the representative of a foreign govern-

ment to communicate with the Supreme Commander for the Allied Powers." As for the content of the letter, I added, "I can only say that it consists of unadulterated twaddle." The communication itself was an endeavor to evade "the searchlight of public scrutiny of the problem of Japanese repatriation."

I doubt that any diplomat under different conditions could have used such blunt language and long held on to his job. But in those serious days of the cold war in Japan the stakes were great and called for strong and decisive action. What I said and how I performed may not always have followed the precepts of the Congress of Vienna, but there was no time to ask for instructions; to have done so could have been dangerous and certainly would have created embarrassment for the State Department. Therefore, we acted, and hoped for the best.

On December 22, 1949, the day following the "repatriation meeting," as we began to call it, some 400 Japanese staged a sit-down demonstration before the entrance to the Soviet Mission in Tokyo. They were orderly, but refused to move until a delegation of eight leaders was received by Derevyanko, to discuss their petition for the early return of the Japanese prisoners. A Soviet staff member announced that some "bright" news on this problem soon would occur, but no such "news" was ever announced. Instead, about a week later, press reports said twelve Japanese were being tried in the Soviet Siberian city of Khabarovsk as war criminals on the charge of conducting "germ warfare." When asked to comment on this report, I voiced skepticism and suggested that both the trial and the charges were fictional. It seemed logical at the time that the Russians would do their utmost through propaganda to overcome the bad taste left by the Council's discussion of the repatriation issue.

Repatriation was continued for five successive meetings on the Council agenda. Derevyanko again walked out of the first two sessions, then boycotted the remainder. When I revived this question for the meeting of May 10, 1950, the Soviets began a six months' boycott of all Council activities, which lasted until

November 8.

With the strong support of the British and Chinese members on this issue, SCAP continued to press the Soviets on repatriation throughout 1950. Although the Korean War stole the headlines and, in truth, became the dominant element in our daily lives, we on the Council were concerned officially only with the affairs of the Occupation. By this time the return of the Japanese prisoners was our predominant issue. For millions of Japanese it was a far more compelling problem than the hostilities on their doorstep.

In January the Soviets unexpectedly asked for vessels to carry an additional 2,500 Japanese from Nahodka. This may have been the "good news" that the Soviet official had promised the Japanese demonstrators in front of the Soviet Mission a month earlier. But it was not repeated.

Several of the Allied governments protested individually and officially to Moscow. Eventually, the diplomatic approach was climaxed by a formal United Nations resolution, on December 14, 1950, demanding the return of the prisoners. Unfortunately, like so many well-meaning United Nations resolutions, this international protest was nullified entirely by Soviet intransigence.

In general, Moscow responded to these pressures with sullen silence. This attitude meant that our most effective pressure was a public display of harrowing facts, pieced together from patient interrogation of returnees. So I continued to reveal more and more evidence of Soviet Russia's callous policy toward its captives at successive Council meetings. The reports did not make pleasant reading.

In a summary of living conditions, for example, I reported an elaborate system of punishments meted out by Soviet prison authorities for "crimes" by the prisoners. One man, I recall, received a sentence of twenty-five years at hard labor for "stealing" an undershirt. By December 20, 1950, we had sufficient information to show that some 8,000 Japanese prisoners had been convicted of various "crimes" in Soviet Russia. Many of the prisoners served their sentences in Russia, then were simply turned loose, without any provision for food, livelihood, or repatriation. Most of them were reduced to abject beggary.

The Japanese Foreign Office collected additional information from four hundred of these once-convicted Japanese prisoners who, somehow, eventually had returned to Japan. In a formal report, the Japanese authorities reported a policy of calculated intimidation, starvation, beatings, and torture against suspected Japanese prisoners, to induce them to confess. The report further showed that the usual trial was a hoax; no defense was provided for the accused, and there was, of course, no appeal. In many cases the charges did not constitute crimes. Punishment universally was extreme.

A special committee of the Japanese Diet investigated various aspects of repatriation and produced its conclusions. Among other documentation, the committee included forty-four affidavits which affirmed that the leader of the Japan Communist party, the late Kyuichi Tokuda, was in direct communication with the Soviet authorities. The affidavits contended that Tokuda specifically had requested that the Soviet authorities repatriate only the Japanese prisoners who had been properly indoctrinated in communism.

On the whole, the Soviet tactics on this issue served, more than anything else, to create unusual harmony and agreement among the other three Council members. We were not always unified, of course, and familiar disagreements reappeared on other questions considered by the Allied body. But in general, the three non-Communist members presented a solid front, on behalf of much of the world, over the subject most challenging to the Japanese. In playing their hand so badly, the Soviets helped to create this situation.

It is difficult to find a parallel circumstance where a great power has endured a position of impotent defensiveness for four years, against unanimous world opinion, without seeking to improve its situation. Although the repatriation question did not set the world afire, it attracted widespread global attention. Within

Japan it was at this period one of the strongest influences restricting the growth of the Japan Communist party and other leftist groups. Moreover, the Soviet government publicly looked foolish on many occasions, a factor which probably had considerable influence in Moscow. While Tass was attempting to explain away the missing Japanese prisoners with scanty facts and shallow claims that all had been repatriated, for instance, the Japanese government, after painstaking research, produced a list of the names of more than 200,000 missing men known to have fallen into Soviet hands.

Although our efforts were only partially successful in accelerating the repatriation of prisoners, in my view untold thousands of Japanese would not have been allowed to return to Japan at all without the pressures generated by the Allied Council. In the end, condemnatory public opinion had its effect.

THE COUNCIL ALSO EXERCISED a considerable influence in the everyday operations of the Occupation. It had only negligible power, because MacArthur and his deputies, who served as chairmen, saw that it acquired none. But the Allied body served as a most useful device to educate the Japanese people in some of the realities of international life, from which they had been separated for more than a decade. The Japanese maintained a continuing interest in the organization, which was reflected by consistently extensive coverage by press and radio. During most of the Occupation, it was the discussion in the Council that rationalized the reasons for unpopular SCAP decisions; not all policies formulated by the conqueror were popular. As a practical matter, there was no other forum in Japan before which SCAP policies could be explained, discussed, and criticized, thus helping the Japanese to understand them. For psychological and other reasons, it was not even possible to do this in the Japanese Diet, where freedom of speech was guaranteed by the new constitution. In this respect, the importance of the Allied Council cannot be overestimated.

Moreover, as chairman I was in a position to give voice to a future Japan which I believed would arise out of the debacle of war and the buffeting of the Occupation. I did this often, especially in refuting criticism of SCAP policies which were liberal, constructive, and far-reaching in effect. MacArthur once told me during a discussion of how I could help build a solid foundation for the future: "You are the conscience of the Japanese people. No one else can or will do what you are doing."

Consequently, I was often distressed by MacArthur's sensitivity to the Council's discussion of his policies. He appeared to be particularly irritated when the British Commonwealth member asked pertinent questions, which by implication were critical. I felt that honest criticism was constructive and, in the long run, beneficial for our effort. The chairman, I believed, could turn aside criticism voiced only for its own sake or unfair remarks or propaganda. After all, he occupied a high position in the Occupation, and, if necessary, could call upon the entire bureaucracy of Headquarters for information and assistance.

Yet MacArthur ignored the Council for two years rather than risk having unsympathetic comments reported by the world press. Try as I might to obtain MacArthur's concurrence in an attempt to put life into the Council during this period, he was adamant in his refusal, to the point where further pleading on my part became self-defeating. To my mind, this was time lost. I felt that we should have used those two years to explain and justify United States policy which was not always clear or understandable to the depressed Japanese people.

8

War Crimes Trials

THE ALLIES FOUND THEMSELVES far more united in punishing
Japan for its past than in plotting its future. For more than two
years judges from the eleven nations which had curbed Japan's
expansion sat in solemn judgment on the actions and policies of
twenty-five men accused of primary responsibility for nearly two
decades of aggression. Although there were disagreements over
whom to prosecute and what charges to make, a façade of agreement was preserved with remarkable continuity. To the Japanese,
the outside world appeared to be totally aligned against them on
the question of "war guilt," for reasons they could not always
understand.

The major, or Class A, "war criminals," as they were called,
were tried under modified Anglo-Saxon law through the elaborate
machinery of the International Military Tribunal for the Far East
(IMTFE). Prosecution and defense spun out a long, confused,
and wearying story of intrigue, conquest, and brutality from the
mid-twenties to 1945. It was undeniably a bloody and shocking
epoch. But the validity of the trial itself doubtless will be long
debated, as will the wisdom of using a court process to reveal this
military past to the Japanese.

I witnessed the beginning and, unfortunately, the end of this
lengthy ordeal. It began with an ostentatious display of righteous

151

international indignation, which I attended as an interested spectator. It ended with the hanging in obscurity and secrecy of seven of the most prominent defendants, before a small group of official witnesses. Much against my personal desires, I was among them.

The twenty-eight original defendants in this top category of war criminal suspects, the actual leaders and alleged conspirators in the imperialistic era, were arraigned before the IMTFE on May 3, 1946. They had been selected from scores of wartime military and civilian leaders who had been arrested and interrogated by Allied agents during the early days of the Occupation. Only a few of the top militarists had died in action or had committed seppuku, the traditional warrior's disembowelment. One of the major civilian leaders died by suicide, Prince Fumimaro Konoye, a former prime minister accused of furthering Japanese militarist power.

Therefore, the Allies took into custody most of the men considered primarily responsible for nearly twenty years of Japanese aggression. Quite literally, the Allied case was based upon the premise that less than thirty leaders had succeeded in turning an entire nation toward conquest.

The arraignment was intended to be dramatic, but I fear it became only garish. It turned out to be a social event of such importance that anyone who was "somebody" in the Occupation attended the invitational affair. We trooped into an elaborate courtroom which had been constructed from the auditorium of the Japanese war college, located on a fairly high hill near the center of Tokyo. The college, taken over by the war ministry in the closing phases of the war, escaped damage during the fire-bomb raids on the capital. Most of the surrounding residential area of private homes had been destroyed.

Huge floodlights daylighted the courtroom constantly, for movie and still photographers. The large room was rimmed with glassed cubicles, for press and radio representatives and official translators, and the glass glittered in the harsh, white light. To the left of the entrance the courtroom was dominated by a long, polished bench for the judges. It was raised so high that the court indeed appeared to be overpowering. Directly across the room, the prisoners' dock was a plain, three-tiered compartment. Near the center of the room, a witness box stood alone, in the British fashion, surrounded by long tables for lawyers and court attendants.

Official spectators sat in soft theater seats behind a railing near the front of the auditorium. The seats were equipped with earphones and switches for simultaneous translation in Japanese and the main Allied languages. The prisoners had similar equipment. The technique of simultaneous translation, unknown then in Japan, was only one of a number of technical innovations which must have impressed the ex-warlords as they faced trial for aspiring to demonstrate their superiority over much of the world.

The pageantry had a Hollywood touch. The lights and the set were designed to dramatize Japan's perfidy throughout the world. But the Japanese people, who presumably were the prime audience, were limited to a relatively small number of seats in the cramped balcony.

The opening proceedings were delayed for almost an hour, to await the arrival of two of the accused, who were being flown to Tokyo from the south. Finally, the prisoners shuffled into the courtroom, under the stern glances of the judges and the curious stares of the packed spectators' galleries. As they stood blinking in the strong light, guarded by husky and armed young American military police in crisp uniforms, the irony of the setting was complete. The former generals, admirals, prime ministers, and other leaders of Japan wore ill-fitting prison garments. They looked like very ordinary, shrunken old men.

Silence hung heavy over the courtroom, as the accused took their assigned seats in the prisoners' dock. General Hideki Tojo, the prime minister at the time of Pearl Harbor, marched stiffly and defiantly to the front row, looking straight ahead. He managed to retain a semblance of dignity, although the lights were reflected from his bald head and his eyeglasses appeared too large for his lean face. Another ex-prime minister, Koki Hirota, also was stiff and unyielding, but his nondescript clothing made him appear like a down-and-out former businessman. General Seishiro Itagaki, ex-war minister and former commander of the Kwantung Army, came in with a sardonic grin on his sharp face, and kept it there throughout the proceedings. Weazened General Iwane Matsui, whose troops committed the horrible "Rape of Nanking," was fidgety and uncertain. Marquis Koichi Kido, the most powerful civilian in the empire as lord keeper of the Privy Seal, the Emperor's personal adviser, groped myopically for his seat, a moment of indecision for a man whose decisions had helped change the lives of millions.

When they had found their places, the formal indictment was read. In brief, these men were charged with varied degrees of responsibility for what the prosecution contended was a deliberate conspiracy to commit and perpetuate military aggression against much of the world. They were charged also with "crimes against humanity," based on the brutalities which distinguished the overseas reign of Japanese military forces. It was, in essence, the indictment of an epoch and of a nation, under the leadership of unchecked militarists and their civilian collaborators. Tension dominated the courtroom as the charges were enumerated, for nearly everyone present felt he had a personal stake in the proceedings.

Although I was familiar with many of the sordid events covered in the indictment, my instinct told me that, on the whole, it was a mistake to hold the trial. I was not in sympathy with the theory that the victor should try the vanquished for deeds which, in the context of international law at that time, were not crimes, however abhorrent or deplorable they might have been from the viewpoint of philosophical concepts of right and wrong. Contrary arguments of considerable persuasiveness have been made, of course, and history may prove them correct. But my feelings on this point were strong; so strong, in fact, that I felt uneasy throughout this first theatrical court session and I never returned to the courtroom. I did, however, follow the course of the excessively long proceedings until the end.

The trial itself stemmed from a decision reached by the heads of government of the United States, Great Britain, and China at their meeting in Cairo in 1943. They announced on December 1 that "The Three Great Allies are fighting this war to restrain and punish the aggression of Japan." The point was reaffirmed nearly two years later in the Potsdam Declaration. "There must be eliminated for all time," the Declaration said, "the authority and influence of those who have deceived and misled the people of Japan into embarking on world conquest." It added, at another point: ". . . stern justice shall be meted out to all war criminals including those who have visited cruelties upon our prisoners."

With this and other Allied-dictated legal authority, SCAP approved and published the charter of the IMTFE on January 19, 1946. It was patterned after the charter of the military tribunal for the German trials at Nuremberg, and employed some of the identical language. The IMTFE charter named Tokyo as the permanent seat of the Tribunal and specified that SCAP would appoint between six and eleven members from names submitted by signatory nations of the surrender document and by India and the Philippines. The charter also provided for the organization, quorum, voting procedure and practice, and similar operational matters.

As to jurisdiction, the Tribunal was given power "to try and punish Far Eastern war criminals who . . . are charged with offenses which include Crimes against Peace." These were defined, along with conventional war crimes and crimes against humanity. The charter further specified that the Tribunal was not bound by technical rules of evidence. Any evidence which it deemed of probative value was admissible, as were "all purported admissions or statements of the accused." It had the power to impose upon the prisoners, on conviction, death or other punishment which it determined to be just. The Supreme Commander was designated as the reviewing authority, with power to reduce or otherwise alter the sentences, except that he could not increase their severity.

SCAP selected an eleven-judge tribunal and, under his authority, appointed the Australian member, Sir William Webb, as the president.[1] Sir William was a large, florid man, with the bold nose of a Wellington. He had been a distinguished member of the Australian bar since 1913. At appropriate times he was capable of adopting the gravest judicial solemnity or the most urbane type of eye-twinkling wit. Sir William, at fifty-nine, already had been a judge of the Supreme Court of Queensland, Australia, for twenty-one years, and chief justice of Queensland from 1940 to 1946. Subsequently, he was a justice of the High Court of Australia, from 1946 until his voluntary retirement in 1958.

Before coming to Tokyo, Sir William had served for two years as a war crimes commissioner, charged with investigating Japanese war crimes in areas where Australians had taken part in the Pacific War, including New Guinea and Papua. This fact prompted some of the defense counsel for the Japanese prisoners to question whether he should disqualify himself. Nothing came of this move, however, and Sir William presided over the Tribunal with great distinction and dedication throughout its life.

At the outset Sir William told me in an informal conversation that the principles of Anglo-American justice would control both the procedural and the substantive law of the trial. This was probably a wise decision. Seven of the eleven judges on the Tribunal were from jurisdictions in which English law was traditional. The language of the court was English, and most of the defense lawyers were American, with Japanese co-counsel. To attempt the adoption of some hybrid system of law might have led to interminable wrangling, in view of the different systems represented on the bench. There was little precedent for this unusual court proceeding, at best, and many questions remain unanswered, even today.

The prosecution, of course, had a distinct advantage, because it was supported fully by SCAP. Each of the eleven nations supplied a prosecutor who worked under the chief of counsel, Joseph B. Keenan, of the United States.[2] Keenan, a florid, aggressive, but not unkindly man, indicated the extent of the prosecution's case, on the opening day, by reading a statement which was more than twice as long as the indictment itself. It totaled thirty-seven printed pages, with another forty pages of supporting appendices. The indictment covered seventeen pages and fifty-five counts. Through SCAP support, the prosecution was able to call upon Headquarters for full administrative help—translators, stenographers, clerks, and other essential personnel for such a complicated proceeding.

The defense, on the other hand, was loosely organized and often complained of receiving inadequate assistance from SCAP. The diversity of the charges against the accused Japanese meant that the defense was incapable of acting as a unit. At the outset, Captain Beverly M. Coleman, USNR, and John W. Guider, both classmates of mine at the Naval Academy, attempted to organize the defense counsel so that, at least, they would not work at cross-purposes. They found, however, that individual defense lawyers brought out from the United States under a hastily improvised recruiting program had different ideas. Further, SCAP Headquarters was adamant in its refusal to give what Coleman considered was necessary logistic support to enable the defense to carry on properly.

At one point Coleman and Guider called on MacArthur, at the General's request, to discuss this question. When they were unable to obtain what they considered essential help from MacArthur, the lawyers submitted their resignations; these were promptly accepted. Despite these troubles, the Japanese prisoners were all represented by counsel in due course.

These complex considerations understandably created concern among friends of the accused, who worked assiduously to obtain appropriate counsel for them. Several approaches were made to me in the hope that I would defend one or several of the prisoners. In the uncertainties of the moment, before the trial opened, the Japanese feared many more major war criminal suspects would be brought to trial. So, in one instance, I was asked to represent Gisuke Aikawa, the former head of the Manchurian Heavy Industries Company, the industrial monopoly in Manchoukuo. Aikawa had been imprisoned, but never was tried.

In all instances, of course, I explained promptly that, as an official of the Occupation, I could not accept such a legal case. The Japanese probably turned to me because of my prewar legal practice in their country. It was never clear, however, whether they expected me to resign in order to become a defense counsel or whether they thought I could hold both positions, conflicting as that would be.

The long and often tedious trial recapitulated, in somber legal fashion, an incredibly crowded period of Japanese history. The details are too voluminous to recount here. The story of conquest stretched from the period in the twenties, when the militarists revived their attempts to nibble away China, to the flaming finale of World War II. Step by step the prosecution attempted to unravel the complicated intrigues, the bluff, and the bloodshed which marked this drive for Asian hegemony. It recounted the penetration, subversion, and final conquest of Manchuria in 1931, and Japan's defiance of the League of Nations and world opinion. The account showed the steady chipping away of China, through the conquest of Inner Mongolia and adjacent areas. Then came the Sino-Japanese War, which exploded in 1937 on a startled world. Steadily, the facts showed, Japan was pointed more and more irrevocably toward war with the United States, as its troops bogged deeper into the morass of China.

The prosecution described a coterie of Japanese militarists and their civilian supporters who operated abroad as almost an independent government. Less belligerent Tokyo authorities could not control them, even when power nominally belonged to officials elected through parliamentary methods. Eventually, the ultranationalists captured open power in Tokyo, through assassination and intimidation. The control structure which had been

perfected in Manchoukuo was then transferred to Japan to dominate the populace. By the time of the Pearl Harbor attack, the
prosecution contended, Japan itself was virtually as completely
enslaved as Japanese-occupied areas abroad; more so, perhaps,
because the Japanese people did not actively oppose their militarists, as the Chinese did through guerrilla warfare.

The long record was spattered with cruelty and disdain for
human life. These constant elements in all Asian warfare were
particularly abhorrent to Western morality, and the prosecution
dealt at length with "crimes against humanity." They ranged in
degree from the calculated brutality used by the kempeitai to
break the spirits of Allied and Asian prisoners to the mass hysteria
and license which had destroyed Nanking in an orgy of pillage
and rape. This was a violent and repulsive chapter, but it was so
diluted in the telling, by the awkward requirements of legal
evidence, that the expected impact upon the Japanese people
probably did not occur.

The prisoners charged with responsibility for this epoch—
which took two years to outline in court—were men of greatly
diverse talents and characters. Tojo, whose mental agility earned
the lifelong nickname of "The Razor," remained dominant
throughout the trial, both as the principal defendant and as the
most defiant. Three others were former prime ministers. They
included Koki Hirota, head of government in the mid-thirties
when the militarists began to assume open control, and who re-
emerged from retirement in 1945 to make fruitless peace overtures to Russia. Of the remainder, only seven were civilians; but
no industrialists were tried before the Tribunal. The balance were
former generals or admirals. In the tightly linked Japanese power
hierarchy, these militarists were the survivors of a relatively small
group of officers who had held the most influential military positions for twenty years. They included Yoshiro Umezu, the thin-
lipped, sullen man who as army chief of staff had signed the final
surrender with the Allies, and Sadao Araki, the onetime fiery
jingoist who had infected a nation as a war-preaching education

minister, now a scrawny 71-year-old, forever protesting his innocence.

They were mostly old men in fact as well as appearance, partly because the Japanese veneration for age meant that youth could not attain such power. When the trial ended, the youngest, at fifty-three, was former General Kenryo Sato, the shrewd, calculating ex-chief of the Army's Military Affairs Bureau, one of the three positions of top authority in the Imperial Army. The fabled Kenji Doihara, whose intrigues across the continent had brought him the title "Lawrence of Asia," was sixty-five years old. The oldest was Kiichiro Hiranuma, eighty-one, a former prime minister. He was a relict of the past who habitually spoke in such classical Japanese that the commoner had difficulty understanding him.

Two prisoners, star defendants in a way, died after arraignment but before they could be brought to trial. One was Yosuke Matsuoka, the ambitious, American-educated civilian foreign minister who, among other actions, had concluded the wartime neutrality pact with Stalin. The second was ex-Admiral Osami Nagano who, as navy chief of staff, had cast the decisive vote for the attack on Pearl Harbor.* A third member of the original group of prisoners, the expansionist author Shumei Okawa, earned a moment of notoriety by slapping Tojo on his bald head during a court session. He was considered too psychotic to stand trial, and was committed to an institution. The surviving twenty-five defendants continued in the dock until the end.

The lengthy and repetitious recital of the prisoners' alleged crimes was a wearisome business for all concerned, including the Japanese people. Preoccupied as they were with the ordinary problems of trying to live, the Japanese masses were almost totally unconcerned and uninterested in the fate of their former leaders. In any event, it was traditional for the average Japanese to follow his leaders with implicit faith, since they made the deci-

* Nagano told me in an interview that his decision broke a deadlock between admirals urging the Hawaii assault and others who wanted to bypass the United States for an attack on Southeast Asia.—R.B.

General Hideki Tojo immediately after having attempted suicide by shooting himself. He recovered and stood trial as a major war criminal. Top right, Russell Brines, representing AP. September 11, 1945.

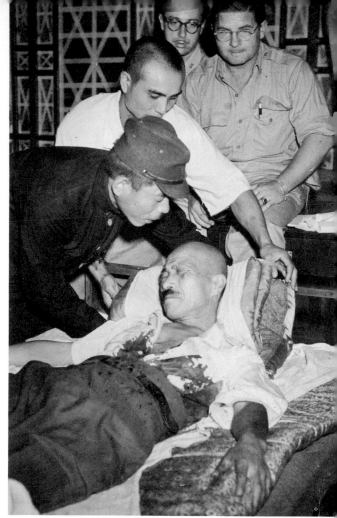

At an 8th Army review: *left to right* — Maj. General Paul J. Mueller, Chief of Staff, GHQ, Far Eastern Command and SCAP; Lt. General Walton H. Walker, Commanding General, 8th Army; William J. Sebald, Chief, Diplomatic Section, GHQ, SCAP. December 22, 1948.

At Haneda Airport, Tokyo, awaiting the arrival
of the Korean President, Dr. Syngman Rhee.
Left to right — Colonel Sidney Huff, General MacArthur,
Ambassador Sebald, Mrs. MacArthur, Colonel Laurence E. Bunker.
Below — Dr. Rhee and the Ambassador at a reception held
later the same day in the President's honor. October 19, 1948.

General MacArthur reviewing a parade of the 8th Army at the Imperial Palace Plaza. Tokyo, July 4, 1949.

Below, right — Prime Minister Hitoshi Ashida with Lt. General Robert L. Eichelberger, Commanding General, 8th Army, at General Eichelberger's residence in Yokohama. August 1, 1948.

The members of the Allied Council during the chairmanship of Ambassador George Atcheson, Jr. *Left to right* — Lt. General Chu Shih-ming, Member for China; Lt. General Kuzma Derevyanko, Member for the USSR; Ambassador George Atcheson, Jr., Chairman and Member for the U.S.; W. Macmahon Ball, British Commonwealth Member.

Ambassador Sebald greeting the Joint Chiefs of Staff in Tokyo.
Left to right — Admiral Forrest P. Sherman, General J. Lawton Collins,
General Hoyt Vandenberg, General Omar N. Bradley, Ambassador Sebald.
Below, left — Ambassador and Mrs. Sebald with Secretary of the Army
Kenneth C. Royall. Tokyo, February 3, 1949.

Ambassador Sebald addressing the graduating class of
Saint Joseph's College, Yokohama, June 25, 1950.

Ambassador William J. Sebald, deputy for SCAP, Chairman and Member
for the U.S., delivering a statement at the Allied Council meeting.
The British Commonwealth Member, Ambassador W. R. Hodgson
at right (smoking cigarette). December 20, 1950.

The Soviet Delegation to the Allied Council for Japan,
headed by Lt. General Kuzma Derevyanko, walking out of the Council,
refusing to discuss the subject of repatriation of Japanese
prisoners of war from Soviet-controlled areas. January 4, 1950.

His Imperial Highness Prince Takamatsu and John Foster Dulles. June 23, 1950. *Right* – the final discussion between John Foster Dulles and General MacArthur before Dulles' departure from Haneda Airport: *left to right* – Dulles, Herbert R. Matthews, General MacArthur, Carl McCardle, Ambassador Sebald. Tokyo, June 27, 1950.

General MacArthur as Commander-in-Chief, United Nations Command, turning over the city of Seoul, recaptured from the North Koreans, to President Syngman Rhee in the National Assembly. Seoul, September 29, 1950, two weeks after the Inchon landings.

General MacArthur, returning from a visit to the Korean battlefront, met by Mrs. MacArthur and his personal aide, Colonel Sidney Huff, at Haneda Airport.

General MacArthur, departing for the Wake Island meeting with President Truman, with Russell Brines prior to boarding plane. Ambassador Sebald on left. October 14, 1950.

General MacArthur returning to Tokyo from the Wake Island meeting
with President Truman: *left to right* — Lt. General Stratemeyer,
Ambassador Sebald, General MacArthur, Brig. General Courtney Whitney,
Maj. General Doyle O. Hickey, Colonel Laurence E. Bunker.
October 15, 1950.

John Foster Dulles, Prime Minister Yoshida, and Ambassador Sebald
at a reception in Tokyo. January 31, 1951.

A group of Japanese leaders at a reception to meet John Foster Dulles. *Left to right* (inner circle) — Prime Minister Shigeru Yoshida (back to camera), John Foster Dulles, Eisaku Sato, Kozen Hirokawa, Katsuo Okazaki, Ambassador Sebald, Kijuro Shidehara (directly behind Ambassador Sebald). Tokyo, January, 1951.

The command post of the 23rd Regimental Combat Team near Inje, Korea.
Left to right — Lt. General James A. Van Fleet, Commanding General, 8th Army;
Colonel John Chiles, Commanding 23rd RCT;
General Matthew B. Ridgway, Commander in Chief, United
Nations Command; Ambassador Sebald. May 28, 1951.

General Matthew B. Ridgway with his senior commanders near
the front line in Korea: *left to right* — General Ridgway,
Maj. General W. M. Hoge, Lt. General James A. Van Fleet,
Maj. General Blackshear M. Bryan, Ambassador Sebald. May 29, 1951.

The signing of the Administrative Agreement between the U.S. and Japan. *Left to right* — Assistant Secretary of the Army, Earl D. Johnson; Assistant Secretary of State for Far Eastern Affairs, Dean Rusk; U.S. Political Adviser to SCAP, Ambassador Sebald, February 28, 1952.

The MacArthurs' departure from Japan. *Left to right* — General and Mrs. MacArthur, Colonel Huff, Arthur MacArthur, Lt. Colonel Story, Maj. General Doyle O. Hickey. April 16, 1951.

sions and accepted responsibility for the affairs of state.

The military men and civilians in the dock may have made mistakes and fatal errors, but in the eyes of most Japanese their actions were within the areas of their responsibilities. Under the Japanese code, the offense was not that the leaders acted wrongly but that they failed. The average Japanese had suffered decades of struggle and deprivation by relying upon these men. Now he, and the nation, were far worse off than before. But he was unable to realize that perhaps some of the blame for what had happened rested upon himself. Many of the more thoughtful Japanese, of course, felt a sense of guilt or shame on learning the painful story of Japan's descent to international irresponsibility, but they were a small minority.

Very often, too, articulate Japanese were openly puzzled by the prosecution's painstaking search of the past. The men and the events of the twenties and the early thirties predated many of the Japanese intellectuals and frequently meant little to them. "Why, he is too old and too impotent to mean anything," they said of men like former General Jiro Minami, a white-haired 74-year-old, who sat each day in the dock in apparent bewilderment, shaking his head constantly from a nervous tic. But Minami had been a vigorous and powerful war minister in his earlier years and, before becoming enfeebled, had helped shape the nation's destiny. Although strongly conscious of history, the Japanese in this instance were unable to see one essential point of the prosecution's case: the direct, perhaps inevitable, link between the first successful theft of Manchuria and the Pearl Harbor attack.

When the testimony was completed in April, 1948, the Tribunal recessed to write its judgment. Later, during the summer, rumors began to circulate through Tokyo that the Emperor was planning to abdicate when the judgment was announced. The ruler, it was said at various times, wanted to share responsibility with his subordinates. Others claimed he could not condone the loss of face if, as appeared likely, officers would be hanged for actions conducted in his name. The atmosphere was tense, and abdication would have been explosive. The effect of such an act upon the Japanese nation could not be anticipated. At a minimum, I felt, it would undermine the discipline of the Japanese people under the Occupation, for much of their obedience was based upon the Emperor's acceptance of SCAP authority.

Accordingly, I made discreet inquiries about the validity of the rumors as they became increasingly persistent. The response was typically indirect. One of my informants, who was close to the imperial household, answered in the abstruse terms of a Japanese poem. "The Japanese people," he said, "are fond of voicing their thoughts regarding the full moon and what it represents to them. The moon, however, expresses no opinion and is silent." This referred, of course, to the Emperor, from whom came neither comment on the rumors nor denial. The same informant, perhaps with this situation in mind, told me that the Emperor's entourage felt that General MacArthur was "friendly" in his attitude toward the Emperor. The Government Section, he said, was "unfriendly."

In October, with the reports still strong, the subject came up after a dinner with Dr. Hitoshi Ashida, who had resigned as prime minister two days earlier. Dr. Ashida, an urbane, Westernized Japanese, spoke fluent English and was regarded as perhaps the most logical of the early postwar leaders, in the American sense. Over coffee and cigars, he brought up the abdication problem. "The question of the Emperor's resignation," he said, "would be inextricably interwoven with the war crimes verdicts, and pressures for abdication would become very great." He added that the Emperor had told him only a few days previously that he would remain in Tokyo until the verdicts were announced, although even this was doubtful. Thus, by tone of voice and demeanor, Dr. Ashida implied without saying so, in the Japanese way, that the great step was possible.

Toward the end of October the subject arose during one of my conversations with MacArthur. The General promptly expressed doubt that the Emperor had any such intention. Referring to the forthcoming judgment of the IMTFE, however, he added: "One can never foresee what might happen when one sets off a ton of dynamite." He said, when the Emperor next called on him, he would advise that abdication would be foolish and preposterous and would be a great disservice to his people.

Nevertheless, the rumors mounted and so did the air of expectancy in Tokyo. One of the capital's most influential papers, *Yomiuri Shimbun,* gave major prominence on November 1 to a story by INS which reported a direct connection between abdication and a series of calls which Prime Minister Yoshida made on the Emperor and his brother, the late Prince Chichibu. For verification, I turned to Terry Terasaki, my friend who served as liaison between SCAP and the imperial household ministry. He expressed belief that the article was entirely speculative, but said he felt it was dangerous, because it built up the possibility of the Emperor's withdrawal.

In agreeing, I told Terasaki the time had come for a specific stand to be taken on this momentous question. "Speaking entirely in my personal capacity," I said, "abdication would be politically disastrous. I also feel that this would be the position of Washington. And, further, I have good reason to believe that the Supreme Commander would share this view." He listened to me gravely, an old-young man with an intelligent face already graven by the great responsibilities of his position, which placed him midway between the traditions of the court and the innovations of SCAP. I added that, if desirable, he was free to pass along these views to the Emperor and his advisers.

New speculation was stirred, in this atmosphere, by a written opinion set down by Sir William Webb. The president of the Tribunal added to the formal judgment his own views on the Emperor's role. The ruler, he said, was not relieved "from responsibility as a leader of the nation for the events for which the defendants were convicted." Sir William had not consulted with the other members of the Tribunal on this opinion and offered it entirely as his own. He said the evidence showed that the Emperor "never wanted war and sometimes acted on advice against his better judgment." But, the Australian added, the Emperor's "authority was required for the war. If he did not want war he should have withheld his authority. It is no answer to say he might have been assassinated. That risk is taken by all rulers who must still do their duty." Sir William wrote, however, that he did not "suggest that the Emperor should have been prosecuted" because he had been given immunity at the outset of the trial "in the best interests of all the Allied Powers."

In fact, Joseph Keenan, the chief of counsel, formally had absolved the Emperor of involvement in the conspiracy to wage war at the outset of his case. Far earlier, the continuity of the Throne and the continued rule of Hirohito himself had been assured, for all practical purposes, by a provision in the Initial Post-Surrender Policy for Japan sent to SCAP at the beginning of the Occupation. It specified in effect that the Japanese themselves would have the authority to determine the type of government they desired. By the time the war crimes trial started, it was clear that the overwhelming majority of the Japanese wanted their monarchy, and even the Communists had ceased to demand its abolition. By the time the Tribunal rendered its judgment, the Throne not only was secure but was established as an invaluable adjunct of SCAP.

Sir William's action in offering his independent opinion, therefore, was a strange procedure which raised many questions. It seemed to be entirely gratuitous under the circumstances. MacArthur told me he thought Sir William Webb was playing cheap politics; an obvious reference to Australian opinion at the time. Inevitably, the statement intensified the speculation about abdication.

Consequently, I was gratified when Terasaki came to my office a few days later and told me the Emperor had written to General MacArthur to say he would not abdicate, regardless of the sentences handed down by the Tribunal. Sir William's opinion, of course, had become known before the lengthy reading of the judgment was completed and before the prisoners actually were sentenced. Although the Emperor's message to MacArthur was never made public, the rumors quietly died down and the possibility of abdication was not seriously raised again.

It is fruitless to speculate on the factors producing the final decision or on the probable consequences if the Emperor had abdicated. But it should be mentioned, from hindsight, that the disaster which I predicted when the rumors were strong most probably would have resulted if the step had been taken. Abdication doubtless would have left the Throne intact, under Crown Prince Akihito, then fourteen years old, aided by advisers sharing views similar to those surrounding Hirohito. Yet the whole system of authority and control, symbolized by Hirohito's relationship with MacArthur, might have been destroyed suddenly, creating chaos or, at least, great opportunities for chaos. Among other considerations, this situation would have given the Communists their most favorable moment to ignite turmoil, at a period when they were approaching the peak of their postwar strength in Japan.

THE FORMAL JUDGMENT OF THE TRIBUNAL, a massive document covering more than 1,200 pages, was read in open court from November 4 to November 12. This, too, became both a solemn and a wearisome ceremony. The lengthy trial itself provided a transcript of 48,412 pages. A total of 419 witnesses had testified in court, and another 779 persons provided depositions and affidavits. In all, 4,336 exhibits were admitted to evidence.

Finally, in a courtroom once more crowded, tense, and hushed, the international court announced the sentences on November 12, 1948. One by one the prisoners, looking even more pitiful, arose in the dock, in the glare of lights, to hear their fate. Each one stood pinned to the courtroom by thousands of eyes— some friendly and sympathetic, the majority stern and uncompromising. Sir William read the Tribunal's findings and sentences quickly, then waited gloweringly for the next prisoner to arise. At the end, the former Japanese leaders responded in their own individual ways. All strove to preserve a mask of impassiveness, but not all succeeded. Several bowed formally to the court, after receiving sentence. The defiant ones remained defiant. Itagaki sneered at a death sentence. Tojo did not even bother to wear his earphones for the translation of "death by hanging."

In all, seven were sentenced to death. Besides Tojo and Itagaki, they were the ex-generals Doihara, Matsui, Muto, and Heitaro Kimura, a former vice minister of war who had wielded great backstage power; and one civilian, Hirota. Sixteen of the prisoners were sentenced to life imprisonment; one to twenty years, and one to seven years.[3] The lightest sentence was given to Mamoru Shigemitsu who, it was generally believed, had been brought to trial only because of vigorous Soviet insistence. He was the civilian signer of the formal surrender document, a former foreign minister and, perhaps more importantly, a onetime ambassador to Moscow.

No one can read the judgment of the IMTFE and not be impressed, indeed shocked, by the story of Japan's spiritual and moral deterioration during the decade prior to Pearl Harbor. The historical portion of the judgment is a lucid and objective summary of the Japanese actions, both external and internal, which provided the basis for assessing the responsibilities of the convicted ex-leaders. It is a history of the gradual capture of all the organs of the state by ambitious military leaders in order to prepare the minds of the Japanese people for war and for military rule. Nothing was left to chance. The judgment is replete with examples of how the tentacles of the military, aided and abetted by civilian counterparts, gradually strangled public opinion, parliamentarianism, and all sense of international decency.

There can be no doubt, as the historical section of the judgment demonstrates, that the accused were the motivating forces behind Japan's aggressive actions during this 20-year period. It was they who made the decisions and who rationalized their policies, often by falsehood when this became necessary. But these men also were influenced by the increasingly immoral world in which they lived. One of the tragedies of the record is the influence, both direct and indirect, which Hitler had upon the destiny of Japan. The German victories in 1940 and 1941, for example, prompted Yosuke Matsuoka and Hideki Tojo to speed up their plans to conquer Southeast Asia lest Hitler beat them to this rich area.

The section of the judgment concerning conventional war crimes—cruel and inhuman treatment of prisoners of war and civilians—covers more than forty pages. Here, international law was well-established, and Japan officially had announced it would adhere to the Geneva Convention of 1929 governing the treatment of war prisoners. It is not clear whether any of the Class A war criminals directly participated in committing these crimes. The Tribunal found, however, that the Japanese leaders could not escape guilt, because the pattern of cruelty was practiced by Japanese armed forces in widely separated areas and because orders for this procedure originated from authority higher than field commanders. Consequently, each of the seven sentenced to death was found guilty of either count 54 (conventional war crimes—atrocities) or count 55 (disregard of duty to secure the observance of and to prevent breaches of the laws of war). Of the seven, Matsui, former commander in chief in Central China, apparently was sentenced to hang solely because of his responsibility in failing to check his troops during the Rape of Nanking.

MACARTHUR, as the designated reviewing officer of the proceedings, began preparations for this procedure several weeks before the Tribunal's judgment was ready. During our conversations on this question, he told me he had decided to call in the representatives of all the eleven countries concerned with the trial. In a plenary meeting, he proposed to ask each representative for his views on the verdicts. MacArthur then would base his decision upon these comments. I was to lead off by giving the views of the United States government. These presumably were to be grounded upon instructions from Washington, which I would request and hopefully expect to receive before the consultative meeting, on November 22.

In my request to Washington for instructions I suggested making a comment upon what I considered as Sir William Webb's gratuitous and politically damaging opinion on the Emperor. The State Department replied with a somewhat discouraging reaction to this proposal, however, and I decided to limit my official comment to a mere "I have no change to recommend." Without a strong opinion on this topic in Washington, it seemed pointless to invite a possible verbal joust with Sir William.

On the day for review, representatives of the other ten FEC nations gathered somberly in a large waiting room in that Dai Ichi building. The usual friendly banter of assembled diplomatic colleagues was missing when I led them into MacArthur's office. The General greeted each diplomat as he entered the room, which was lined with chairs facing the big uncluttered desk. When all were seated, MacArthur returned to his leather desk chair, gravely looked at us and briefly sketched the purpose of the meeting. He asked each man for comment on the sentences. I was called upon first, presumably on the theory that I would set the pattern by being succinct and unequivocal. Loudly and clearly I said: "I have no change to recommend."

These were the other recommendations:

Representative and Country	Recommendation
MR. PATRICK SHAW, *Australia*	*No change, but would not oppose reduction in sentences.*
MR. E. HERBERT NORMAN, *Canada*	*Not opposed to reductions in sentences.*
GEN. SHANG CHEN, *China*	*No change.*
LT. GEN. Z. PECHKOFF, *France*	*Officially, no change; personal appeal for clemency.*

Representative and Country	Recommendation
MR. B. N. CHAKRAVARTY, *India*	*All death sentences to be commuted to life imprisonment.*
BARON LEWE VAN ADUARD, *Netherlands*	*Mitigation of sentences: Umezu and Hata, life to 20 years; Shigemitsu, 7 to 2 1/2 years; Togo, 20 to 10 years; Hirota, death to life imprisonment.*
SIR ALVARY GASCOIGNE, *New Zealand*	*No change.*
DR. BERNABE AFRICA, *Philippines*	*No change.*
LT. GEN. K. N. DEREVYANKO, *U.S.S.R.*	*No change.*
SIR ALVARY GASCOIGNE, *United Kingdom*	*No change.*

The next day I again called on MacArthur for a further conference on this problem. I recommended that, if any hangings occurred, all photographers should be barred. The General immediately concurred, saying photographs "would violate all sense of decency."

Then MacArthur asked me to listen to his review of the sentences, a decision which he proposed to make public the next morning. The review was written on a number of small pieces of paper, the size of an ordinary scratch pad, in his own handwriting, with interlineations and corrections.* The General upheld all the Tribunal's sentences, with no changes, and he had assembled his reasons for this position. He read them to me in a slow, measured, solemn tone, as if I constituted an audience of several thousand. He spoke in a low voice, but with emphasis and intonation. It was a moving performance which affected me deeply; my reaction was a mixture of sadness, sympathy, admiration, and impending doom. In conclusion, MacArthur said the Commanding General Eighth Army, Lieutenant General Walker, would be instructed to carry out the sentences at any time *after* one week from November 25. No announcement of the date of execution

* See Appendix D.

would be made beforehand. The procedure, he added, would be similar to that carried out in the cases of other war criminals, convicted as lesser ranking officials. The property of the condemned men would be returned to their families.

The General obviously was deeply affected and moved by the decision he had made and which, apparently, I was the first to share with him. I had not seen him display such deep emotion before. In almost a whisper, he said: "Bill, that was a difficult decision to make."

That night, unable to sleep for thoughts of MacArthur's decision, I tried to analyze the possible effects of the executions on the Japanese people. Perhaps, I conjectured, it might have been wiser to reduce the sentences in one or two cases, thus tempering justice with mercy. This would have saved Japan's national face. But could there be a commutation of sentence without undermining the integrity of the Tribunal? Unable to answer this question to my own satisfaction, I was thankful that the decision was not mine.

MacArthur's timetable for the executions was postponed when defense attorneys for seven of the convicted Japanese filed motions on November 29 and December 2 with the United States Supreme Court for leave to file petitions for writs of habeas corpus. Three of the petitioners, Tojo, Doihara, and Hirota, had received death sentences, while life imprisonment had been given the others, Kido, Oka, Sato, and Shimada. All of the executions were postponed, upon MacArthur's order, pending the disposition of these petitions, a normal procedure in such cases.

Similar petitions on behalf of German war criminals previously had been denied by the Supreme Court, by a 4–4 decision. Justice Jackson had disqualified himself, however, because of his position as a prosecutor at Nuremberg. In this instance, Jackson participated in the Court's deliberations, since he had not been involved in the Tokyo trials, and voted with Justices Black, Douglas, Murphy, and Rutledge on December 6 to hear arguments on the questions presented.

While Tokyo remained in suspended animation, the arguments were made before the Supreme Court in Washington on December 16 and 17. Three days later, the Court denied the petitions, stating:

> . . . General Douglas MacArthur has been selected and is acting as the Supreme Commander for the Allied Powers. The military tribunal sentencing these petitioners has been set up by General MacArthur as the agent of the Allied Powers.
> Under the foregoing circumstances the courts of the United States have no power or authority to review, to affirm, set aside or annul the judgments and sentences . . . the motions for leave to file petitions for writs of habeas corpus are denied.[4]

On December 6, MacArthur told me he intended inviting the members of the Allied Council for Japan to act as official witnesses to the hangings. Because of the time differential, this was before the Supreme Court had agreed to hear arguments on the Japanese petitions. In any case, MacArthur seemed to feel confident that the Court could not take jurisdiction to review the judgment of an international tribunal such as the IMTFE. He told me that a letter would be delivered to each member of the Council during the afternoon before the hangings. I was then to collect the members and take them to the prison. Noting my reaction, the General added he would not insist on my carrying out this assignment, for he knew it would be an onerous and distasteful task.

The day after the Supreme Court decision, on December 21, 1948, MacArthur handed me four identical letters, each addressed to a member of the Allied Council. The body of the letter read:

> The war criminals condemned to death by the International Military Tribunal for the Far East will be executed at Sugamo Prison on Thursday, December 23, in the early morning hours.
> Inasmuch as the execution will carry out in pertinent part the judgment of the Allied Powers represented on the Tribunal, I request your attendance thereat as official witnesses for the said powers in order that you may thereafter certify to the executions of that phase of the Tribunal's judgment.

The details of arranging and assuring the presence of the members were left to me. The hangings were to begin at 12:01 A.M., December 23. As I was leaving MacArthur's office, I said, "General, from here on, I presume I am on my own?" He replied: "You are on your own. Use your own discretion." Then, approaching me, he patted me on the back and remarked: "Bill, this is a tough assignment." It was.

The Allied Council held a regular meeting on the morning of December 22 and afterward I quietly made appointments to see each member between five and six that afternoon. Calling at their residences, I handed each of them the General's letter. Upon reading it, Pat Shaw swallowed hard, turned pink, and said, "Let's have a whiskey!" General Derevyanko merely said, "Yes, I will come." He readily agreed to be alone, although I had never seen him previously without an aide or an interpreter. General Shang turned a bit pale but said, "Of course I will come. What shall I wear?" I suggested that he wear his uniform.

IT WAS NECESSARY to go to a dinner party that evening, but I had difficulty in following the chatter. My mind was on the time and on how soon I could quietly leave for home to change clothes and prepare to receive the other Council members for the night's ordeal. On the plea that my wife was very tired, we quietly slipped out at 10 P.M., followed by Pat and Helen Shaw, who were at the same dinner. At home, while changing my clothes, a Major Morrisson arrived with two sedans and a jeep carrying armed military police. The jeep was an extra precaution which I had requested from Eighth Army, in the event of some unforeseen incident. The secrecy surrounding the executions had been carefully planned, in case any Japanese might be plotting to interfere, and I considered it prudent to assume the secret might leak out.

The other diplomats soon arrived, and we greeted each other almost in whispers. Drinks were served, to relax the tension. We stood awkwardly with them for a while, then it was time to go.

The two sedans and the jeep formed into a melancholy convoy and hurried the short distance to Sugamo Prison. The night was cold and crisp, and tires crunched on spots of frost. The dark streets were empty; our little caravan proceeded unnoticed.

Sugamo rose in squat ugliness against the night, preserving the architecture of hopelessness which the Japanese had copied from European prisons. Inside, Colonel Handwerk, the American commandant, greeted us, and again we talked in whispers. Promptly at 11:50 P.M., we left the light and warmth of the main building and plunged into the cold darkness outside, for a five-minute walk to the death house. No one spoke, as we plodded, single file, through the shadows.

A door opened, and we entered a well-lighted room. We were directed to a low, narrow dais along one wall. We faced a long wooden platform, over which were suspended five ropes, each ending in a noose. They hung stiff, without the slightest motion. Each was numbered, from 1 to 5. The platform itself was reached by an open stairway of thirteen steps, apparently a traditional number.

As the official witnesses, we were asked merely to stand on the dais and to observe the proceedings. A number of American army officers, who proved to be doctors, and soldiers were in the room. They waited for the grim proceedings to begin. There was absolute quiet.

Outside, I heard shouts of "Banzai!" from many voices, and the cry seemed to ricochet through the hush. This traditional Japanese yell has a meaning much broader than our "hurrah," with which it is sometimes compared. It is used to express triumph, joy, sorrow, or resignation. On this occasion it probably was meant primarily as a farewell to the Emperor and his people, and secondarily, as a symbol of determination and defiance; for the shout came from the men about to die. I learned later it was led by former General Matsui who, at seventy, was the eldest of the doomed group and therefore was entitled to the honor of leading the banzai.

Seconds after midnight, four of the prisoners entered the death house, each flanked and assisted by two American soldiers. An officer preceded them. The Japanese entered in this order: Doihara, Matsui, Tojo, and Muto. The prison chaplain walked alongside them, praying in a low voice. The condemned men were muttering what I presumed were Buddhist prayers. Each was identified as he entered the chamber and passed directly before us, within a few feet. They wore United States Army salvage clothing, devoid of insignia, the most shapeless covering imaginable. It helped to make them all look old, very old, helpless, pitiful, and tragic. They seemed to shuffle as they walked, and each face was a vacant stare as it passed me.

They mounted the stairs to the platform, then walked in turn to each of the first four trap doors. They stood there, facing us, in the heavy silence. Another identification was made. Black hoods were placed over their heads. The ropes and nooses were adjusted. Then the chief executioner reported that the condemned men were prepared for execution. A single word crackled: "Proceed!" Instantly, the four traps were sprung simultaneously, with a sound like a rifle volley.

One doctor immediately attended each body and, with stethoscope, listened for heart action. The senior doctor was called successively to each corpse and, in turn, reported: "I declare this man dead"—Doihara at 12:07 1/2; Tojo at 12:10 1/2; Muto at 12:11; and Matsui at 12:13. The bodies were placed in plain wooden boxes and carried off by two men to each box. The bodies were to be cremated and the ashes scattered, so that graves of the executed leaders could not be canonized in the future.

In the presence of this man-made death, I felt very humble. These men, who had wielded such enormous power and influence, died secretly and alone, surrounded by former enemies. There was something inexorable in this finale, for the mode of death, not the fact of death, was impressive to fatalistic Japanese. Each of these former generals had survived combat, and Tojo had recovered from a postwar attempt to shoot away his own life, only to dangle from a rope. This was indeed a final insult for a Japanese military man. How and why should it have transpired that I, of all people, was a witness to this event?

The second group of three prisoners was escorted into the death chamber in the same manner as the first, in this order: Itagaki, Hirota, and Kimura. There was the same shuffling walk, the same quiet, unidentifiable mumbling, the same hopelessness. As they passed me, Hirota turned his head and looked straight into my eyes. It was an exchange of glances in which he seemed to appeal to me for sympathy and understanding.

With clocklike precision, the traps were sprung and the final verdict of the senior medical officer spoken: "I pronounce this man dead"—Itagaki at 12:32 1/2; Hirota at 12:34 1/2; and Kimura at 12:35.

We hurried back to the main prison building, still silent, and walked to the Officers' Club, where the commandant thoughtfully had laid out refreshments. We each had a drink, straight whiskey, I noted, and soon left the prison in our army cars. Derevyanko rode with me, as he had in going to the prison, an arrangement I made because the Republic of China and the U.S.S.R. were not on speaking terms, and because Shaw wanted to hurry home. The Soviet General, who by then understood a passable amount of English, accepted my invitation to have a nightcap at my residence. An hour later I took him home, slightly worse for the evening's experience. Perhaps incorrectly, I derived some satisfaction in surviving this unwanted ordeal in better shape than my colleagues, judging by their reactions and appearance.

In the Japanese tradition, several of the executed war leaders wrote classical poems, describing their feelings, shortly before the executions. Dr. Shinsho Hanayama, the Buddhist priest who spent the last hour with the condemned men, made public the following poems, which he said were given to him just before the final walk to the death house:

By Hideki Tojo:
>Farewell to all,
>For today I cross the earthly mountains
>And gladly go
>To the folds of Buddha.

By Iwane Matsui:
>Without hatred of Heaven, earth, and men,
>But with strong faith in Buddha
>I calmly go
>To the great Beyond.

By Seishiro Itagaki:
>Humbly do I kneel
>In front of our great God
>And beg forgiveness
>For all my sins.

During the morning hours following the executions the bells of Buddhist temples and Shinto shrines and Christian churches summoned their members to prayer. What the faithful said, God alone knows.

9

Korean War

ALTHOUGH KOREA WAS NOT the direct responsibility of MacArthur or SCAP Headquarters until after the outbreak of hostilities in 1950, the affairs of that unhappy peninsula became a constant preoccupation for the command in Tokyo. The United States command in Korea reported directly to the Joint Chiefs of Staff in Washington, but kept MacArthur intimately informed of developments, in his role as the major commander in the Far East. POLAD also received regular information copies of many political reports sent to Washington by civilian United States officials in Korea, and one of my responsibilities was to keep abreast of developments in this field.

Even without such specialized information, however, it was clear in Tokyo that Korea was destined, from the beginning, to occupy a troubled and significant position in postwar Asia. The nation was divided in 1945 at the 38th parallel, and its internal affairs soon became almost chaotic. The United States and Soviet Russia became involved in a dispute over the continued division of the peninsula. As the cold war grew more intense, we could see that this impasse resulted from standard Soviet tactics. Finally, turmoil grew more pronounced in Korea and, to use a word popularized much later, the confrontation of Washington and Moscow hardened into implacability. In retrospect, the Korean War appears as the logical finale for a political conflict which was no less significant because it occurred before an inattentive world audience.

By their brief war against Japan, the Soviets were able to accomplish, with relative ease, what the czars had been unable to achieve in a century's effort: absolute control over a portion of Korea. Their advance was slowed but not halted when the Allies and Japan ceased hostilities on August 14. The Soviets, in fact, continued fighting until August 31, and stopped their offensive with obvious reluctance.[1] At this point, the expediency of dividing Korea at the 38th parallel was adopted as a means of establishing temporary zones of responsibility between Soviet and United States forces in accepting the surrender of Japanese forces. This division was made on the initiative of the United States, with British and Soviet concurrence. At that time the "line" was considered as nothing more than a minor nuisance.

Hastily assembled and prepared for a short occupation, troops of the United States XXIV Corps, under Lieutenant General John R. Hodge, entered Korea early in September, 1945. Their task was to accept the Japanese surrender, as agreed upon with the Russians, and to oversee the southern half of the peninsula. The situation, as seen from afar, was illuminated by President Truman's statement of September 18, promising the eventual independence of all Korea, which had been pledged earlier by the Allies.

Immediately, however, it became apparent that agreement with the Russians in the north was necessary for the creation of any kind of acceptable national government. This realization started the long diplomatic effort to unlock the 38th parallel. The first effort was a decision, at the Foreign Ministers' Conference in Moscow during December, 1945, to establish a Joint United States–U.S.S.R. Commission over Korea. Representing the two commands, the Commission's task was "to assist the formation of a provisional government," as explained in the communiqué issued December 27, 1945. Moreover, the foreign ministers agreed to establish a four-power trusteeship over Korea "for a period up to five years."

For nearly two years the United States tried to use the Commission to establish some basis for agreement, but Soviet intransigence was consistent, and no decisions were possible. With the Commission unable to operate effectively or, indeed, to exercise its legal authority to supervise North as well as South Korea, the United States finally placed the issue before the United Nations. On November 14, 1947, the General Assembly adopted two resolutions. The first established the United Nations Temporary Commission on Korea (UNTCOK). The second provided terms of reference for this Commission, including authority to visit North Korea. More importantly, it also made specific recommendations for establishing a Korean national government and, when this was accomplished, for the withdrawal of both American and Soviet occupation forces.

The United States consistently had advocated the end of all foreign occupation in Korea. Restating this position, it said officially on September 20, 1948, "that the best interests of the Korean people would be served by the withdrawal of all occupying forces from Korea at the earliest practicable date." This was a political decision based upon a Joint Chiefs of Staff study which concluded that Korea was of little importance in global strategy and that the American forces there could better be employed elsewhere. Even MacArthur, who was not one to withdraw in the face of pressure, told me at that time he considered a United States pullout sensible, because Korea was militarily indefensible. In an interview on March 1, 1949, with G. Ward Price, the British journalist, MacArthur was quoted as saying:

. . . our line of defense runs through the chain of islands fringing the coast of Asia.

It starts from the Philippines and continues through the Ryukyu Archipelago, which includes its main bastion, Okinawa. Then it bends back through Japan and the Aleutian Chain to Alaska.[2]

That this was firm United States policy was clearly indicated by the remarks of Secretary Acheson in his famous speech before the National Press Club in Washington on January 12, 1950. Speaking from informal notes and not a prepared text, the Secretary outlined the "defensive perimeter" of the United States in words almost identical with those attributed to MacArthur in the Ward Price interview nearly a year earlier. Although the omission of Korea from the line of defense as defined by both MacArthur and Acheson was cited by critics as one factor triggering the North Korean attack in June, 1950, neither of them necessarily ruled out the United States defense of Korea against aggressive attack. Korea simply was not mentioned.

Faced with the consistent Soviet refusal to adjust or to abandon the supposedly temporary division of Korea, the United Nations tried to patch together an alternative. The General Assembly voted on December 12, 1948, to recognize the government of South Korea as the only legal regime in the peninsula. Based upon this United Nations action, the United States on January 1, 1949, extended full recognition to the government of the Republic of Korea. The withdrawal of American troops was begun immediately, and only a regimental combat team was kept in the peninsula until June, 1949, at the request of President Syngman Rhee.

Rhee had been elected the first president of the newly independent republic in July, 1948, and the young-old nation had declared its independence as of August 15. The Soviets quickly followed by proclaiming a People's Republic in North Korea on September 7. Moscow announced that Russian occupation troops would be withdrawn by the end of the year. The Koreans were to be left to solve their problems themselves—or so it appeared.

Moscow had trained and activated a North Korean people's Army of three divisions by 1948. This had been increased to ten divisions by the spring of 1950, plus several additional infantry regiments, an armored brigade, and a small air force and navy. By 1950 the South Korean Army totaled eight organized divisions, aggregating about 100,000 men. Because of Rhee's constant belligerency, United States advisers refused to give this force tanks, medium or heavy artillery, or military aircraft. It was feared that, properly armed for offense, Rhee promptly would punch northward across the 38th parallel. The ROKs, as the Republic of Korea soldiers were known, also lacked training in large-unit maneuvers and had no defense against tanks. The United States Korean Military Advisory Group (KMAG), which supervised the training, expressed confidence, however, that the ROKs could handle the continuing threat from the north. When United States combat units withdrew, they left behind arms for about 50,000 men. The small KMAG unit was still in Korea at the outbreak of hostilities.

From the thirties, when I had crossed the country six times, I had retained the impression of Korea as a nation of sad people—oppressed, unhappy, poor, silent, and sullen. The postwar circumstances and President Rhee's harsh character made the Koreans even more flinty and trying for a number of United States political advisers to the American commanding general. These men and other United States officials assigned to Korea visited our POLAD office during their various trips through Tokyo, and we came to know them well.

The special representative of the President to Korea, John J. Muccio, bound for Seoul on what proved to be a historic assignment, arrived in Tokyo on August 14, 1948. I persuaded him to stop over for almost a week in order to meet General MacArthur and to familiarize himself with the Headquarters staff. We both felt this indoctrination would be useful, for no one could foresee when or how the Far East command might be drawn into the Korean problem. MacArthur was careful to stay in proper channels on Korean affairs, but as the theater commander he inevitably would become directly involved should hostilities break out on the peninsula. Without actually anticipating the Korean War, we expected an indefinite prolongation of the tension and small-scale guerrilla action which had become commonplace in Korea.

During the years before the Korean War I absorbed many of the peninsula's problems and challenges through the constant flow of officials and commissions through Tokyo to Seoul and through my relations with the Korean Mission in Japan. Within Japan, officials of the Korean Mission constantly sought help in handling the sometimes volatile affairs of the large Korean community in Japan, which was sharply divided between pro-Rhee and pro-Communist factions. Unfortunately, a succession of heads of mission for the Republic of Korea, with one exception, vied with each other for ineptness and mediocrity. The exception was Chung Ham Pun, who had the rank of ambassador. Educated in the United States, Chung spoke English with a Boston accent.

Late in October, 1949, Chung brought his minister of defense, Sihn Sung Mo, to call upon me. Sihn, slight and gray, puzzled me at first by speaking with a marked English accent. It seemed that he held a master's license in the British merchant marine; when he learned of my naval background, he asked me to address him as "Captain." I received the impression that Sihn was somewhat out of his depth in the position of defense minister, but he made a brave effort to live up to expectations, partly by speaking confidently of the South Korean Army's fighting ability.

One night during a diplomatic dinner, however, he confided in a moment of privacy that much work remained to be done before the ROKs could match the North Koreans. On the same occasion, ironically, much of the evening's conversation was monopolized, in different tones, by Brigadier General William L. Roberts, commander of the KMAG unit in Korea. Roberts, who accompanied Sihn to Tokyo, was talkative and confident on the subject of South Korea's defenses. He spoke, proudly, of "my army" and "my forces" and emphasized that "I can hold the Commies" if they attack. I could hardly imagine a more vociferous advocate of South Korean military prowess. Notably, Sihn Sung Mo said nothing during the general conversation about the deficiencies he had mentioned to me.

Despite the constant verbal war between North and South Korea and an enlarging series of small attacks and probing actions, I found a considerable amount of confidence in Seoul at the start of 1950. Visiting Korea with Philip C. Jessup, President Truman's roving ambassador, I attended a series of formal briefings in which the possibility of war was largely ignored. Instead, I received the impression that, five months before the conflict, United States and South Korean officials regarded inflation as their major problem. On defense matters, General Roberts and other officers told us the ROK Army was excellent, but needed some antiaircraft guns; also needed were a few fast naval vessels for coast guard patrol, and a dozen planes of the caliber of the old P-51 fighters.

THE DAY OF THE COMMUNIST ATTACK, June 25, 1950, was a bright, comfortable Sunday in Tokyo, as Pearl Harbor day had been in Washington so long before. During a leisurely breakfast, Suzu, an old retainer of my wife's family, casually mentioned that the Japanese radio had reported a North Korean attack against the South, with heavy fighting apparently continuing. I hurried to the office, but found nothing to confirm the report. Little news came to us during the next few hours. From all we could learn, it appeared as if an attack had been made but that it was no more serious than a number of border clashes during the past weeks. Available information was sufficiently reassuring, in fact, so that I proceeded to give a long-scheduled Commencement Address to the graduating class of St. Joseph's College in Yokohama.

Several hours later I was handed a note to call the "Washington operator." Since the military circuit to Seoul, which we constantly used, was confusingly called "Washington," I immediately telephoned Ambassador Muccio. The chief operator of the "Washington" circuit, recognizing my voice, explained hurriedly that Muccio was unavailable, then assured me he was "all right," even though "things over here are a bit messed up at the moment." There had been no call from Seoul, however, so my message could only have originated in the State Department; an indication that Washington, D.C., was seriously concerned by the Korean situation.

Before I could contact the department, it was time to meet John Foster Dulles at Haneda Airport, upon his return from a weekend sightseeing trip to Kyoto. Dulles had arrived a few days earlier as a special envoy of the State Department to explore the feasibility of negotiating a formal peace treaty with Japan. He emerged quickly from the plane, looking somewhat harried, and we immediately departed for Tokyo. Dulles had heard of the North Korean attack from a news correspondent who had been in touch with Tokyo from Kyoto. Since neither of us had further information, we drove directly to the Dai Ichi building to see General MacArthur.

The General did not appear unduly concerned by the reports of the fighting which had been received up to that hour, nightfall on the first day of the conflict.* Instead, speaking with the contagious enthusiasm which he so often showed, MacArthur expressed confidence in the ability of the South Korean Army to brace itself and hold, once the initial shock of the Communist attack had worn off. If anything, Dulles seemed more apprehensive. During the meeting he stressed the hope that strong United States support could be given to South Korea. MacArthur made the point that Korea was outside his area of responsibility, but quickly added he was sending munitions to the beleaguered nation, as already requested by Washington. These were to be carried in World War II LSTs (Tank Landing Ships) under cover of American fighter planes. Thus, within a few hours the United States began to help defend a nation which, not long before, had appeared to some to have been written off as both indefensible and outside American strategic requirements.

After we had left the buoyant General, Dulles drafted a telegram to Secretary of State Acheson, which I filed for him. In it

* My wife told me later that she had been invited to tea by Col. and Mrs. Sidney Huff during the afternoon but had arrived early. The Huffs and several others were sitting near the embassy swimming pool, a typical Sunday afternoon gathering. My wife casually mentioned the North Korean attack of which she had heard from Suzu. Col. Huff, the personal aide to MacArthur, excitedly asked whether Edith was sure of her facts, and when he learned that the story had been broadcast over the Japanese radio, hurried off to inform General MacArthur.

the special envoy urged strong United States action in support of South Korea. Otherwise, he told Acheson, our entire position in the Far East would crumble. Meanwhile, I had spoken by telephone to Dean Rusk, Assistant Secretary of State for Far Eastern Affairs, in Washington. Rusk asked that I do all possible to encourage SCAP to supply necessary munitions. I was able to indicate that the request was already being fulfilled by MacArthur, but it was clear from this conversation that Washington was better informed about the hostilities than we were in Tokyo, ten thousand miles closer to the scene. Rusk also told me that the Communist attack had been placed before the United Nations Security Council on Sunday afternoon, Washington time.

Dulles and his wife spent the evening with us, and the "family" dinner that night was nervous and uncertain. We talked to Muccio by telephone and were told that the situation in Korea was deteriorating rapidly. Muccio said that he was about to order the evacuation of the rather sizable number of American civilian and military dependents in Seoul and adjacent areas. Although this was a normal precautionary measure, Muccio's decision served to emphasize the seriousness of the situation.

The news was no better the next day, and the reports we received were conflicting and misleading. Dulles was particularly concerned by the hostilities for a number of reasons, in addition to what appeared to be their growing severity. To some extent he felt personally involved, because he had just visited Korea and had been on the "line" of the 38th parallel less than a week previously. Moreover, a major conflict in Japan's front yard could easily disrupt the negotiations Dulles was about to begin for a Japanese peace treaty.

We called again on MacArthur and found him still confident that the South Koreans could hold. He had been informed, however, that Korea might be placed under his responsibility. In that event, he told us, he proposed to fly immediately to the battle area to size up the situation. Despite his years, the General seemed impatient for action.

Events moved rapidly in the three main areas of activity—Korea, Washington, and Tokyo—and by June 28 the whole nature of the conflict had changed. Upon authorization from Washington, MacArthur swiftly followed his first shipment of munitions with other military equipment. He was directed also to provide ships and aircraft to evacuate American civilians from Korea. A small Norwegian freighter at Inchon, the port of Seoul, was loaded with women and children and sailed for Kokura, on the Japanese island of Kyushu. American air cover was provided, as necessary, for the three-day voyage, marking the first direct United States involvement. Further, an American Air Force airlift was inaugurated on June 26 between Kimpo, the airport for Seoul, and Itazuke Airfield, Kyushu. As soon as the United Nations Security Council voted to support South Korea, the United States responded with dispatch. While at the airport on June 27 to see off Dulles, who had been requested to return to Washington, we discussed the situation with MacArthur. The General and Dulles both were pessimistic, and MacArthur even spoke of writing off Korea—a complete reversal of his previous optimism. Later in the day MacArthur was directed to assume command of all military personnel in Korea, as the situation deteriorated hour by hour. President Rhee and most of the Korean government had left Seoul. The next day word was received in Tokyo that President Truman had ordered the use of the United States Air Force and Navy to drive the enemy back across the 38th parallel. One American foot already was on the battlefield.

The members of the United Nations Commission on Korea (UNCOK), who were in Tokyo, had been instructed to determine whether aggression had been committed, but they were most reluctant to return to Korea. Under our prodding, a seven-man group from this body agreed to go by air to Pusan, the southernmost port in Korea, and to proceed farther north, if possible, to investigate the situation. Eventually, this group reported to the General Assembly that "The invasion of the territory of the Republic of Korea by the armed forces of the North

Korean authorities was an act of aggression initiated without warning and without provocation, in execution of a carefully prepared plan." UNCOK reminded the Assembly that it had submitted a report on the day preceding the North Korean assault which said an inspection of the entire 38th parallel showed the South Korean forces were in no condition to launch a major attack northward. Now, it said, fresh investigation confirmed that, in fact, the South Koreans had not attacked. Instead of suddenly mobilizing to repel a border incursion, as they claimed, the North Koreans had launched an invasion under conditions indicating "a long-premeditated, well-prepared and well-timed plan of aggression." This was the first of several official reports which documented the consistent United Nations policy of branding North Korea and eventually Red China with aggression in Korea.

As depressing news continued to reach a tense and apprehensive Tokyo, Muccio telephoned me on June 28 from the small and then little known city of Taejon, near the center of South Korea. Speaking in an almost unintelligible garble of double-talk, to preserve security on a line that enemy agents could tap, the ambassador finally was able to inform me that President Rhee was with him in Taejon. This city was well south of the Han River, the first natural defense line which had been expected to delay the North Korean advance. The call, therefore, confirmed the critical turn of events which other reports had indicated. I was not surprised, then, when MacArthur told me later in the day that he would fly to Korea the next day, with a selected staff, to inspect the situation.

The General's plane took off early on the morning of June 29 for the relatively short flight to the battle area. It landed at Suwon Airfield, twenty miles south of Seoul, and MacArthur immediately went into conference with Rhee, Muccio, and with Brigadier General John H. Church, who had been sent ahead to survey the situation with a party of American military technicians. The result of this meeting was a strong recommendation by MacArthur that American ground troops be employed to shore up

South Korea's defense. After the MacArthur party had left Suwon, Muccio telephoned me. He said: "The Big Boy [Mac-Arthur] had a lot of guts and was magnificent." From this I assumed that the group had been under fire and, knowing of Mac-Arthur's intrepidity in these situations, I could well believe Muccio's report. *

The next day, June 30, Muccio telephoned again, reporting that the situation was growing desperate and that he feared panic among the Korean leadership, particularly members of the National Assembly, many of whom were at Taejon. The North Koreans had captured Seoul with such swift power that ROK forces abandoned the capital in great confusion. When the Communists plunged with little pause across the Han, the retreat grew more frenzied. One of the most formidable battlefield jobs is to regroup a losing and frightened army. What was needed, Muccio said, was a development to give the South Koreans confidence that the tide would soon turn. He hoped the "bold plan" of MacArthur could be adopted. I assumed that this phrase, a necessarily obscure part of our almost telepathic conversations, meant the commitment of American forces in strength.

Less than twenty-four hours later the first American combat troops landed in Pusan by air from northern Kyushu. The steady deterioration of the situation had made it necessary for President Truman to authorize the use of American ground troops. Five days later this advance group, the 1st Battalion, 21st Infantry, known as Task Force Smith, was under fire from strong North Korean forces and almost destroyed. The rest of the 24th

---

* As one of the four newspapermen accompanying MacArthur on this trip, I can affirm that the journey entailed a certain amount of danger and that the General, as in World War II, carried himself with calm disdain for the risk. Communist Yak fighter planes were still active, and one had to be driven off by U.S. fighters escorting the unarmed *Bataan* on the flight to Korea. The Suwon airfield was bombed shortly before MacArthur landed and, again, a few minutes after the *Bataan* took off for Japan, late in the day. While MacArthur was aground, his pilot, Major Anthony Story, flew the *Bataan* back to Japan for safety, returning to Korea in time to pick up the General's party. During the visit, MacArthur drove through the swirling, defeated South Korean Army and masses of bewildered, pathetic civilian refugees for a firsthand look at the battlefront along the Han River.

Division, commanded by Major General William F. Dean, also had to be committed piecemeal, through the unfortunate urgency of the situation, and it suffered accordingly.

Press reports from the battle zone soon indicated that the American Occupation troops from Japan were soft, inadequately equipped, and lacked the discipline to stand up to the trained, battle-hardened, and well-armed North Korean Army. It was not that our troops were less brave; they simply were unprepared to fight a war on such short notice. As MacArthur had predicted some three years earlier, Occupation duty had taken its toll.

The Chinese (Nationalist) Mission in Tokyo sent me a formal note on July 2, offering three combat divisions to the United Nations cause in Korea. I took this offer to the Chief of Staff, Major General Almond. His tentative reaction was that the logistic problems of such a force would be too great to make the proposition practicable. General MacArthur, to whom we referred the offer, thought it necessary to let Washington decide. Several days later MacArthur told me the proposal had been declined, although it was not clear who had made the final decision. The General said he had discussed the difficulties with General Ho Shai-lai, the chief of the Chinese Mission, and that Ho understood the reasons for the rejection. The proffered Chinese divisions would have been without artillery, armor, transport and logistics, and short of ammunition. In essence, then, they would constitute only additional manpower, and there was an ample number of South Koreans.

TOKYO BECAME A WAR CENTER almost in stride. By 1950 the capi-

Throughout the journey, the convoy constantly risked enemy air action, against which it had no adequate protection. Remaining in the battle area for an hour, MacArthur surveyed the situation from a hill within one mile of the front lines, which even then were wavering and were in danger of collapse. The crump of mortars was loud and clear, and the North Koreans could have seriously endangered the party with gunfire from only moderately heavy artillery. During this period, his staff later said, MacArthur conceived several strategic moves, including the subsequent "end run" landing at Inchon, to split North Korean forces. He gave no indication of the enormity of these plans or of any concern for his own welfare as he stood, thoughtfully, on the barren hill, watching the gunfire.—R.B.

tal already was overcrowded and bustling with the nervous energy of revival. Outwardly the Korean conflict made little change, except to increase the sense of apprehension which almost was endemic in that period. A heavy influx of officers and officials was reflected immediately, however, by cramped space in the limited accommodations available for Americans and other foreigners. Many of the dependents evacuated from Korea remained in Japan, and a number of staff personnel from the United States Embassy in Seoul and the Economic Cooperation Administration (ECA) also arrived hurriedly among us.

My office was also engulfed by a number of special diplomatic problems springing from a limited war so close to the established international community of Tokyo. It became a clearinghouse for information and the contact center for all types of unusual assignments. Visitors of all nationalities constantly called upon me for details of the fighting, which they could not always obtain clearly from news dispatches or official communiqués. On one occasion Frederick Bieri, the delegate of the International Red Cross, came to me for introductions to officials in Korea who might be able to assist in contacting North Korean leaders. He was seeking their pledge to respect the terms of the Geneva Conventions governing the conduct of hostilities and the treatment of prisoners. United Nations commanders promptly agreed to uphold these humanitarian conditions and did so, with considerable scrupulousness, throughout the conflict. The Communists, however, made their own rules.

The Japanese attitude toward the conflict was voiced strongly one day by Ichiro Ohno, vice minister of foreign affairs. He assured me that, as he put it, 99 percent of all Japanese supported the Korean operation, despite a widespread antiwar sentiment which was apparent throughout the country. We received assurances of similar popular support from representatives of all nations involved in the United Nations operations in Korea and a large number of other countries.

Contrarily, a colonel from the Soviet Mission sought to use

our office for another purpose during the early stages of the conflict. Identifying himself as Colonel Nikolai V. Smirnov, he asked one of our officers for several maps "which show the location and types of bridges from Kamakura northward to Mito." The area included the main communications around the industrial complex of the heavily populated Tokyo-Yokohama region. We assumed that Smirnov's mission was to engage in a not-too-subtle bit of psychological warfare, by suggesting reprisals against Japan, if the American saturation attacks in Korea continued.

On the bright sunlit afternoon of July 14, when the Korean campaign was still in its initial panic-stricken stages, a historic ceremony was held on the roof of the Dai Ichi building. General J. Lawton Collins, the U.S. Army Chief of Staff, formally presented the United Nations flag, symbolizing the first United Nations command, to General MacArthur as commander in chief. MacArthur, who looked tired and ashen-gray in the harsh light, was alert to the importance of the occasion. "I accept this flag with the deepest emotion . . ." he said. Standing with a small group of official observers, I could see clearly that the General meant his words. This was the first time the United Nations had at its disposal actual and potential forces sufficient to withstand naked aggression.

During the difficult days of July, August, and the first half of September, 1950, I attended many of the GHQ daily briefings on the Korean War. These briefings, essential to understanding the fighting, were conducted professionally on a General Headquarters level by high-ranking officers of exceptional experience. They included Major General Charles A. Willoughby for intelligence; Brigadier General E. K. Wright, for operations; Major General William A. Beiderlinden, for personnel; and Brigadier General H. E. Eastwood, for logistics. The Navy and Air Force also presented a day-by-day account of their operations.

At this top level, as well as in the foxholes, the Korean War was a heartbreaking, frustrating campaign. In the beginning the retreat of our forces, which so shocked the world, was necessary to trade space for time. The first piecemeal commitments of American forces enabled the United States Eighth Army and the reconstituted ROK Army of two corps to form the ultimate defense at the southern tip of the peninsula. This position, east of the Naktong River, was known as the Perimeter and was designed for a hold-or-die defense.

The Perimeter was manned by eight below-strength divisions —three American plus the 8th Regimental Combat Team from Hawaii, and eventually a brigade of U.S. Marines, and five ROK divisions. But there would be no further retreat. MacArthur had decreed that this line must hold while American forces, arms, and equipment were funneled into Pusan, the chief port at the southeasternmost end of the peninsula, as rapidly as availability and transport would allow.

Once stung and alerted by the initial Communist attack, the United States swiftly provided the men and equipment which were lacking at the outset of the war. The buildup was so fast that, by the end of August, the attacking North Korean Army around the Perimeter was outnumbered by the Americans and ROKs in both men and guns. The United States also held complete control of the air and the sea. But this preponderance was not enough, by itself, to determine the outcome of a war which primarily was confined to the mountains, hills, and valleys of a primitive and almost roadless country.

Despite the buildup, the North Koreans continued to hold the initiative throughout the summer along the hot, dusty front of the Perimeter. Their attacks were bitter, hard, and determined. In Tokyo, as we followed the desperate, seesaw battles across the sea from us, it seemed that the late Lieutenant General Walton H. Walker was holding back the Communist tide by sticking his fingers in the dike of the Perimeter. Walker commanded the Eighth Army with gruff and fearless intensity. The battle zone, a rough rectangle in the extreme southeastern corner of South Korea, was so small that it could be traversed quickly by jeep. And so the squat, heavy-chested figure of the commanding general usually materialized out of the choking dust at every spot where the pressure was most intense. By his personal example Walker spurred on the United Nations forces during this critical period, for the numerical superiority of the defenders did not completely replace the shock of the initial retreat; nor did it mean that they had enough men for the task of holding a front of some 125 miles against tank-equipped attacking forces, who appeared unconcerned by their losses. Walker had served during World War II as one of General Patton's senior commanders during the armored dash across Europe, and he had retained Patton's belief that generals were most useful at the front. Walker was dogged, stubborn, often blunt and direct, and a thoroughly professional field commander.

The details of the fighting are beyond the scope of this book and have been recounted with dramatic accuracy in a number of histories.[3] Watching from the vantage point of my position in Tokyo and with the information provided by the GHQ briefings, however, I acquired sidelight knowledge and impressions which bear on the main story. It will be recalled that the defense of the Perimeter was only the first major phase of a campaign that lasted for twenty-one bitter months. The defensive war ended with the brilliant Inchon landing in mid-September, 1950, and the simultaneous breakout from the Perimeter. Then came the recapture of Seoul, and the drive northward across the 38th parallel, with advance United Nations units reaching the Yalu River. Here the Chinese Communists entered the war in force, drove back into Seoul and deep into South Korea before they were stopped. The United Nations counterattack again recaptured the capital. The war finally ended along a line roughly approximating the 38th parallel, after the Chinese had fought costly, if limited, engagements for political objectives during the protracted truce negotiations.

The bloodiest fighting in this entire campaign took place around the Perimeter during the first two weeks of September, 1950. Without discounting the ferocity and importance of later engagements, or the heroism they produced, it was also apparent at Headquarters that the Perimeter was the most important single phase of the war. If the defenders had not held their barren and scrubby beachhead, and held it with forces inadequate for the immensity of the job, South Korea would have fallen. The chances of recapturing it would have been small indeed, and would have required immense power. Whether the United Nations would have paid the cost of returning in arms to South Korea, after once being driven from it, remains disputable.

The vast number of men required to fight even a so-called brush-fire war was astounding. This point was emphasized, time and again, by statistics concerning the manpower situation of the U.S. Army during GHQ briefings. There were many days, especially during the period of severe fighting, when G-1 reported that casualties exceeded the replacements. But new units continued to arrive.

This seemingly insatiable need for men raised the question of creating a complete United Nations multinational force in Korea. In due time the peak strength of all contingents other than South Korean and American totaled only about 40,000 men. Of these, the British Commonwealth Brigade was the main force, although the units of fourteen other countries fought bravely and contributed much.

Although their activities were little publicized, many United Nations officials, and particularly several connected with the Secretariat, helped to solve some of the difficult problems of coordination between Tokyo and New York. Many of them worked closely with our office. In particular, Colonel Alfred Katzin of the United Nations Secretariat played a substantial role in handling the medical and other supplies which had been contributed to the war effort by nations which, for various reasons, were unable to send fighting troops. Colonel Katzin also was helpful in solving the problem of transportation for the members and staff of the United Nations Commission (UNCOK) who traveled between Korea and Japan. He did this by the simple expedient of leasing a C-47 plane which made a daily round trip between the airports at Haneda and Pusan. The plane was clearly marked "UNITED NATIONS" in bright blue letters. Katzin was confident it would not be shot down by mistake, although others were more skeptical. The shuttle run continued throughout the conflict, providing the means for United Nations observers to obtain firsthand information on the hostilities. Fortunately, the plane was unmolested, and the possibility of an accident which could have created a grave crisis for the international organization was averted.

At the end of July, 1950, a member of my staff returned from a visit to Taegu with discouraging observations of United States forces in that hot spot. The man, who was not a career Foreign Service officer, reported that the general morale of our "citizen" soldiers was very low. He said the men failed to understand why they were involved in such a dirty war and usually considered it better tactics to withdraw rather than to stand and fight. This dismal picture was in sharp contrast to the air of confidence which I noted around Headquarters and which was reflected in many official statements. The report, however, corresponded to our historical experience of allowing the Army to deteriorate to the point where soldiers forget that their mission is to fight. Time, more experience, and battle requirements would change all this soon enough, but as of midsummer 1950 the prospects of fighting a bitter war against a determined and ruthless enemy were not good.

MacArthur, of course, was aware of this problem. Talking with me on August 1 he wondered aloud what had happened to the many billions of dollars which the United States had spent since World War II on its armed forces. A large portion of these appropriations, he mused, had been wasted upon frills and fancies which, in turn, militated against producing good soldiers. Nevertheless, he emphasized, the last withdrawal had taken place in Korea and the Perimeter would hold. Even so, the General felt that he would not have too many troops for this assignment.

During August MacArthur's chief of staff, Major General Edward M. Almond, disappeared frequently from his desk in the Dai Ichi building. The reason was that a new force, the X Corps, was being formed, with Almond as the commander. The chief of staff was a vitriolic man, who customarily discussed even the weather with impatient energy, and his absence from his scrupulously neat desk was almost as revealing as a public announcement of his whereabouts. Despite tight military secrecy, the existence and purpose of the new force must have been known by hundreds of Americans and Japanese. Its mission was to launch an amphibious landing at Inchon, the port of Seoul, deep in the rear of North Korean forces battering away at the southeastern Perimeter. Before the landing, the impending operation and even the fact that Inchon was the target became almost an open secret in Tokyo. It was miraculous that the network of spies, which North Korea was known to maintain in Japan, did not alert the Communist capital of Pyongyang. Yet the landing, when finally made, achieved tactical surprise. A short time before the invasion fleet departed from various ports in Japan, Almond disappeared completely from his desk job, which was taken over by his deputy, Major General Doyle O. Hickey.

The Inchon landings—there were two of them—became one of the most incredible operations in modern military history.[4] The spring tides at Inchon, lasting only three days but essential for an assault over the beaches, ran to thirty-one feet, leaving long and deep mud flats at the ebb. With the tide in at dawn on D day, September 15, a battalion of Marines went ashore at Wolmi Island, a small wooded and rocky, triangular-shaped islet guarding the entrance to the harbor and on which the North Koreans maintained artillery. Once ashore, the Marines were cut off from reinforcements by the rapidly receding tide. The enemy then knew that a second landing would be made at sunset, when the tide next was at flood, in order to capture Inchon itself and surrounding areas. Within three days, supply operations were well in hand, and with the end of the spring tides on D plus 3, adequate logistic support was assured through superb organization and teamwork.

Despite staggering difficulties, the operation was a complete success, and the port was quickly secured by U.S. Marines, supported by a vast array of naval gunfire and airpower. MacArthur had won a daring gamble, with the strategic concept he had conceived on his first wartime trip to Korea and which he had pursued in the face of almost unanimous opposition by the top commanders of all services, culminating in conferences lasting two days in the Tokyo Headquarters. This "brilliant and audacious" stroke, as it was called, was correlated with a simultaneous breakout from the Perimeter by the Eighth Army. Tired and worn troops in the south, who had been subjected to weeks of pressure and heavy fighting, turned upon the North Korean Army, pushed it northward and, in an incredibly short time, nearly destroyed it. There is no better tonic than success for a dispirited army.

Within a fortnight MacArthur and his top generals were in recaptured Seoul. In a dramatic formal ceremony, the General turned control of the capital over to the aging, wet-eyed President Rhee. The North Koreans were fleeing northward and, it was hoped, the war soon would be over. In the circumstances of the campaign at that time, MacArthur's thrust at Inchon had achieved its purpose of breaking the backbone of the North Korean military force. Seoul was the hub of all communications southward, and its recapture cut off the outflung North Korean forces from all supplies. They had to pull back northward from the Perimeter to re-establish communications, and in the process of doing this they were smashed as an army.

PROBABLY THE GREATEST HELP which Japan gave to the United Nations and to SCAP at this time was its prompt agreement to establish an internal security force. This was provided for in a letter from MacArthur to Yoshida dated July 8, 1950. SCAP authorized the Japanese government to form a national police reserve of 75,000 men and to increase the Maritime Safety Board, which patrolled the coasts, by 8,000 men. These increases were necessary, because Japan was about to be virtually denuded of American troops and needed protection against both external and internal aggression. In due time the police reserve became a "self-defense force" which permitted development of a defensive army, despite the constitutional provision outlawing arms or the waging of war. Several judicial interpretations of this clause by Japanese courts have upheld the legality of ensuring the defense of the country, as, indeed, practicality requires. The "self-defense force" was organized into five divisions and, in time, was supplied with heavy weapons, including tanks. Several thousand members of the police reserve were used for guard duties over Occupation installations, storage depots, and munitions dumps. They were armed with American rifles and pistols.

The new Japanese Army, in fact, looked as though it had been made in the United States. On a visit to one of the training camps, I thought at first I had stumbled into an American base, for everything from guns to fatigues was GI. Only when I saw the Japanese soldiers eating with chopsticks did I fully realize that these were, indeed, soldiers of another Japanese generation, with a new mission. I was struck by the zest of the drills, the high morale, and the energy demonstrated by officers and men. Even so, it seemed somewhat anomalous that we Americans should be teaching the Japanese how to be soldiers.

With MacArthur's urging the Japanese government took steps at the start of Korean hostilities to curtail Communist party activities, but the danger of sabotage and disruption was constantly present. Probably because of the expanded police reserve, however, no major instance of sabotage occurred during the Korean War.

The Japanese also provided a considerable amount of backup support for the war effort. American planes and ships operating from Japanese airfields and ports were dependent, in large measure, upon Japanese labor. Japanese industry supplied the equipment and skilled personnel for all types of repairs on army and naval equipment. Mountains of supplies moved through Japan for the Korean fighting fronts. Remote sections of Japan provided staging areas for further training of fresh American troops from the United States. Almost half of the 7th U.S. Army Division, which was part of the X Corps, was composed of Koreans who were brought to Japan and integrated with American soldiers.

Less well-known, perhaps, is the close front-line support furnished by the Japanese. A large portion of available Japanese shipping was mobilized and used to transport men and supplies to Korea. Almost a third of the 120 vessels used to transport X Corps to the Inchon landings was manned by the Japanese. Some twenty Japanese-manned minesweepers, operating under contract, were utilized to sweep both coasts of Korea. Several hundred Japanese stevedores were brought to such front-line ports as Inchon, Wonsan, and Hungnam to assist in handling cargo.[5]

In short, it was apparent at the time that Japan was in full accord and sympathy with the United Nations action in Korea, and both the government and the people responded as fully as the situation required. This infuriated the Soviets, of course, and not surprisingly they protested publicly at a meeting of the Allied Council. General Kislenko, then the Soviet member, succeeded in making public a long bill of particulars concerning Japanese co-operation with the Korean War effort. Although he evidently expected to create an adverse reaction in Japan strong enough to raise demands for strict noninvolvement, he received no support whatsoever from the Japanese press or public.

The partial destruction of the North Korean Army in South Korea immediately raised the question whether United Nations forces should cross the 38th parallel. On September 27, 1950, MacArthur received authorization from the Joint Chiefs of Staff to do so, in order to complete the destruction of enemy forces. This permission was conditioned, however, by the basic assumption that no major Chinese or Soviet forces would have entered North Korea. The General's orders also stated that no United Nations forces were to violate the Yalu River border between North Korea and Chinese and Soviet territory. Furthermore, Washington specified that only Korean ground troops were to operate in this border region. This injunction soon was modified.[6]

On October 1 MacArthur broadcast a demand for surrender addressed to the commander in chief of the North Korean forces, but there was no answer. On the following day the General told me that United Nations forces already were across the parallel. He said the North Koreans probably would be fooled by their Communist friends into refusing to surrender, and thus would be destroyed. During the night of October 4 I was awakened from a sound sleep and handed an "urgent telegram" from Washington. It contained a report of a conversation between Ambassador K. M. Pannikar, the Indian envoy to Peking, and Chou En-lai, the Chinese Communist foreign minister. Chou had given a strong indication, the message said, that a crossing of the 38th parallel by United Nations forces would be considered dangerous by the Chinese People's Republic. The inference was that, in this event, Chinese troops would be sent into North Korea. Although this message originated in the State Department, it was sent through army channels to Tokyo and was, therefore, disseminated in the General Headquarters.

Five days later, on October 9, MacArthur issued a second call for the surrender of North Korean forces. This time the broadcast message was addressed to "The Premier, Government of North Korea." I told MacArthur's aide, Colonel Bunker, that this mode of addressing the political authorities of an unrecognized government was irregular and might cause embarrassment in the future. Bunker replied that he had no advance knowledge of the broadcast.

It was after this sequence of events that the momentous conference between President Truman and General MacArthur was held on Wake Island, October 15.* In the President's public statement on the meeting no mention was made of the crossing of the parallel or of the possibility that Chinese or Soviet troops might intervene in Korea. Indeed, in his memoirs, President Tru-

* See pp. 217ff.

man states that MacArthur "also informed me that the Chinese Communists would not attack." [7] The President, however, commended the "very complete unanimity of view which prevailed" and "the excellent coordination which has existed between Washington and the field, to which General MacArthur paid tribute." If there was, or had been, any friction or misunderstanding or hard feelings between Tokyo and Washington, the Wake Island statement made no note of it. Instead, the announcement seemed to wipe the slate clean.

In the field, the United Nations forces were operating under a new plan which MacArthur had given to his commanders at the end of September. The strategy called for Eighth Army to advance northward along the western flank through the North Korean capital of Pyongyang. The X Corps, composed of Marines and infantry, was to make a ship-borne landing at Wonsan, on Korea's east coast, and from there was to move westward to join up again with Eighth Army. At the same time, the United Nations General Assembly adopted a resolution calling for steps to ensure conditions of stability throughout Korea. This seemed to give another green light for MacArthur's plan of attack in North Korea. Accordingly, it was carried out, but with some changes. The X Corps landings were delayed six days, until October 25, while Wonsan harbor was swept of mines. Then the Corps, instead of heading westward, advanced generally to the north, in accordance with changes dictated by fresh dispositions of the remaining North Korean Army.

Among other considerations behind this strategic concept was MacArthur's concern over the administrative complexities and confusion resulting from the occupation of North Korea. He told me in several conversations there were too many United Nations commissions, such as UNCOK, UNCURK, and UNKRA, all dealing with Korean problems. Furthermore, he said, the immense task of rehabilitating the north, which had been devastated by air attacks, was complicated by difficult Korean personalities and by confusing and conflicting policies regarding unification of the country. The General felt that the only realistic solution would be to allow the ROK government to "spill over" the parallel, letting nature then take its course, with an election to be held as soon as practicable. However, he continued to maintain contact with the chairmen of the main United Nations organizations dealing with Korea.

From August through October, 1950, antiaircraft fire from the Manchurian side of the Yalu River and captured prisoners within Korea indicated the involvement of Chinese Communist forces. By October 30 it was clear from all available intelligence that Eighth Army was faced by major Chinese Communist forces in North Korea. In retrospect, however, I cannot recall that MacArthur showed concern during this period over the possibility that Peking would enter the war. To the best of my recollection, the subject was not mentioned during several conversations between the General and me at this time, the latest being on October 27. Perhaps there was no reason why the General should have indicated concern or mentioned the subject to me. But for several weeks General Willoughby, during intelligence briefings, had pointed out the capabilities of the Chinese Communist Army and had provided identifications of its major formations in Manchuria.

MacArthur sent a special report to the United Nations on November 5, detailing the evidence of Chinese participation in the Korean conflict. In another report, on the following day, he pointed out the seriousness of the military position created by the Chinese intervention. This, he said, is the "present situation": (1) Although the North Korean forces had been destroyed, "a new and fresh army now faces us," backed by large alien reserves in Manchuria, "beyond the limits of our present sphere of military action"; (2) it remained to be seen whether these reserves would be moved forward to the battle area and this was "a matter of the gravest international significance"; (3) for the United Nations, the "present mission is limited to the destruction of those forces now arrayed against us in North Korea.

At the regular GHQ briefing during the morning of November 7, 1950, General Willoughby gave a clear and succinct analysis of the order of battle of the Chinese Army engaged in North Korea. He also provided identifications, tentative in some cases, of a large number of reserve divisions still north of the Yalu. I specifically asked Willoughby at that time whether his identifications and unit locations were firm. His answer was an unequivocal affirmative. This exchange was to come back to me many times, when it appeared later that the United Nations forces were "reeling" from the "sudden onslaught" of the Chinese Communist forces and when charges were made in the world press that intelligence was taken by surprise and hence was the cause of the United Nations "defeat" in the first Chinese offensive. The years have not dimmed my belief that, contrary to achieving tactical surprise, the Chinese movements were well known to the United States intelligence officers.

ON NOVEMBER 14, I had a lengthy interview with General MacArthur during which he explained his concept of the Korean campaign. In brief, he said his immediate objective was to destroy the bridges across the Yalu River and thus isolate the area between the United Nations forces and the North Korean border. He said orders had been given to his forces, including the Air Forces, that the border must be scrupulously observed. All built-up areas in North Korea between the United Nations lines and the border were to be destroyed. The General indicated that preparations were being made for an offensive to drive the Communist forces across the Yalu River, although the United Nations forces were to stop at the border. In the event of failure of this offensive, MacArthur saw no alternative, from a military point of view, to bombing key points in Manchuria. He hoped this would not be necessary, as "the fat would be in the fire" should such bombing bring counteraction by Soviet Russia. The General felt, however, that Soviet Russia was not taking a direct part in the war and that the Chinese had intervened on their own responsibility.

With the Chinese entry into Korea there was increased impatience and frustration among the high command in Japan over the restrictions placed on United Nations military operations by policies of the United States government and, later, those of the United Nations itself. Lieutenant General G. E. Stratemeyer, Commander of the Far East Air Forces, told me in mid-November, for example, that he could flatten China with his airpower if authorized to do so. He was not alone in his fierce determination to conduct hostilities as fully as seemed necessary to the military commanders directly involved.

MacArthur and several staff officers flew to Korea on November 24, ostensibly to open the offensive which would end the war. But the whole complexion of the conflict changed when the Chinese launched a major assault on November 25 against Eighth Army in the west, and two days later against the Marines in the east. Through a special communiqué on November 28, MacArthur announced that Chinese armed forces "in army, corps, and divisional organization of an aggregate strength of over 200,000 men are arrayed against the United Nations forces in North Korea." With heavy Chinese reinforcements within the "privileged sanctuary" of Manchuria, MacArthur pointed out that "we face an entirely new war." An additional paragraph to this communiqué was issued about an hour later, stating that the problem created by this Chinese force posed issues which were beyond the authority of the United Nations military command.

The GHQ briefing on the following day, November 29, reflected a grim situation in Korea. The Chicoms, as the Chinese forces were known in military parlance, had folded up the entire right wing of the United Nations forces in the center and west and had practically annihilated the ROK II Corps on the right of Eighth Army. This forced the withdrawal of the left wing of the United Nations forces to the Chongchon River line. Two days later a Japanese newspaper "extra" on the streets of Tokyo reported President Truman had told a news conference that the question of using the atomic bomb in Korea or elsewhere against the Chinese Communists was under active consideration, but he hoped it would not be necessary to do so. This, plus continuing bad news from Korea, seemed to indicate an increasingly serious world crisis which conceivably could trigger World War III. Or so we, in Japan, thought at the time. In a call on MacArthur later that day I found him deeply preoccupied with the military situation and concerned with the task of stopping between 200,000 and 300,000 troops.

In this deteriorating situation, I was confronted by the possibility that the evacuation of all or part of the Americans in Japan might become necessary. Our roster showed some 30,000 dependents of American military and civilian officials, plus about 10,000 nonofficial American residents. Previously, I had discussed the evacuation problem with Headquarters and had urged precautionary plans to establish priorities, to locate collection centers, determine procedures, and outline the responsibilities and tasks of the government authorities involved. Consequently, members of my staff worked with appropriate Headquarters officers and in a few days had drawn up complete plans to meet various emergencies arising out of war, natural calamities, and other crises. The plans, fortunately, did not have to be used.

Tokyo anxiously watched the 1st Marine Division of the X Corps conduct its epic withdrawal from the Chosin Reservoir area to the port of Hungnam during the first ten days of December. The Marines fought against vastly superior forces in bitterly cold weather, aided by superb air support from Marine air and carrier-based navy planes. Despite the collective heroism and skillful leadership of the Marines, the operation created an unfortunately strong undercurrent of criticism and some defeatism among those in Tokyo who should have known better.

Among other black rumors, reports grew that United Nations forces would evacuate Korea and return to Japan. MacArthur told me on December 12, however, that this would not occur and that our forces would hold. This conversation arose out of a message I had received from the State Department complaining about the defeatist tone of press dispatches from Tokyo and Seoul. It was not difficult to understand the reasons for newspaper pessimism. A strategic withdrawal is a difficult maneuver and, to succeed, it must be conducted with as little publicity as possible. The reasons for pulling back, consequently, cannot be explained publicly until after the event. Our troops on both fronts were on the defensive, a situation particularly distasteful to American soldiers. Correspondents with the troops naturally heard, and often reported, the griping which this kind of unpleasant war usually produces among men and officers alike. Other circumstances added to the gloom. President Truman declared a "national emergency" on December 17, an act which seemed to impress soldiers and civilians near the front with added discouragement. Visitors from Washington who called on me reported a bad case of "nerves" in the United States, with visible fear and concern over the possible widening of the Korean hostilities. Several Americans from Seoul met with me just before Christmas and expressed considerable pessimism about our ability to hold in Korea, despite the optimism which had been expressed publicly by United Nations leaders.

In this atmosphere the sudden death of General "Johnny" Walker was a particularly serious blow to morale. He was killed in a jeep accident while en route to a front-line position. On a cold day, December 30, his remains were placed aboard a special plane at Haneda Airport for return to the United States, in the presence of General and Mrs. MacArthur and the entire diplomatic corps. The General's widow and son also departed aboard the plane, at the end of a brief ceremony which seemed to epitomize the irony and frustration of the conflict in Korea.

The withdrawal of the United Nations forces continued, and Seoul was abandoned on January 4, 1951. Eventually, a continuous front was established farther south across the peninsula, and the Chinese drive was halted. During early February, MacArthur told me the war had changed so much that he lacked precise instructions on his current mission in Korea. He felt that

United Nations resolutions calling for reunification of the country could no longer be implemented.

The dispirited and uncertain United Nations troops were stirred alive and welded into a newly invigorated fighting unit by the new Eighth Army commander, Lieutenant General Matthew B. Ridgway. Ironically, it was Ridgway who proved the value in combat of the particular flamboyance made famous by Walker's former mentor, General Patton. Instead of pearl-handled pistols, Ridgway wore two live hand grenades on the lapels of his battle fatigues, as he strode through the lines like the paratrooper he was. Ridgway arrived in the right uniform for the occasion.

During the next several months a series of operations carried the United Nations line northward to the vicinity of the 38th parallel. Seoul was recaptured March 15, and the new line was established nearly straight across the peninsula, northward of the capital. This was the relative position of the front when I made my first visit to the battle area, on May 28, as the guest of General Ridgway, who had become SCAP. The General still wore his same battle dress, even though by then he was supreme commander. The Eighth Army had been taken over by Lieutenant General James Van Fleet. Before leaving Tokyo, I was lent a field uniform, without insignia or rank, and equipped with heavy boots, a pistol, and a canteen.

The long-somnambulant peninsula was crowded and alive with the men and machines of war. The enormous energy required by combat became apparent from the air. Everywhere we saw crisscrossing lines of trucks, bulldozers, jeeps, helicopters, camps, dumps of all kinds, and on the ridges of barren hills, foxholes and trenches. Against the backdrop of growling gunfire, the land, it seemed, was being dug out and reshaped with furious speed. The panorama sharply illustrated the huge effort and the large number of men required behind the lines to support the actual fighters.

When I returned to quiet and peaceful Haneda Airport, shaking off the dust and the noise and tensions of Korea, I found a deep new respect for our army. During my brief but extremely crowded visit of three days I had seen enough of the conflict— from the front lines to the rear areas—to obtain a new realization of the formidable task of fighting a war on the ground.

ON JUNE 23, 1951, NEW YORK TIME, the Soviet delegate to the United Nations, Yakov A. Malik, suggested in a speech that negotiations for an armistice would be welcomed.

Initially, the State Department in Washington adopted what it described as a position of "extreme caution" in commenting on Malik's proposal, a reflection of the general suspicion in official quarters over Soviet motives. This only served to intensify the air of uncertainty and confusion, particularly among the large and aggressive press corps operating out of Tokyo. In an effort to clarify the situation, my public affairs officer, Saxton Bradford, prepared with my authorization a statement explaining Washington's position.

The result was almost disastrous. Instead of accepting the statement on Brad's terms, many correspondents read a deeper meaning into it, and in some stories it was interpreted as a denial of Malik's offer. The confusion heightened, and Washington quickly reacted to the repercussions. I received an urgent call from Dean Rusk for clarification, for he said "great embarrassment had been caused to the Department" by the press release. Even General Hickey, the even-tempered SCAP chief of staff, contacted me several times during the day for an explanation.

Like many similar "press hassles," this result of inaccurate reporting had no appreciable effect on the effort to conclude a truce. Presumably the Communist side—Russian, Chinese, and North Korean—all wanted armistice negotiations for their own purposes and were unwilling to be diverted. General Ridgway was instructed on June 30 to broadcast an invitation to meet with Communist leaders aboard the Danish hospital ship *Jutlandia* in Wonsan harbor. The invitation was accepted on the following day, but with the suggestion that the meeting be held at the little village of Kaesong. This led to the long and tortuous quest for a truce. In the light of all that has happened in the past thirteen years, I have often wondered whether the confusion and doubt created by Brad's press release were prophetic.

Several lengthy planning sessions in Tokyo and more minor misunderstandings preceded the departure of the United Nations negotiating team for Kaesong. Paul Nitze, head of the Policy Planning Staff of the State Department, arrived in the Japanese capital, and I joined him for long conferences with General Ridgway. Nitze contributed valuable suggestions for what we all knew would be difficult negotiating sessions with the Communists. Another suggestion, which might have had significant influence, was made by Governor Thomas E. Dewey of New York. Reaching Tokyo on a Far Eastern tour, the former presidential candidate called on Ridgway. At this meeting, which I also attended, Dewey strongly advised the General to avoid participating personally in the truce talks. He recalled the difficulty that President Wilson had encountered at the Versailles Peace Conference, to settle World War I, when the President's presence weakened his bargaining power.

The late Vice Admiral Charles Turner Joy was named chief negotiator on July 8, when the United Nations armistice team was announced. Ridgway made no attempt to take part in the truce negotiations, although he was in Korea when they started at Kaesong on July 10.

Fighting in Korea did not cease until more than two years later, when the cease-fire agreement was finally signed at Panmunjom on July 27, 1953. They were years which produced some of the most savage combat of the entire war, with tens of thousands of casualties. The battle names were sadly descriptive of the frustration over last-minute campaigns, launched for political advantage by the Chicoms or to gain a military adjustment on the line—Bloody Ridge, Heartbreak Ridge, Baldy, Whitehorse, Pork

Chop Hill. There was also unbelievable destruction by tremendous and continuing air bombardments, and the Navy was never busier.

Thus, by some strange quirk of fate, I was spared involvement in the tensions and infuriations which plagued the true negotiators during this long period.

10

Dismissal of MacArthur; Ridgway as Supreme Commander

THE ABRUPT DISMISSAL of General MacArthur from all his commands in April, 1951, was a climax which had been developing slowly for five and one-half years. During the Occupation, as we have seen, a low-key, smoldering state of misunderstanding was almost continual between Tokyo and Washington. This resulted in occasional resentment on both sides. The Korean War added virtually intolerable burdens. Early in that struggle the President and the General fell into a collision course. It was surprising that the showdown did not occur earlier.

During this long and troubled period the absence of any misunderstanding between MacArthur and Washington would have been most unusual under any circumstances. MacArthur handled his various command responsibilities and the innumerable challenges of the situation in a characteristic way, long familiar to Washington. With his sense of history, experience, seniority, reputation, and temperament, he did not easily compromise when his judgment or his decisions were questioned. Although he knew when to conform to specific superior authority, he did not hesitate to advance his views vigorously. He was never reluctant to interpret his authority broadly or to make decisions and act quickly—arguing the matter later. Many in Washington remembered these same qualities from World War II and resented them even more in the semipeace of the postwar era.

During the Occupation period, before the Korean War, some of the misunderstandings were critical enough to cause concern. Washington authorities were particularly aroused by instances when, without consultation, MacArthur pursued his own plans until a specific project became a fait accompli and had to be accepted by Washington. I was well-aware of these feelings through my several trips to the capital. The results sometimes made it appear as if the two major centers of Occupation authority were working against each other.

In the Tokyo Headquarters the reaction to Washington policy and guidance often was a sense of frustration. Most SCAP officials believed that Washington did not understand the situation in Japan and that all they needed to complete the Occupation task adequately was clear-cut authority to conduct affairs. There was, of course, some appreciation in Tokyo of the global responsibilities which the United States had assumed and which often governed or influenced the specific policies preferred by Washington. Tokyo was convinced, however, that it felt the cold war more keenly and understood it more thoroughly than did Washington.

This latter point was understandable and, at least until 1948, probably correct. SCAP was confronted at the outset of "peace" by a combination of Soviet power and chicanery which appeared only vaguely recognizable in Washington. The power was visible, for Soviet military force bristled on the nearby mainland and came within sight of Japan Proper, through the occupation of the Habomai Islands, three miles from Hokkaido. In addition to holding hundreds of thousands of Japanese war prisoners, Moscow demonstrated this power by the frequent arrest of Japanese fishing boats near the Habomai and Kurile islands. Along with developments on the continent, these actions provided constant evidence that the might of Soviet Russia stood ready to fill any vacuum created by American misstep or default.

Politically, we had to contend with the ceaseless propaganda and subversive activities of the oversized Soviet Mission. Furthermore, the political pressures and machinations of the Japan Communist Party were a persistent and real threat to the peace and tranquillity of Occupied Japan.

This basic situation became more acute because of the appalling military and political problems of the Korean War. Frustration grew into a sense of futility in both Tokyo and Korea. This stemmed chiefly from the assignment of fighting a "limited" war with patently insufficient forces and under restrictions preventing the full employment of the available power.

Serious misunderstanding between MacArthur and Washington probably began with the General's unannounced journey to Formosa on July 31, 1950.* The trip did not appear to produce any alterations of policy, yet it was a conspicuous point of irritation with Washington. Part of this was caused, I believe, by MacArthur's failure to give due weight to the fact that, under our system of government, foreign policy is made by the President, and that the Department of State recommends and implements this policy. Public dissent with State Department direction, therefore, was in fact a public disagreement with the President. Despite the apparent lack of results from the Formosa visit, MacArthur made it at a time of his own choosing, at a particularly delicate moment, and on the basis of only a very general suggestion from Washington.

The Administration's policy—that is, the policy of the United States government—was to prevent any fighting between Formosa and Mainland China. This was designed to prevent the spread of hostilities in the Far East. It was hoped thereby to give practical evidence that the United States wanted to localize the Korean conflict and, if possible, to contain it below the 38th parallel, as demanded by some friendly governments, notably India. President Truman had ordered the United States Seventh Fleet on June 27 to patrol the Formosa Strait and to prevent any

* See pp. 214ff.

military action from either the Communist mainland or Formosa. In MacArthur's view, this neutralization actually "protected" Communist China from any attack by the Chinese on Formosa, despite the opportunity for such action created by the Korean conflict. The General believed that this "protection" enabled Peking to release two field armies from defense positions in South China and to send them to Manchuria during the summer and early autumn of 1950. These same two armies spearheaded the Chinese Communist attack in Korea.

The neutralization policy raised serious questions and provoked considerable debate, both public and private. Encouraged by Washington's concern over the island and by press speculation that he might visit Formosa to study the situation, MacArthur decided to do so at the first opportunity. This arose on July 31, when United Nations forces in Korea were still locked behind the Perimeter and when intelligence knew that the first of the Chinese Communist units were moving from South China to Manchuria. The offer of three combat divisions for Korea by the Republic of China had been declined more than three weeks earlier.

Immediately upon concluding his visit to Taipei, MacArthur issued this statement:

My visit to Formosa has been primarily for the purpose of making a short reconnaissance of the potential of its defense against possible attack. The policy has been enunciated that this island, including the Pescadores, is not under present circumstances subject to military invasion. It is my responsibility and firm purpose to enforce this decision.

My conferences here on all levels have been most cordial and responsive in every respect. Among the problems which were discussed was the prompt and generous offer of the Chinese Government to send troops to join the United Nations forces in Korea. The belief of all concerned however was that such action at this time might so seriously jeopardize the defense of Formosa that it would be inadvisable.

Arrangements have been completed for effective coordination between American forces under my command and those of the Chinese Government, the better to meet any attack which a hostile force might be foolish enough to attempt. Such an attack would, in my opinion, stand little chance of success.

It has been a great pleasure for me to meet my old comrade-in-arms of the last war, Generalissimo Chiang Kai-shek. His indomitable determination to resist Communist domination arouses my sincere admiration. His determination parallels the common interest and purpose of Americans, that all peoples in the Pacific area shall be free—not slave.

This statement visibly upset Washington, because of its clear political implications and its promise of close American and Chinese cooperation for the defense of Formosa. Secretary of State Acheson's instruction to me to ask for more details, therefore, was understandable and was hardly satisfied by the General's reply that, in effect, his "military conversations" were none of the State Department's business. Although MacArthur said he had reported fully to Washington through his own channels, it was never clear in Tokyo whether the State Department was adequately informed of the Taipei talks. In any case, Harriman's visit to Tokyo on August 6 indicated concern on the highest level that MacArthur and Chiang Kai-shek might take action, on their own responsibility, thereby upsetting the careful and delicate balance which the Administration was trying to maintain.

If anything, MacArthur added to this uncertainty by his press release of August 10, issued primarily to answer newspaper speculation that he had a particular purpose in failing to take me with him to Taipei. Emphasizing the military nature of the journey, MacArthur ended his statement with this controversial paragraph:

This visit has been maliciously misrepresented to the public by those who invariably in the past have propagandized a policy of defeatism and appeasement in the Pacific. I hope the American people will not be misled by sly insinuations, brash speculations and bold misstatements invariably attributed to anonymous sources, so insidiously fed them both nationally and internationally by persons 10,000 miles away from the actual events, if they are not indeed designed, to promote disunity and destroy faith and confidence in American purposes and institutions and American representatives at this time of great world peril.[1]

These were MacArthur's sincere sentiments and those of the overwhelming majority of his staff officers at that period of frustration in the Korean War. Washington was sufficiently concerned, however, so that on August 14 Secretary of Defense George C. Marshall sent specific instructions to MacArthur, forbidding authorization of any Nationalist Chinese attack on the mainland. Marshall based the order on the contention that "the most vital national interest requires that no action of ours precipitates general war or gives excuse to others to do so." MacArthur replied that he fully understood the presidential decision of June 27 "to protect the Communist mainland."

The relationship between MacArthur and the Administration changed markedly, if temporarily, after the Inchon landing. The bickering and occasional flashes of temper which had occurred on both sides calmed. The military operation vindicated MacArthur's judgment against all advisers, including most of the Joint Chiefs of Staff. He had demonstrated that a bold policy against the Communist aggressor, by the skillful use of available means, would win. Even President Truman basked in the sunlight of MacArthur's tremendously successful strategic and tactical stroke. It was followed by the crossing of the 38th parallel, the Wake Island meeting, and the entry of powerful Chinese Communist forces into the war.

Although the decision to cross the 38th parallel resulted from apparent total agreement between MacArthur and Washington, fundamental differences of viewpoint over the Korean conflict remained. In particular, they disagreed over the relative importance of Europe and Asia in global strategy, a controversy held over from World War II. MacArthur firmly believed that the Communists would conquer Europe through Asia unless stopped in the Far East. He believed also that both Europe and the United States were shortsighted in failing to accept this premise. The Administration, on the other hand, clearly was following a global strategy. Despite the demands of the Korean War, Washington was increasing and strengthening United States forces in Europe. To a considerable degree, this policy was feasible only if the Korean conflict remained localized and limited, thus requiring fewer American troops.

President Truman apparently initiated the Wake Island meeting with MacArthur, on October 14, 1950, largely to clarify these misunderstandings. It seemed likely the President also wanted to emphasize again the need for the General to conform to fundamental Washington policy, while simultaneously establishing closer rapport with the Far Eastern commander he had never met.

MacArthur, on the other hand, made it clear to me that he as attending the conference reluctantly. On this occasion I had called on him to protest exclusion from his party, which was limited to his immediate aides. The General answered, in effect, that I would be better off to escape the implications of the meeting. He said Japan probably would not be discussed and Formosa, if it arose during the session, would be highly controversial. Political affairs relating to Korea were to be handled by Ambassador John J. Muccio, whom Washington had invited. MacArthur clinched his argument by saying he regarded the Wake Island trip as only a political junket.

During our conversation MacArthur compared his forthcoming meeting with President Truman to his World War II journey to Pearl Harbor for a major conference with President Roosevelt. Although the Navy was preparing to thrust directly across the Central Pacific, MacArthur convinced Roosevelt to authorize a return to the Philippines, which the Navy proposed to bypass. On that occasion, the General reminisced, he also had gone alone to meet the President.[2] Now it was evident that MacArthur, with his usual sense of the dramatic, was deliberately underplaying his visit to Wake by appearing as a simple soldier, without advisers for the meeting with the President and his large official and press party.

The General was not alone in anticipating a stormy session. He read me some of the numerous cables he had received from individuals throughout the United States, warning him about the State Department, President Truman, and in some instances, "the

Communists." The wires urged MacArthur to "Keep a stiff upper lip!" and to "Be on guard against evil people still in control."

MacArthur and three aides left Haneda Airport at 7 A.M. on Saturday, October 14, and returned at 4:02 P.M., Sunday.[3] This was indeed a brief absence, the minimum that courtesy to the President seemed to demand. MacArthur gave no details of the conference, not even to his headquarters, and he said nothing publicly beyond expressing his satisfaction over meeting Mr. Truman. Muccio, who returned to Tokyo in MacArthur's plane, told me the General and the President had conducted themselves magnificently during the meeting. They had held a one-hour private session which, at the time, seemed to promise a better working relationship, based on mutual understanding, between the two leaders. Other than these signs, we had no means of evaluating the Wake Island conference. Since Washington did not fill us in on the meeting, I was obliged to pass along rumor and secondhand information to the numerous foreign diplomats who besieged POLAD for information.

The central problem of Chinese Communist intentions made the Wake meeting a historic occasion and, in some respects, a historic mystery. MacArthur had brushed aside the probability that the Chinese would enter the Korean conflict in force, although he stated that some 300,000 Chinese troops were in Manchuria. His reasons were not made public at that time. As to the Russians, the General expressed the belief that they would be unable to spare ground troops for Korea; there was the possibility, however, that Russian air strength could support Chinese ground troops. This contingency seemed highly unlikely.

As we have seen, twelve days later firm evidence of Chinese involvement in Korea was available. ROK forces began meeting heavy resistance on October 26. By October 30 Chinese prisoners of war were being captured. By the beginning of November there no longer was any doubt that Chinese troops in great strength were in Korea. On November 6 MacArthur sent Washington his report regarding the entry of "an alien army." Yet, on November

24, a United Nations offensive "to end the war" was launched, its mission being to clear Korea of the enemy. This attack was approved by the Joint Chiefs of Staff. They specified, however, that certain precautions be taken to minimize the risk of a more general involvement. MacArthur had other ideas and said so. His plan was to consolidate along the Yalu River, then turn over these advanced positions to the ROK Army. American troops would be withdrawn to Japan, leaving matters in the peninsula to the South Korean government, assisted by United Nations authorities.

The Chinese counteroffensive not only wrecked this strategic plan but revived stronger Washington-Tokyo tensions. The Chinese attack, forcing the withdrawal of Eighth Army and X Corps and the temporary loss of Seoul,* was regarded in Tokyo as a serious reverse. This belief produced increased strain and shortness among SCAP personnel. Worse, it was clear from various indications that serious misunderstandings and distrust between Washington and Tokyo had blossomed again with the failure of the United Nations offensive. This had exposed the relative lack of strength with which the avowed drive to the Yalu had been undertaken. The outcry in the world press, particularly in the United States, was loud, long, and bitter. It placed the Administration in a difficult position, and this embarrassment made itself felt across the Pacific.

MacArthur and his staff explained subsequently that the November 24 offensive was undertaken with full knowledge of the risks involved. They contended that only a strong forward movement would determine accurately whether the Chinese were in Korea in strength. An immediate orderly withdrawal was planned, they said, if full-scale Chinese intervention was discovered. Critics deny this explanation, which they claim is an afterthought. Whatever the facts, relations between MacArthur and Washington quickly reached a new low.

Although it was not apparent at the time, the failure of this offensive and the world reaction to it actually opened the last

* See p. 206.

phase of the Truman-MacArthur affair. The frustrations on both sides of the Pacific became more evident and the attempt to overcome them contributed directly to the final showdown. In retrospect it appears clear that by late 1950 the Administration and MacArthur were committed to two irreconcilable viewpoints. Washington was seeking an honorable end to the conflict. MacArthur wanted victory.

During December, 1950, and the next January, the search for a new and effective policy for Korea produced an extensive interchange of communications between Tokyo and Washington. As part of this effort, the chiefs of the Army and Air Force, Generals J. Lawton Collins and Hoyt Vandenberg arrived in Tokyo on January 14 on a swift and semisecret exploratory mission. Immediately upon arrival they conferred with MacArthur, the session lasting until almost midnight. The two generals proceeded to Korea the following day. As usual in the case of military conferences, I was not informed officially about the Tokyo meeting. In an effort to smoke out some information, I asked General MacArthur the next day whether the conference had considered the Japanese peace treaty, a subject which fell within my province. He replied that the treaty had not been discussed, but offered no further enlightenment.

The Collins-Vandenberg visit to Korea, I learned later, gave these top commanders a more optimistic view of the conflict than Washington generally held at that time. The generals found the United Nations Army in good shape, despite the previous belief in Washington that evacuation of these forces from Korea might become necessary.

Confusion over the purposes and prospects of the Korean campaign continued. It was spurred, no doubt, by a rash of newspaper articles originating in Tokyo. As one result, two directives were issued in Washington to tighten control over official statements. One provided that all speeches, press releases, and other statements concerned with foreign or military policy must be cleared beforehand with the State or the Defense Department.

The second directive specified that all officials overseas, including military commanders and diplomatic representatives, should exercise extreme caution in making public statements which, in any event, were to be cleared with the appropriate department before becoming public. These directives applied to all of us in Japan and Korea, including General MacArthur.

When I called on the General early in February, 1951, he looked tired and gave me the impression of being depressed. For once, he failed to contribute his customary ebullient views on a subject which the Soviet member had placed on the agenda of the Allied Council. Later in the month, on February 21, the same mood persisted when I made a farewell visit to MacArthur before one of my periodic trips to Washington. He lacked even his usual capacity for incisive comments, both pro and con, concerning the chief personalities in the capital. When I asked if he wished to be remembered to anyone, he replied: "If you see my nephew, please give him my best wishes." This referred to Douglas MacArthur II, later ambassador to Tokyo. The General's response indicated his intense preoccupation with other matters, for normally he seemed to relish the opportunity to send greetings to friends.

In Washington I conferred with many officials on the troublesome problems of that period. Although these conversations have become blurred with time, I recall several instances in which MacArthur's exact status as a public official became a prime topic. In the light of subsequent events, there was more than academic significance to the question whether the General was acting purely as an American official in his positions of SCAP and United Nations commander or whether he was an international officer. In the prevailing Washington view, MacArthur was an American official and subject to all the requirements of such a position. Although exercising the functions and some of the prerogatives of an international official, it was argued, MacArthur nevertheless was appointed by the President of the United States, was paid by the United States government, and was a United States Army officer, subject to the limitations and restrictions that

221

his oath of office implied.

The General had different ideas. During a conversation on March 21, following my return from Washington, he expressed the opinion that SCAP was an international officer. He could be called to account, MacArthur added, only in consequence of an agreed Allied position. When I repeated the Washington attitude on this point, the General called it incorrect. But we dropped the subject, much to my relief.

It was against this background that the climax of the Truman-MacArthur controversy was reached during the third week of March, 1951. In Washington a carefully worded statement was being worked out by the State and Defense Departments to explore the possibility of ending the war through diplomatic means. President Truman was to have issued the statement on behalf of the Allied nations involved in the struggle, and the concurrence of these powers had been obtained. On March 20 MacArthur was advised that the presidential announcement was imminent and that no further major advance beyond the 38th parallel was contemplated, pending a reaction from the Communist side. He was asked for recommendations that would permit him "sufficient freedom of action for the next few weeks to provide security for the United Nations forces and to maintain contact with the enemy." MacArthur replied that current directives covered the situation, since he lacked the forces to clear North Korea of the enemy, but requested that no further restrictions be placed on his operations.[4]

The heart of the proposed Washington statement, which was not issued publicly at that time, was that the fundamental task of "repelling the aggressors" against South Korea had been accomplished. Now, it said, every effort should "be made to prevent the spread of hostilities and to avoid the prolongation of the misery and the loss of life." The United Nations command "is prepared to enter into arrangements which would conclude the fighting and ensure against its resumption. Such arrangements would open the way for a broader settlement for Korea, including the withdrawal of foreign forces from Korea."

MacArthur, however, issued a statement on March 24, Japan time, which had the effect, unfortunately, of telling the Chinese Communists that they could not win the war and, therefore, should come to terms. Failing to do so, he implied, would broaden and accelerate the war. "The enemy," he said, "must by now be painfully aware that a decision of the United Nations to depart from its tolerant effort to contain the war to the area of Korea, through an expansion of our military operations to its coastal areas and interior bases, would doom Red China to the risk of imminent military collapse." At best it was problematical whether this kind of statement would cause the Chinese to negotiate a truce; at worst, it was an ultimatum which they could not accept. Nevertheless, it was broadcast to the enemy commander, in addition to widespread and thunderous press distribution.

President Truman said later that the MacArthur statement "was so entirely at cross-purposes with the one I was to have delivered that it would only have confused the world if my carefully prepared statement had been made." So the Washington document was withheld.

"This [MacArthur statement] was a most extraordinary statement for a military commander of the United Nations to issue on his own responsibility," President Truman said in his *Memoirs*. "It was an act totally disregarding all directives to abstain from any declarations on foreign policy. It was in open defiance of my orders as President, and as Commander in Chief. This was a challenge to the authority of the President under the Constitution. It also flouted the policy of the United Nations.

"By this act MacArthur left me no choice—I could no longer tolerate his insubordination." [5]

But the finale was still not completely clear in Tokyo and, in fact, was not generally expected. The extent and seriousness of the controversy were fully recognized, of course, but in SCAP Headquarters there was little tendency to believe that MacArthur could be punished, let alone dismissed, for his actions. Instead, there were many who thought, or hoped, that Washington could be converted to MacArthur's view. These were military officers, for the most part, involved in what certainly was one of the most disheartening campaigns in American military history. When MacArthur protested the restrictions on his operations and demanded the chance to win a victory of arms, he spoke generally for most of the officers in his command.

General MacArthur's personal aide, the late Colonel Sidney Huff expressed the mood to me two days before the dismissal order. Discussing the "current controversy" between MacArthur and Washington, Sid said frankly that he hoped the General would be recalled to Washington "for the purpose of clarifying some of the fuzzy thinking there." I reminded him that the issue also involved American politics and the complexities of the world situation, and voiced the opinion that MacArthur had underestimated the importance of these factors. "Do you think," I asked, "that the 'old man' could stand the public criticism he would get, if he pushed his ideas publicly at home?" Huff saw no difficulties and said the General could easily handle these problems in his stride. Sid had served MacArthur faithfully for fifteen years and had come to believe implicitly in the General's capacity to overcome any challenge. He had been one of the small staff serving with MacArthur in Manila before Pearl Harbor and had followed him through the retreat from Corregidor to Australia and the eventual return to the Philippines. This was, in itself, a curious career for the relaxed and affable Huff, who had become a full colonel, for he had once been a naval lieutenant and had been retired for medical reasons. Nevertheless, I was less sanguine about MacArthur's grasp of the political complexities of his situation and relayed my doubts to Huff. Ironically, it was his job— two days later—to deliver the cable of dismissal to the General.

MacArthur had his supporters in Washington, of course, particularly among certain members of Congress. Two of these, Representatives O. K. Armstrong of Missouri and W. J. Bryan Dorn of South Carolina, respectively, Republican and Democrat, were in Tokyo at that time. They called on me on the afternoon of April 6, after a conversation with the General. The congressmen made it amply clear that they endorsed two proposals that Mac-Arthur made to them in their meeting—the bombing of Manchuria and the use of Nationalist Chinese forces in the "war," as they termed it, against Red China. My reaction was cautious. I argued that the American people were not ready psychologically for a general war, if this resulted from the proposed bombing of the "Manchurian sanctuary." Neither, I contended, was the United States industrially geared for such a conflict, and time would be necessary for industrial mobilization. Instead, I tested the congressmen on the theoretical tactic of first separating the Chinese Communists from Moscow, before risking all-out war, a possibility that a number of experienced Asian diplomats had suggested at that time. The legislators replied that this would be impossible.

On April 5, Washington time, Representative Joseph W. Martin threw gasoline on the public flames of the controversy by revealing a letter to him from General MacArthur, dated March 19. Martin was Republican leader in the House of Representatives and an active critic of President Truman's Korean policies. Replying to an earlier communication from the congressman, Mac-Arthur restated views which already had become public. He agreed with Martin's contention that Nationalist Chinese troops should be allowed to enter the conflict by establishing a front on the Chinese Mainland, thus relieving the pressure in Korea. Once again the General contended that the future of Europe depended upon victory or defeat against communism in Asia.

The letter created a public furor, but President Truman has revealed that he already had decided to relieve the General before it was made public. Nevertheless, the publication of this latest document provided the basis for the President to canvass the views of his Cabinet and military leaders. When, after studying the situation, even the most reluctant agreed that MacArthur should be dismissed, the President told them that he had determined to do so on the basis of the General's March 24 statement.[6]

In his *Memoirs,* Mr. Truman rejected MacArthur's Asia-first analysis of the Communist attack by referring to Moscow's pressures on Europe and such events as the guerrilla war in Greece. "Communism was capable of attacking not only in Asia but also in Europe and . . . this was one reason why we could not afford to extend the conflict in Korea," the President said. These points had been made to MacArthur in a presidential letter dated January 13.[7] The President also said that eight months earlier MacArthur had endorsed the decision to avoid using Chinese Nationalist troops.

Tokyo was flooded with press reports indicating "an open break" between MacArthur and the Administration. In this atmosphere Secretary of the Army Frank Pace arrived for an unexplained visit which, however, we generally assumed was connected with the controversy and, particularly, the Martin incident. The Secretary himself said nothing about it during a conversation with me on April 9. The occasion was ironic. He was the guest of honor at a luncheon given by General and Mrs. MacArthur. The affair went off smoothly, and Pace departed soon afterward for Korea, apparently unaware of the storm clouds, indirectly involving him, which were growing in Washington.

Shortly after this luncheon, the final decision to remove MacArthur was reached, and Pace was elected to deliver the verdict to the General. But Pace was at the Korean front and could not be located. An impending newspaper "leak" of this momentous story caused the President to move quickly. "That was when I decided," he wrote in his *Memoirs,* "that we could not afford the courtesy of Secretary Pace's personal delivery of the order but that the message would have to go to General MacArthur in the same manner that relieving orders were sent to other officers in the service." [8]

Meanwhile, the Japanese were becoming increasingly bewildered by the whole affair. In the hurly-burly of practical politics, most Americans doubtless understood the stridency of the debate, as reflected in this statement by the late Senator Robert S. Kerr, Democrat of Oklahoma: "MacArthur's prolonged . . . one-man act," he said in a comment well-publicized in Tokyo, "is wearing the patience of the rest of the team mighty thin. . . . In fact, it is getting about as threadbare as the General's much touted Oriental prestige. The time may be nearer than we think when the over-all cost of keeping MacArthur as theater commander will be greater than the value of his 'position' with the Asiatics." The Japanese simply could not understand this kind of attack on a man who, indeed, did have a unique prestige among them. Most of them were deeply concerned by the whole incident. Moreover, to the Japanese this public airing of high policy was not only unusual, it was dangerously confusing.

It was against this background of contention, misunderstanding, action and reaction, as well as the more serious resentment caused by MacArthur's seeming refusal to carry out Administrative policies, that the blow fell. President Truman made the news public, through his press secretary, at an unusual 1 A.M. news conference, April 11, 1951.* A report based upon this conference gave SCAP Headquarters its first firm information that the President was ending the career of General of the Army Douglas MacArthur by unceremoniously and peremptorily stripping him of his commands and authority. Colonel Huff later delivered the official orders to the embassy residence in a plain Manila envelope.

In many respects April 11 started out very much like many other days under the Occupation of Japan. There was the usual biweekly meeting of the Allied Council, *pro forma* and brief. MacArthur was giving a small luncheon for Senator Warren G. Magnuson, who had arrived five days earlier to investigate shipping problems. My wife and I had accepted an invitation from Prime Minister Yoshida to attend the season's first garden party at his official residence. The weather was good, although somewhat cool for early spring, and the cherry blossoms were firm and

* Thirteen years later, on April 11, General MacArthur's body was laid to rest in the MacArthur Memorial in Norfolk, Virginia. Together with many of those mentioned in this book, including former Prime Minister Shigeru Yoshida and his daughter Mrs. Aso, I attended the funeral services in St. Paul's Episcopal Church of Norfolk.

not yet quite in full bloom.

We arrived at the prime minister's garden party at 3:45 P.M., slightly late, as I had been delayed at the office. This was three-quarters of an hour after the beginning of Press Secretary Joseph Short's 1 A.M. news conference in Washington, and I had not yet heard the news. But the party buzzed with it. Mrs. George E. Stratemeyer, wife of the commander of the Far East Air Forces, told me the news had been broadcast a short time earlier. Then Prime Minister Yoshida called me aside and asked whether I could confirm the report. I replied that I had no official information but would return immediately to my office.

On the way I stopped at the Dai Ichi building to see Colonel Bunker, the General's aide. He confirmed the dismissal of Mac-Arthur and the appointment of Lieutenant General Matthew B. Ridgway, Eighth Army commander in Korea, as his successor. At my own office I was told that an urgent telegram from Washington was being decoded. This contained instructions to call immediately on Prime Minister Yoshida and to inform him that the change of commanders in Japan in no manner signified any change in United States policy toward Japan, the impending peace treaty, or the Far East.

When I returned to Mr. Yoshida's residence I was received in his upstairs study. The prime minister had changed to Japanese dress which, I thought, somehow added to his dignity and authenticity as the head of the Japanese government. We were seated on opposite sides of his foreign-style desk, the prime minister awaiting my report with serious intensity. I conveyed the message from the Secretary of State, while he nodded slightly. On my own responsibility, I added the hope that neither the prime minister nor his cabinet would resign because of this incident. This would have been the traditional Japanese gesture of responsibility for MacArthur's relief, particularly in view of Yoshida's close association with the General. I emphasized that, despite tradition, it was imperative that the government continue to function and to furnish the necessary leadership to the people. Governmental calm was necessary, I added, to bridge over any possible crisis from a development which I believed would profoundly affect the Japanese people. Yoshida was visibly shaken, but he expressed gratitude for my message and its assurance. He said there would be no resignation.

Then I went to Headquarters and called on MacArthur. As I had done so often before, I walked directly into the General's plain office without formality. The General rose and met me with a smile. I was so keyed that I was unable to speak. A tear rolled down my cheek. MacArthur offered me a cigarette and lighted it for me, as we sat down at our usual places in the worn leather furniture at the far end of the room. For a moment the silence was oppressive, then, with some difficulty, I remarked: "General, you are a much better soldier in this business than I am." While not a profound remark, it broke the tension.

MacArthur replied in his most earnest and telling manner. He expressed irony and bitterness over the *method* that had been used to send him home. "Publicly humiliated after fifty-two years of service in the Army," he said somberly. As a soldier, he added, he would have retired without protest, if the President had given the slightest intimation that he wished him to do so. This proud, sensitive, and determined man, who had followed a destiny which now had evaporated, was deeply hurt and, perhaps, momentarily defeated. Watching and listening to him was the most painful interview I have had.

Referring to the Japanese situation, I asked MacArthur to include in any statement that he might make an admonition to the Japanese people to support and cooperate with General Ridgway. MacArthur replied that he would make no statement. I asked him to reconsider, saying: "After all, the present state of Japan is a monument to you and I would hope that everything possible could be done to preserve it." The General made no comment on this point, but he talked on, as if compelled to talk, and I felt this was a good sign. He spoke of his removal as part of a plot in Washington which, he said, would result in the eventual crumbling of the entire United States position in the Far East. He denied disobeying any orders from Washington. As for the letter to Representative Martin, which had assumed such public importance, the General said he did not even remember writing it. When it was published, a copy had to be fished out of his files to refresh his memory. In any event, MacArthur added, it was a personal letter, which certainly was not meant for publication, as the text itself would indicate.

The conversation then veered toward my own future. The General predicted I would be "eased out" at the first convenient opportunity and assigned to some innocuous post. My reply, that I hoped this would not happen, was based upon the conviction, as I told him, that I should remain on the job, at least temporarily, for the sake of continuity. I assured him I would do everything possible to help carry on the operation in Japan. MacArthur's parting words were: "Bill, the weakness of your position is that you have been too loyal to me. You may have to pay for that loyalty."

I left him, standing erect and alone in the office which had dominated his life for more than five years and from which this general in three wars was about to make his only permanent retreat.

The incident, quite naturally, dominated the emotions of Japan and filled the newspapers. Press reports, widely published, said a great public debate and emotional outburst were occurring in the United States, a development that further confused the Japanese. Part of my job immediately required an analysis of the reaction to the "new" situation in Japan, and I busied myself with numerous telegrams to the State Department on this subject. As a reminder that the Occupation had to function, despite the interruption, Secretary Pace telephoned me on the day after the dismissal, suggesting that I might wish to think about a public statement for General Ridgway upon his arrival in Tokyo. Accordingly, I prepared a suggested statement and kept it ready for the new SCAP's perusal and possible use.

Ridgway arrived at Haneda Airport from Korea at 9:09 P.M. on

Saturday, April 14, 1951, three days after his appointment as SCAP. In an air of intense curiosity and some uncertainty, which had built up in Tokyo, the new commander's manner of arrival and his first public statements and actions were matters of some moment. Not knowing exactly what to expect, the chief of staff, Major General Doyle Hickey, who had served MacArthur in this vital position since the formation of the X Corps, and I waited somewhat impatiently to greet Ridgway at planeside. When the aircraft had landed and had taxied to the appropriate spot, the General quickly appeared—and the reality of the new regime was established immediately.

General Ridgway was dressed in a field uniform, with overseas cap and live hand grenades, the battle dress that had become his trademark in Korea. Fifteen years younger than MacArthur and physically a handsome man, he gave the impression of boundless energy, restlessness, frankness, and a desire for team operation. MacArthur, of course, had gone everywhere dressed in a rather faded, sometimes patched, set of khakis, wearing his famous and somewhat shapeless "scrambled egg" officer's cap from World War II. He was no less restless and energetic than his successor, but on public occasions of this sort MacArthur generally gave the impression of relaxed confidence. Even upon return from the Korean War front he made it a point first to greet Mrs. MacArthur, whenever she was at the airport; then he turned to business. Ridgway, on the other hand, was all business as he hurried General Hickey and me to a waiting limousine for the trip to Tokyo.

We went to the Imperial Hotel, where Ridgway was to be billeted until the MacArthurs left Japan, and immediately started work on an arrival statement which the new SCAP wished to make. MacArthur, as a rule, made his own statements, often writing them in longhand during a flight back to Tokyo, and seldom conferred on them with his subordinates. MacArthur also turned immediately to the waiting newsmen, after greeting his wife, on occasions when he had a particular point to make. On this first occasion, Ridgway did not talk to the press.

In the Imperial Hotel we went over the draft of my proposed arrival statement and another one which Ridgway's staff had prepared for him. I found parts of this objectionable, in the political climate of the moment, although some points were excellent. We decided, therefore, to combine the two versions in a third draft for Ridgway's approval. My public affairs officer, Saxton Bradford, had alerted the Japanese, as well as the foreign press, to the impending announcement, which was primarily designed for the Japanese Sunday morning papers. The newsmen were waiting while we worked.

We sat down to go over the final version, with Ridgway eager and alert. When he came to the phrase, "with due humility," which I had inserted, the new SCAP promptly crossed it out. "I am not humble in this job or any other," he explained. "I am humble before God, but no one else." The rest of the statement passed general muster, and an acceptable draft was finished and distributed to the press by 10 P.M. The work done, Ridgway invited me to have a drink with him. This was, incidentally, my first drink with either the old or the new Supreme Commander for the Allied Powers.

Silently I expressed my strong hope that the new regime would fare well. Not only were the interests of Japan deeply involved; the position, influence, and prestige of the United States also could be profoundly influenced by the manner in which the new SCAP carried out his responsibilities.

The Ridgway statement was given prominent play in the Japanese press, but editorial comment was restrained. It was obvious that, before committing themselves, the Japanese would wait and see what the new SCAP was like and how he would fit into the huge gap left by General MacArthur. The Japanese people deeply respected MacArthur; he had managed with his superb instinct to act with restraint and deftness in the exercise of the unparalleled power of his position. The Japanese were particularly impressed by MacArthur's subtle relations with the Emperor, for whom they

retained a deep and rather complicated reverence, despite strenu-
ous official SCAP efforts to eliminate the aura of "divinity" from
the Throne. MacArthur's contacts with the Emperor were formally correct and were carefully handled to avoid any suggestion
of undermining the monarch's person or position. At the same
time, his method of approach emphasized the point that the new
constitution severely limited the power and authority of the Emperor. An essential part of this elaborate duality was made possible by the aloofness with which MacArthur handled his duties
and his restricted pre-Korean War routine of limiting himself to
the route between the Dai Ichi building and the American Embassy. These traits were often criticized, but not by the Japanese,
who understood or respected the need for aloofness. The critics
generally were non-Japanese writers and reporters who had no
responsibility for the Occupation and little understanding of Mac-
Arthur's methods of dealing with a unique, sensitive, and alien
people.

General Ridgway's approach to the position of SCAP was
much more conventional. As an active and forceful commander
who relied more upon the outward signs of authority, Ridgway
felt the need to see and to be seen, and to experience his problems
at first hand. Once when I remarked on the way MacArthur had
handled a particular situation, Ridgway told me he was no General MacArthur and, indeed, would not attempt to become one.
Instead, he said he would carry out his responsibilities by his own
methods and techniques. MacArthur worked extensively through
his staff and acquired an amazing knowledge and feel of the
situation by listening to informal verbal reports and by wide reading of formal documents. Ridgway, on the other hand, traveled
extensively throughout Japan, met local commanders, and relied
to a greater degree upon formal briefings. Further, he was more
disposed than MacArthur to listen to all sides of a problem as
presented by his staff. These features were not apparent, however, during the early days of his regime, and only time would
clarify the differences between the two commanders.

233

On April 15 my wife and I joined with other Americans in calling at the Embassy to say "good-by" to Jean MacArthur. During this last occasion, an informal "at home," Mrs. MacArthur, as usual, was gracious and friendly, without the slightest hint of bitterness or resentment. Rather, she greeted each caller with an infectious smile, dissipating awkwardness and lugubriousness. The large embassy residence, which the MacArthurs had occupied for more than five and one-half years, looked bare and empty, with their personal possessions gone. Jean talked of returning "home" after such a long absence and of the problems she would face, as if this were simply another military transfer. As usual, she was concerned almost exclusively with "the General" and his welfare. This self-effacement was genuine, as all who met her quickly realized. In her own quiet way Jean MacArthur became to the Japanese people a symbol of the wifely devotion which they considered a paramount virtue among women.

The following day we arose at 5 A.M. in order to reach Haneda Airport before the MacArthurs were scheduled to arrive, two hours later, for the brief ceremonies preceding their departure for the United States. The streets to the airport were lined by available American troops, sailors, and airmen, and by Tokyo municipal and rural police, when we set out on this melancholy journey. Thousands of Japanese waited patiently for a glimpse of the man they still called *"Makassa Gensui"* (literally, Field Marshal MacArthur). Many of them had come to see him for the first time. MacArthur's honor guard, a platoon of select troops, was drawn up at the airport. The young soldiers stood stiff, hiding any emotions they might have had on this occasion. The whole affair was a military operation, well-planned and precise, from the carefully arranged places for senior commanders and civilian officials to the snapping flags in the morning breeze. At one side, MacArthur's plane, the *Bataan*, was waiting, well ahead of time, for a quick getaway. It was as if military brusqueness was designed to serve deliberately as a means of hiding the intense emotion of the occasion.

My wife joined the ladies, and I stood with a group of tense officers awaiting the MacArthurs' arrival. Included were Vice Admiral Turner Joy, the senior U.S. naval officer, Lieutenant General Sir Horace Robertson, commander of British Commonwealth forces, Lieutenant General George E. Stratemeyer, Commander of the Far East Air Forces, and many others. Little was said, beyond greetings, as we waited in the chill morning air. Promptly at 7 A.M., a limousine drew up and the MacArthurs alighted.

While Jean, smiling, walked toward the wives of Occupation officials, General MacArthur reviewed the guard of honor, striding purposefully and with set face past the young men who had served under him. As customary, he ended the brief and ritualized review by shaking hands with the guard's commander. Then he walked quickly to the senior officers and shook hands with each of us, always with a smile, a penetrating glance, and frequently, a word of personal intimacy. The farewells were an ordeal. Many of the women were sobbing openly, and a number of the battle-hardened men had difficulty in suppressing tears.

In the meantime, the small personal staff accompanying the MacArthurs to the United States quietly boarded the plane. They included Major General Courtney Whitney, Colonel Huff, Colonel Bunker, and Lieutenant Colonel C. C. Canada. Ah Cheu, the Chinese amah who had been with the family since the days of the Philippines, chaperoned little Arthur to the aircraft, talking to him constantly. The pilot was Lieutenant Colonel Anthony Story, who had flown the General to the Korean War fronts, among other trips.

Finally, Jean pulled herself away and, assisted by the General, climbed the ramp and turned for a final wave. The couple stood immobile, but visibly saddened, as a 19-gun salute rolled across the airfield. Then, with a quick gesture, MacArthur guided his wife into the plane, the door was shut, and the aircraft taxied away. Soon it was airborne, and the chilling moment was over. Officers and their wives slowly trooped away, the flags were furled, the troops dismissed—and the working day began.

A short time later General Ridgway held his first Tokyo staff meeting, at GHQ. He was firm, succinct, and forceful. There was no doubt among those present about who was boss of the Occupation at this point. For me, this was an impressive beginning.

But, naturally, the new SCAP had his problems in assuming the unfamiliar and clamorous problems created by the dual task of directing affairs in one foreign country while continuing to fight a war in another. Some of the complexities began to emerge that afternoon. John Foster Dulles and his party were returning to Japan for further work on the Japanese peace treaty. While standing with General Ridgway on the apron of the runway, awaiting the Dulles plane, I was told by a member of my staff that three top-ranking Japanese had been barred by the American military police from entering the field. They were Katsuo Okazaki, the chief cabinet secretary, and Sadao Iguchi, the vice minister of foreign affairs, who had come with their wives, and Hisato Ichimada, governor of the Bank of Japan. Quickly, I instructed my aide to tell the MPs to pass the Japanese, all of whom were important officials.

Shortly afterward they approached us in a group. General Ridgway, who had not heard my instructions, immediately called to the nearest MP officer to "get on the job," indicating that the Japanese were to be ordered from the field. Fortunately, I was able to explain the situation in time and to smooth over the affair before any harm was done. I introduced my Japanese friends to the General who, in these rather strained circumstances, had his first chance to meet high Japanese government officials.

During these initial days Ridgway took advantage of as much advice as was available to familiarize himself with some of the intangibles with which he would have to deal. Thus, for example, he sent his deputy chief of staff, Major General Alonzo P. Fox, to see me for guidance on how SCAP should deal with the Japanese, both officially and otherwise, a type of inquiry which had not been made before. The complexities are indicated, perhaps, by the advice I felt compelled to offer at that time. I suggested that General Ridgway should confine his dealings with the Japanese government to the highest levels—prime minister, chief justice, heads of the two houses of the Diet, and possibly a few others. This would not prevent him from receiving groups of Japanese, such as athletic teams proceeding to the United States. On his visits around Japan, I suggested it would be proper for the General to meet leading local officials, although he should normally have no official dealings with them. The purpose of all this, of course, was to preserve the identity and proper status for the office of the Supreme Commander, a unique and unprecedented institution.

Less than two weeks after MacArthur's departure, General Ridgway invited me to accompany him on a brief visit to Hokkaido, the northernmost island of Japan. The journey gave us an excellent opportunity to discuss some of the problems which soon would demand a SCAP decision. For one thing, the Japanese Federation of Labor Unions (Sohyo), the largest and most predominantly leftist labor organization in the country, had demanded permission to hold a May Day demonstration on the Imperial Palace Plaza. The Japanese government had rejected the demand, and Sohyo had appealed to SCAP. There also were protocol problems involving the Emperor, an impending move to soften the impact of the political and economic purges, and similar basic questions. During the flight I found Ridgway relaxed, attentive, and interested in the discussion of these matters, but noncommittal. He did, however, reflect sympathetic understanding of official United States policies, as formulated by the Department of State.

On the ground in Hokkaido, Ridgway became the Commanding General, in fact as well as name. I was impressed, for instance, by the manner in which he dealt with a certain amount of slackness that he observed among the officers of a newly arrived

United States division. His leadership, forcefulness, clarity of expression, and ability to project his viewpoints were remarkable.

As the finale to our airplane conversation, Ridgway upheld the Japanese government decision to bar Sohyo from the proposed May Day demonstration. This was announced April 27, after the labor leaders had been informed in advance. Ridgway also agreed to ameliorate the purge, as it had been carried out by MacArthur under SCAPIN 550. In effect, the new SCAP order brought the purge into line with policies advocated by the Far Eastern Commission. This was done by depurging, or removing from the restrictions, all military and naval officers who had entered the service subsequently to 1937, among others. This was, I told the General, a major step forward which would greatly help to remove a major irritant in United States–Japan relations.

On April 30 Prime Minister Yoshida called on General Ridgway to arrange a visit for the Emperor on May 2. When asked my advice on the best procedure for SCAP to follow, I suggested an attitude of informality, commensurate with dignity, friendliness, and cordiality. The meeting was held, on schedule, in one of the apartments in the American embassy compound. I met the Emperor upon his arrival and conducted him to General Ridgway, who was waiting at the top of the stairs, on the second floor. The two principals then retired for a one-hour conversation, alone except for an interpreter. I spent the time chatting with my friends, Grand Chamberlain Mitani and Grand Steward Tajima, who had accompanied the Emperor.

The tempo of Japanese life, at this period, seemed to be returning quickly to normal. Times were relatively good, spurred by huge United States expenditures in Japan for the Korean War. The people, at long last, appeared to be relaxing from the fierce stresses of the long war and the strains of the postwar years. They reflected this mood by pouring out by the thousands to celebrate a national holiday, Constitution Day, with a mass rally on the Imperial Palace Plaza, May 3, 1951. The occasion commemorated the Occupation-inspired constitution which, among other innovations, sharply restricted the Emperor's authority. When the Emperor and the Empress appeared, however, the throng gave them a throaty "Banzai!" full of genuine affection, however much the awesome reverence of the past might have been diluted.

LIFE FOR ME under the new regime was more brisk than previously, if for no other reason than the reliance which General Ridgway placed on my advice regarding Japanese affairs. Events moved along so rapidly that even the State Department became anxious over the pace of depurging, whereas previously it had been concerned that the purges under SCAPIN 550 had gone too far. The new attitude reflected a certain disquiet in the Far Eastern Commission over the decision to restore to active political and economic life some of the Japanese who had been disbarred. Some member nations of the FEC refused to reconcile themselves to the forthcoming peace treaty conference. Another change in Occupation policy also occurred during this period. Effective July 1, 1951, all Occupation personnel, including foreign diplomatic missions, were no longer furnished household servants at the expense of the Japanese government. The free ride was over.

With all the changes, however, there was also a notable social relaxation in Tokyo, in comparison with the MacArthur regime. Mrs. Ridgway arrived in Tokyo, and with her husband began to accept social invitations and to entertain. The Ridgways created a precedent when they invited a number of Japanese leaders and their wives to a reception at the American Embassy.

During this period the parade of foreign visitors to Tokyo continued, bringing to the busy capital such diverse personalities as Secretary of Defense George C. Marshall, Andrew Cordier of the United Nations Secretariat, Paul V. McNutt, the handsome Indiana Democratic leader and former High Commissioner to the Philippines, Vice President Alben W. Barkley, and former Governor Thomas E. Dewey. It was characteristic of the new mood among the Japanese that the Emperor gave audience to a considerable number of these visitors, and it was my duty to escort them to the palace. One of the most memorable was Dewey's meeting with the Emperor, held in the imperial household's office building, a portion of which had been converted to an audience chamber. The interview began with rather stiff formality, until Dewey began to discuss his New York farm and its problems. The Emperor's face lighted, and thereafter the audience was relaxed and friendly. I was impressed by Hirohito's knowledge and deep interest in various aspects of agriculture. Question and answer led to a comparison of agricultural methods in the United States and Japan, and the Emperor displayed a surprising knowledge of rural Japanese practices. It was evident that he found genuine pleasure in discussing some of the simple truths which spring from the land.

At about this time I was approached by the late Yasumasa Matsudaira, the grand master of ceremonies, with the suggestion for a planned "accidental" meeting of Ridgway and the Emperor. The ruler was staying at Nasu, a summering place about a hundred miles north of Tokyo. Matsudaira, an alert and dedicated palace official, suggested that, if the General "happened" to be in the neighborhood, it might be convenient for him to call on the Emperor. Although I realized that this undoubtedly was a gambit invented by my friend Matsudaira, I politely replied that the idea probably would be impractical because I was certain General Ridgway had no plans to be in that area in the near future. I suggested it might be easier to arrange a meeting at the American Embassy at any time after the Emperor's return to Tokyo.

When I reported this conversation to Ridgway later in the day, he thoroughly approved of the manner in which I had handled this rather delicate matter. Fortunately, all concerned understood that the recommended procedure was correct. In any event, the Emperor called on the Supreme Commander at the embassy residence on August 27, the second meeting between the two leaders. And on September 18, after the signing of the peace treaty, my wife and I accompanied General and Mrs. Ridgway to a luncheon in their honor at the Imperial Palace. The Emperor and Empress, as host and hostess, were more relaxed on that occasion than I had seen them for a long time.

11

The Peace Treaty

THE FORMULATION OF the Japanese peace treaty involved a tremendous amount of energy, thought, and work during the six years of the Occupation. More importantly, the final document reflected an almost complete reversal of national viewpoint toward the Japanese on the part of the United States and many of its allies. The initial vengefulness yielded eventually to cooperation, and fear of a resurgent Japan disappeared behind the realities of the cold war. The Japanese people themselves contributed immeasurably to this change. But the evolution in the concept and philosophy of peace was a long and sometimes painful process which, inevitably, created divisions among the Allied Powers and even between departments of the United States government. The task of adjusting these differences fell largely to John Foster Dulles and, with MacArthur's strong and constant support, he contributed more than any other individual to the eventual peace settlement between Japan and the non-Communist world. Soviet Russia and other Communist nations have yet to conclude a formal peace with Japan.*

* After a series of negotiations which commenced in London on June 1, 1955, Japan and the U.S.S.R. signed a Joint Declaration in Moscow on Oct. 19, 1956, providing for the normalization of relations between the two countries. It was also agreed that "negotiations for the conclusion of a peace treaty" would be continued after normal diplomatic relations were re-established.

The search for an adequate Japanese peace treaty was continuous from early 1947, although the subject had appeared to command public interest only infrequently. There was in this search considerable byplay, for strong, conflicting personalities and principles were involved. It is my purpose here to relate some of the main background incidents and observations on this subject. The outlines of the story have been told adequately by others.[1]

The first United States draft treaty, completed in March, 1947, was based upon the then prevailing concept that resurgent Japanese militarism was Asia's greatest menace and, to prevent it, Japan should remain indefinitely under Allied control. The draft was produced by a working group in the State Department, headed by Hugh Borton, and this basic psychology was retained in subsequent revisions of August, 1947, and January, 1948. The general approach was that Japan could not be trusted and that every precaution must be taken through the treaty to prevent a revival of Japanese military power. This was to be done over many years, with twenty-five years' surveillance the favored period.

The draft provided for a Council of Ambassadors, composed of representatives of the eleven Far Eastern Commission powers, to maintain over-all supervision over Japan. Beneath this group, a Commission of Inspection was to guard against any possible infractions of the demilitarization provisions contained in the proposed treaty. Japan was to have no military forces, no military or civil aircraft, no stockpiled strategic materials, no scientific research of military potentiality, and no nuclear research. Moreover, the proposed treaty carried over some of the severe provisions of the Initial Post-Surrender Policy, such as exclusion of certain classes of individuals from public office. The Council of Ambassadors was to have final decision over the implementation of many provisions in the proposed treaty and would, therefore, maintain a certain amount of autonomy over Japan's compliance.

This was, in general, a Draconian approach which would have perpetuated the bitterness of World War II. To my mind, the draft was unworkable and self-defeating and made the approach to peace retaliatory. It was the Treaty of Versailles all over again, and this indicated that we had learned little from the experiences of the previous twenty-seven years.

The draft was not made public, of course, but it served as an explicit example of the psychology then prevailing in Washington and in the capitals of most nations which had suffered from Japanese aggression. Ironically, it was at this same time, March, 1947, that General MacArthur brought the question of peace into public view and on terms which, even then, indicated he was more disposed than Washington to move quickly and with comparative leniency toward a settlement. In his press conference * of March 17, SCAP said: "The time is now approaching when we must talk peace with Japan." He divided the Occupation job into three phases—military, political, and economic. The military task was completed, he said. "We have demobilized the troops, demilitarized the country, torn down military installations." Next, he continued, "The political phase is approaching such completion as is possible under the Occupation." As to economics, he said, the Occupation, if continued on its current course, could "only enforce economic strangulation." His clear implication was that Japan must be helped to gain economic viability or the United States would have to pay the cost of preventing widespread starvation. Finally, in a somewhat sweeping statement, MacArthur suggested that the United States exercise control over Japan, a condition that "Japan would be willing [to accept] and would desire it." Asked when the peace treaty should be negotiated, MacArthur replied: "I will say as soon as possible." [2]

To these two views of the subject, a third was contributed by

* My recollection of this press conference, which I attended, is that MacArthur intended it primarily to launch his ideas on a peace treaty. It was, in fact, the only general press conference he held throughout the Occupation, although he saw newsmen individually and, during the Korean War, maintained frequent contacts with the chiefs of the American and British news agencies. The press conference occurred when the General, to everyone's surprise, accepted a standing invitation to lunch with the Foreign Correspondents' Association. Afterward, when MacArthur offered to answer questions—"on the record," for publication—the sur-

the American military authorities in the Army and Navy Departments. They saw a Japan denuded of all military strength and with no possibility of raising adequate forces to defend itself. Under the new constitution, Article 9 provided that "the Japanese people forever renounce war as a sovereign right of the nation." and "land, sea, and air forces, as well as other war potential, will never be maintained." This meant, in the United States military view, that Japan would depend indefinitely upon outside assistance for its defense. The idea that the United Nations could become the nation's protector was considered unrealistic; United Nations strength for this purpose was, actually, the strength of the already widely committed United States. To protect Japan, in face of continued Soviet hostility, unrestricted use of United States bases and freedom to move men anywhere in the Japanese islands or throughout Asia from Japan were considered basic essentials by the United States military authorities. These were, in their view, nonnegotiable requisites for any peace treaty, even though they would consitute a highly irregular basis for formal peace. Therefore, the military departments preferred to drop the idea of a treaty and to carry on the Occupation for the indefinite future.

Before a peace treaty could be concluded or seriously negotiated, however, two basic steps were necessary, in my estimation. First, the Japanese economy had to be allowed to rehabilitate itself. Secondly, some of the excesses of Occupation control, particularly the extensive purges, had to be corrected. MacArthur's views about the economy were simple: Let the Japanese do it. But in 1947 and, indeed, for the next two years, the Japanese

prise was so genuine that many newsmen had neither paper nor pencils. The General's highly articulate and well-prepared comments on a peace treaty were even more astounding, for the Occupation was still too new and too vigorous to permit much speculation or much thought among foreigners in Tokyo over the basis for an eventual settlement. I doubt if any correspondent had spent any time, up to that point, in exploring a peace treaty, amid the other chores of keeping abreast of the fast-moving Occupation. MacArthur's gesture succeeded, however, in implanting the subject so firmly that speculative stories on the peace were not unusual thereafter. I have no doubt that this was his major purpose.—R.B.

lacked both the means and the will to revitalize their economy. This was due, in considerable measure, to the so-called economic "reforms" which, in my view, barred the very men upon whom we would have to rely to improve the economy. Although SCAP moved fairly swiftly to furnish food and some raw materials and other essentials to the weakened populace, he did not alter these restrictive "reforms." It was not until early 1949 that a concerted move was made to change this dangerous situation. The process of removing the purge restraint on Japanese enterprise had hardly begun when MacArthur left Japan.

Having dropped his "time bomb" suggestion for a prompt peace treaty, MacArthur let it ferment in world opinion, with an occasional further suggestion that action was necessary. His own ideas remained consistent. In mid-August, 1949, he insisted again, in a conversation with me, that the United States should call a peace conference "now." He was not sanguine about the possibility of success, however, whether Russia participated or whether it boycotted the conference, as seemed more likely at that time. His thought was that the United States should take the initiative on the peace question. He also proposed that the United States, at the first opportunity, support Japan for admission to the United Nations. In the spirit of the time, this was a rather advanced suggestion, for the idea of fully welcoming Japan back into the family of nations was seldom considered seriously.

This conversation with MacArthur gave me the basis for a long and carefully drafted dispatch to the State Department, adding my own views on the desirability of an early treaty. Contributions to the report were made by the senior members of my staff— Cloyce Huston, Cabot Coville, and Charles Nelson Spinks. Upon conclusion, we all agreed, in the enthusiasm of the moment, that our views and specific recommendations for a liberal peace based on understanding and friendship would make history and would mark a departure point in our policy toward Japan. I doubt that this dispatch was quite so historical or influential, but its realistically based argumentation and recommendations could not be ignored.

My own thoughts were that peace is possible only by removing the causes of war, and this requires a broad and courageous approach. I recorded in my journal that Japan must be allowed to find its own solutions to its many problems. For a proper peace, education was needed and a rising standard of living for the Japanese was essential. If methods to solve these and other problems were foisted on Japan from the outside, they would only create further problems. Moreover, it seemed to me, a punitive and detailed peace made the traditional mistake of attempting to measure events of the future through the device of tying them to an inflexible document. The formal peace, as I envisioned it, had to be based upon a high moral plane which, above all, would restore Japan as a sovereign nation and would give its people the incentive to revitalize themselves.

When I outlined these ideas to MacArthur in late September, 1949, he agreed. The treaty, he added, should be simple and should be written in general terms. The question of Japan's future security, the great problem of the day, "should be arranged by bilateral agreement with the United States," MacArthur said. He did not amplify this thought, but it offered a new solution for the problem; eventually, it became the final solution. Heretofore, security had been considered solely as a matter to be nailed down in the peace treaty itself, and no one had proposed solving the problem through a more easily negotiated separate arrangement. MacArthur ended this conversation by expressing hope that the peace conference would be held in Tokyo, suggesting that, as SCAP, he would not refuse an invitation to act as its chairman.

By the middle of 1949 a firm impasse had arisen between the Department of State and the Department of the Army over the security provisions in any peace settlement. The Army, quite naturally, wanted more assurance of post-treaty control over Japanese security than the diplomats considered wise. But MacArthur threw his considerable influence, on this issue, behind the State Department and never wavered in his advocacy of an early peace. A procession of top Defense Department officials came to Japan during this period, primarily, it appeared, to work on Mac-Arthur in an effort to obtain his support for delaying a settlement, on the grounds of security. Among these delegations, one was led in December, 1949, by Under Secretary of the Army Tracy S. Voorhees and Lieutenant General Alfred M. Gruenther, Assistant Chief of Staff for Operations. They made it clear, in private conversations with me, that the impasse was strong. Although they conferred at length with MacArthur, his ideas had crystallized, and there was no sign the Washington emissaries made any progress whatsoever in altering his views.

On the contrary, by mid-January, 1950, MacArthur was in a mood to suggest to me that the Joint Chiefs of Staff should be overruled on the treaty issue, so that work could begin "within six weeks" on a conference. But the impasse continued.

Meanwhile, a considerable amount of speculation about the treaty issue created more turmoil and uncertainty within Japan. Virtually every foreign correspondent in Tokyo was writing about this subject, and I had a number of background sessions at their request with such men as Tom Lambert of AP, Howard Handelman and John Rich of INS, Keyes Beech, Chicago *Daily News*, and Norman Soong of the China News Agency. My comments, which were not for attribution, followed a consistent theme: The Occupation already was growing stale and its personnel were becoming less and less effective. The only solution, as I saw it, was the negotiation of a treaty. The mood of the period was reflected, however, by the reaction to a story filed out of Manila by Frank White of AP. White, who had served previously in Tokyo, had talked to General MacArthur before undertaking a new assignment in the Philippines. He reported that MacArthur believed there were three requisites for the defense of Japan after it regained independence:

(1) Membership for Japan in the United Nations;

(2) maintenance of United States bases in Japan on a long-term basis; and

(3) protection by United States and other friendly forces.

This touched upon the State-Defense impasse, and the story was somewhat of a bombshell. I was called to the Dai Ichi building to see MacArthur on a Sunday morning, to discuss a telegram which the State Department had sent me, requesting comment on White's story. The General suggested a mild reply, "so that you will not get into trouble." I replied that I would have no trouble, because I had not seen White, other than to say good-by just before his departure. This puzzled MacArthur, who wondered aloud how his views could have leaked out. Apparently he had forgotten his customary farewell conversation with the newsman about a week earlier. Like most of these minor crises, no damage resulted from the disclosure. If nothing else, the "leak" laid the groundwork for what actually transpired later.

Despite the extensive exchanges which had taken place during the previous two years, the State Department retained its punitive attitude toward Japan in its new draft treaty, completed November 2, 1949. To my mind, the document was too long and too complex and its general tone was one of dictation by the victor to the vanquished. MacArthur also told me he did not like the latest version and said he would have written it differently. However, he added, he was not in the treaty-writing business, a function he left to the State Department, and he did not propose to get into an argument with the department. Again, with the assistance of my senior officers, I sent off a lengthy commentary to Washington. Huston was given the job of toning down my language, as I felt rather deeply about the patronizing tone of the draft treaty, and said so.

As international discussion of the peace question continued into 1950, the strictly military view remained rigid. Press reports on April 29 quoted the late Lieutenant General Robert L. Eichelberger, former commander of the Eighth Army in Japan, as saying in a speech: "A peace treaty with Japan would be disastrous to the United States in the Far East at this time." Such a comment in the United States by one of our senior and most respected generals was, to say the least, not helpful, and it served further to confuse the Japanese regarding our intentions.

A number of Japanese expressed general concern over the situation at this period, and prominent visitors came to my office, worrying about the future. Many influential Japanese strenuously advocated the retention of American troops in the islands after the peace became effective. Admiral Kichisaburo Nomura expressed the predominant hope that Japan would be given assured partnership in the Free World. "A neutral Japan," he said, "would rapidly turn into a Red Japan." Governor Tanaka of Hokkaido called with a petition asking for the return of the Kurile and Habomai islands. The disposition of the Kuriles had been decided, of course, at the Cairo and Yalta conferences. The Habomai Group, which lies within three miles of Hokkaido, had not been mentioned at any of the wartime meetings, but Soviet troops had occupied these islands shortly after the surrender and had refused to depart.*

This was the over-all mood when the task of expediting the treaty began in earnest just before the outbreak of the Korean War and during its early hectic days.

Two official groups from Washington, arriving in Tokyo within a few hours of each other on June 17, 1950, carried the State-Defense impasse to the front lines, so to speak. The first party was headed by John Foster Dulles and was bound for Korea for a brief visit before returning to Japan to investigate peace treaty possibilities. The second group included Secretary of Defense Louis Johnson and General Omar Bradley, Chairman of the Joint Chiefs of Staff. Among other matters, the military officials clearly hoped to convince MacArthur that an indefinite delay was vital.

Dulles, every inch the diplomat, strode vigorously from his plane at the unholy arrival hour of 5:40 A.M. He wore a black Homburg and, despite the early morning sultriness, a pin-striped

* The "Habomai Island Group (including Suisho, Yuri, Akiyuri, Shibotsu and Taraku Islands)" and Shikotan Island among others are mentioned in SCAPIN 677 (January 29, 1946) as excluded from the territory over which the imperial Japanese government might have any governmental or administrative authority. This SCAPIN was prepared by Government Section, GHQ, SCAP.

blue suit and vest.[3] A well-built, but slightly stooped man, he moved quickly and purposefully. His rugged face, topped by gold-rimmed bifocals, was strong and intelligent and reflected immense confidence. Dulles smiled at the crowd of welcoming newsmen, greeted me affably, and posed good-naturedly for pictures. With no display of fatigue, he marched into the airport terminal for an informal press conference and breakfast. Mrs. Dulles, who accompanied him, seemed resigned to all this bustle. I found her to be a motherly, soft-spoken, intelligent woman.

Parrying loaded questions with evident enjoyment and skill, Dulles managed to satisfy the inquisitive newsmen without providing much vital information. He reported that he was visiting South Korea at the invitation of President Rhee. In four days, he said, he would come back to Tokyo to inquire "whether it was wise to proceed with a peace treaty." Dulles said he would limit his investigations to political, economic, and social factors, leaving military problems to Secretary Johnson and General Bradley.

Although the great moments of his career were yet to come, Dulles already was well-polished and well-skilled in international affairs. He was the grandson of President Harrison's Secretary of State and a nephew of Robert Lansing, President Wilson's Secretary of State. He knew Europe well and was widely known there. In the United States, his name had become the byword for a highly successful international lawyer. He also was established as a major foreign policy spokesman for the Republican party, a factor which no doubt influenced President Truman's decision to appoint him as a special State Department adviser. Despite this background and experience, Dulles was little known at that time in Japan, and a number of Japanese leaders asked the Diplomatic Section for information about him. During the next fifteen months Japan, too, would come to know Dulles as a hard-working, knowledgeable, and busy emissary who negotiated the peace treaty with the skill of a master craftsman.

The early-morning press conference illustrated Dulles' capacity for handling delicate news with care which he later would demonstrate to a wider audience as Secretary of State. He was patient, courteous, clear, and accommodating, if generally non-committal. He was experienced enough, however, to use the press intelligently to underscore the points he wished to impress on the public mind. In that first meeting Dulles was anxious to make it absolutely clear, to both Japanese and Americans, that treaty negotiations would have to wait unless he was satisfied that the time had arrived to proceed with a settlement.

During the two-hour stopover at Tokyo's Haneda Airport, I was able to go over with Dulles a suggested program for his Japan visit, which would begin June 21. He readily approved the schedule, adding only that he wished to give a speech at a luncheon to be held in his honor by the American Chamber of Commerce. The idea made me wince with the thought of all the wrong things that could be said on such an occasion by a public official who had come to Japan primarily to listen and to learn. This was an unjustified doubt; for I soon discovered through personal contact that Dulles not only had unbelievably broad experience with foreign affairs but that he prepared his public statements with meticulous care and precision. Rarely did he say anything publicly without studied purpose and then only after checking and rechecking his facts.

The Dulles party had scarcely departed for Seoul when I was back on the Haneda runway, awaiting the arrival of the Johnson-Bradley group. The timing of these visits, so close together yet so far apart, made me wonder whether the two delegations had purposely planned to avoid meeting. If so, this would demonstrate the acuteness of the differences over Japanese security. If they ever met as missions during their visits to Japan, I was unaware of it.

The intensity of Secretary Johnson's feelings on the subject soon became apparent to a small group within Headquarters. On an otherwise calm Sunday morning we assembled in the Dai Ichi building for the usual briefing given by SCAP officers for visiting dignitaries. Normally, these briefings consisted of a series of short presentations, illustrated by charts, by key SCAP section chiefs, each detailing his area of responsibility, his accomplishments and problems. On this occasion, however, Johnson took the floor to denounce the State Department and Dulles. Johnson, a robust, heavy-set man, talked and moved with vigorous determination.

This was, however, a particularly unpleasant and, in my view, a completely unjustified episode. In the course of a 15-minute harangue, Johnson attacked "the State Department crowd" in terms which I considered shocking. Discussing the departmental impasse over Japanese security, the Secretary sharply criticized statements which had been made in Tokyo that the Japanese had fulfilled the terms of the Potsdam Declaration. These statements, he said, tended to support the State Department position favoring an early peace treaty and thus augmented pressures to force the withdrawal of all United States troops from Japan. Johnson characterized Dulles as an impractical man who approached the world's problems with a religious, moral, and pacifistic attitude.

Secretary Johnson's main point seemed to be that the security of both Japan and the United States depended upon the continued presence of American troops in Japan. Such an arrangement, he said, would be impossible to maintain if the Potsdam terms were to be considered as fulfilled. It evidently never occurred to Johnson, as it did to MacArthur and Dulles, that United States forces could be retained in Japan through a voluntary agreement with the Japanese government, as eventually was done.

The Secretary must have been upset when later he was given a memorandum prepared by General MacArthur on the peace treaty issue. The memorandum made this fundamental point:

. . . The Japanese people have faithfully fulfilled the obligations they assumed under the instrument of surrender and have every moral and legal right to the restoration of peace. On this point, as before stated, all of the Allied Powers concerned are in full accord and publicly committed and their failure to protect Japan in this right would be a foul blemish upon modern civilization. For this reason and irrespective of the issues joined and ultimate policy objectives, we should not allow ourselves to be deterred from moving invincibly forward along a course which we ourselves and the entire world recognize to be morally and legally right. We should proceed to call a peace conference at once . . .

MacArthur anchored his position more firmly by opening his memorandum with this sentence: "Three years ago I publicly expressed the view to the Allied press in Tokyo that the Allied Powers should proceed at once in the formulation of a peace treaty for Japan."

The memorandum, of course, was written before the Korean War changed the entire world situation. In this atmosphere it was apparent to me, and to many others, that the time was rapidly approaching when we had to formulate a concrete United States position on the treaty. MacArthur once told me that the United States should proceed unilaterally, if necessary, to conclude an early settlement.

When Dulles and his party returned from Korea on June 21, General and Mrs. MacArthur and a number of senior generals were in the airport reception group. MacArthur always was meticulous in the greeting of distinguished visitors, and Dulles in this instance represented both President Truman and Secretary of State Acheson. The General also realized the importance of Dulles' visit, for it was clear his recommendation would carry considerable weight with the Administration.

Dulles and I rode with MacArthur to the embassy apartment which had been allocated to the Dulleses during their stay. The MacArthurs hosted a luncheon in honor of the visitors, then Dulles was given the usual briefing at Headquarters. It was notable how completely the special envoy had done his homework and how skillfully he brought out, through questioning, information of particular concern to him, on such topics as Japan's economic rehabilitation and the domestic political situation. Afterward we sat down to go over MacArthur's peace treaty memorandum.

Although much of this document now is only of academic interest, it represented a serious effort by MacArthur to bridge the gap between the State and Defense Departments. State wanted to proceed with negotiations on the diplomatic level to determine whether a treaty was possible. Defense continued to oppose any negotiations and wanted to halt all peace treaty activity for the time being.

In his memorandum MacArthur took exception to a basic position assumed by the Joint Chiefs of Staff, that no treaty negotiations should be undertaken without assurance that Soviet Russia and Communist China would sign. This position presumably was based on the assumption that the U.S.S.R. and Communist China, as nonsignatories of an Allied treaty, might take advantage of a continued technical state of war with Japan by making unilateral demands upon the unarmed country. Even if the JCS position were correct, MacArthur argued, it did not necessarily follow that no action should be taken until their conditions were met.

MacArthur also rejected two alternative security proposals which the Defense authorities had suggested. One provided for a collective security arrangement, by which the Allies would aid Japan against attack and would help each other against Japanese aggression. This proposal also contained a provision for the continued maintenance of United States bases in Japan, by edict of the treaty rather than by Japanese invitation. MacArthur said this plan would be a step toward "colonization." The second Defense proposal was to restore Japan's sovereignty in every respect except security, with the United States continuing tight control over defense. This would have meant the perpetuation of SCAP, the Far Eastern Commission, and Occupation forces. MacArthur labeled this idea as worse than the Occupation.

The General suggested a broad solution to the security dilemma. United States forces, he said, should continue to occupy "points in Japanese territory" until "irresponsible militarism is driven from the world" and there is no longer any threat to "peace, security and justice." These were the conditions laid down by the Potsdam Declaration, although the threat had shifted from resurgent Japanese militarism to active Communist aggression.

MacArthur had thus offered an ingenious compromise to what appeared an insoluble problem. I doubted that Dulles would accept it completely, but at least the suggestion pointed the way toward a solution. This was, in fact, the genesis of the final disposition of the security question which Dulles later worked out. United States troops and bases were kept in Japan after the treaty, as MacArthur wanted, but not as the result of a dictated peace settlement; this was covered by a separate security treaty, concluded as a contract with, and at the request of, an independent, equal, and sovereign Japan.

In his first speech in Japan, before the American Chamber, Dulles clearly outlined the philosophy which finally governed the peace treaty when it was concluded more than a year later. A draft had been sent to MacArthur and, on the day of the speech, Dulles arrived early at my office to ask: "What does General MacArthur think of my speech?" When the answer came, somewhat later, we were told the General thought it was "tops."

Carefully and thoroughly Dulles built up, in his address, a view of the divided world which still was not clearly apparent to most Japanese—the prime audience he hoped to reach through his appearance before the American business group. His title, "The Free World and the Captive World," coined the concept of the global divisions which later became standard for State Department spokesmen. This was, however, an early date to advance to skeptical people the idea that the cold war was not ideological, as the Communists contended, but a conflict between freedom and captivity. Dulles insisted that the Communist world was "made up of peoples who never chose captivity."

Having laid this foundation, Dulles turned to Japan. "As the surrender terms are fulfilled," he pointed out, "Japan's destiny will increasingly be in her own hands." Japan would have the opportunity of choosing between the Free World and the Captive World. In making the choice, the Japanese "will determine their future destiny," he added.

The purpose of the speech was unmistakable. It gave the Japanese clear reasons for joining the Free World as an equal partner, as opposed to the blandishments and specious promises of the Communist bloc.

Dulles was constantly busy during the six days he remained in Japan on that occasion. Among other activities, he conferred with a large cross-section of Japanese leaders, foreign diplomats and businessmen and others with views about the treaty. This thought-gathering process was topped by what was supposed to be a quiet and unpublicized meeting with Prime Minister Yoshida at my residence. When Dulles and I reached the house from my office, however, at least a hundred reporters, cameramen, and hangers-on were waiting. Dulles eased my embarrassment with a loud laugh, and we agreed that the prime minister's public relations men were on the job.

Yoshida arrived precisely on time, nattily dressed as always and completely at ease. But he was in one of his puckish moods, when in Western terms he refused to talk "sense." Dulles, a man not given to small talk under any circumstances, tried to steer the conversation toward a discussion of Japan's security. Yoshida would have none of this. Smiling and with chuckles, he spoke with circumlocutory indirectness, with vagueness, and with an astute use of parables. He refused to commit himself in the slightest way. "Yes," he said, "security for Japan is possible, and the United States can take care of it. But Japan's *amour propre* must be preserved in doing so." In any event, the prime minister said, Japan could have security through her own devices, by being democratic, demilitarized, and peace-loving and by relying upon the protection of world opinion. Dulles was flabbergasted. He refused to follow this line of reasoning, and finally abandoned all attempts to discuss other matters. Later he told me he felt very much like Alice in Wonderland. I counseled patience, for this was only a "get acquainted" meeting, marking the first round. I did not point out that Yoshida's rationale for security used the very words so often employed in Far Eastern Commission policy decisions.

Although the outbreak of the Korean War diverted thought from the Japanese treaty, I still felt strongly that a prompt settlement was necessary. As soon as Dulles left for Washington, on June 27, I telegraphed the State Department, for Dulles' attention, urging that the Korean situation, serious as it was, not be allowed to delay peace negotiations. It seemed obvious to me that Japan as a sovereign nation allied to the Free World would be a far greater asset than a country remaining under Occupation control of foreign powers, including Soviet Russia.

During the tragic summer of 1950, when the Korean hostilities were so black, Dulles continued his efforts to find a Japanese security formula which would be acceptable to the Defense Department, now doubly concerned for the safety of Japan and the United States. Using MacArthur's original suggestion, Dulles succeeded in working out details of a proposed bilateral United States–Japan security treaty, as a separate document from a peace settlement. Japan would grant the United States the right to dispose forces in and about Japan until it was mutually agreed that a satisfactory alternative solution through the United Nations or other arrangement would terminate the agreement.

This formula was accepted by the Secretaries of State and Defense in early September as the solution to the security problem, and the impasse accordingly dissolved. They recommended to the President that the State Department be authorized to begin diplomatic conversations with Japan and friendly members of the Far Eastern Commission to determine whether the proposed treaty and the accompanying bilateral United States–Japan security agreement were acceptable. President Truman announced on September 14, the day before the Inchon landings, that he had authorized these discussions. The clear implication was that Washington was prepared to pursue the treaty, whether the Soviet Union participated or not, although a final United States decision had not been made on this point. This was real progress

—at long last.

Dulles clarified two major aspects of his thinking during a background press conference in Washington on September 15. He emphasized, first, that there was no intention of turning the United States bases in Japan into autonomous areas for the use of offensive American power in Asia. Secondly, Dulles said the United States did not contemplate any restrictions on the rearmament of Japan, if the Japanese government wished to rebuild its strength.

The latter point, understandably, created resistance among Allied nations which had been occupied by the Japanese. Dulles and his deputy, John Allison, canvassed the Far Eastern Commission nations and Indonesia during the Fifth General Assembly of the United Nations at New York, explaining the American views on the treaty. The Allied delegates also were given a seven-point statement of principles which the United States intended as the basis for the Japanese peace settlement. In addition to opposing Japanese rearmament, most of the Allied nations in Asia also objected to the United States proposal that further reparations be waived, as a means of encouraging Japan's economic rehabilitation. There were indications, however, that opposition to rearmament might be overcome by an adequate United States guarantee for the security of those nations still apprehensive about Japan. Most Asian delegates also realized that it would be difficult to exact additional reparations, beyond the hundreds of millions of dollars already advanced or pledged by Japan, and impossible to collect the total multibillion dollar bill which had been rendered by Japan's wartime victims. A few delegates continued to insist upon maintaining post-treaty controls over Japan.

Yakov Malik, the Soviet representative, indicated that Moscow would object to any treaty language which cast doubt on the Soviet title to southern Sakhalin and the Kurile Islands or on Communist China's sovereignty over Formosa. At the same time, he questioned the right of the United States to exercise trusteeship over the Bonin Islands and the Ryukyu Group, which included the major United States base on Okinawa. Malik contended that these were "small islands to be left with Japan."

Communist China's large-scale entry into the Korean War increased the need for determining the conditions under which Japan would be willing to stand on the side of the Free World. Before this could be done, however, the United States had to make a number of fundamental decisions which would govern the timing of the peace treaty. Thus, State and Defense agreed that only as a sovereign nation could Japan play its full part as an active, contributing member of the Free World. It was further agreed that the treaty could be pursued without fear of impairing Japan's position as the primary and essential base for operations in Korea. If conditions changed, the exact date on which the treaty would become effective could be controlled through the United States constitutional process, since Senate ratification was one of the necessary steps to make the treaty effective. The two departments, whose agreement was essential for final action, also approved the important principle that it was desirable for Japan to increase its ability to defend itself. Finally, it was decided that appropriate security arrangements with certain Pacific nations would be undertaken, with the understanding that they would accept the general basis upon which the United States was prepared to conclude peace with Japan.

On January 10, 1951, Dulles was appointed as President Truman's Special Representative to conduct all necessary negotiations for a peace settlement. He was authorized to visit Japan and all other countries, as required, to complete the mission. Heading a balanced and competent mission, the special envoy reached Tokyo on January 25 and immediately plunged into work.[4] My office had prepared a detailed schedule to give Dulles maximum access to all areas of Japanese thought on the problem, and he went over this and other multitudinous details on the morning of his arrival. MacArthur had designated me, on a staff level, to handle the visit.

Some of the preparations necessarily impinged upon SCAP

prerogatives, and Dulles and I discussed these with MacArthur during a three-hour conference. MacArthur was at his best in this meeting—articulate, explicit, persuasive, and rational in advancing his ideas. One of the major problems to be solved was who, among the Japanese, was to be consulted on substantive provisions of the treaty. Dulles and I agreed that the treaty needed broad support among all major Japanese political parties, since they, like the United States Senate, were capable of raising objections on purely partisan grounds. MacArthur previously had indicated he favored a restrictive approach. In this meeting, however, he told Dulles to proceed on his own responsibility, consulting anyone he wished.

Accordingly, I arranged a series of four receptions at my residence, inviting on each occasion between twenty and twenty-five Japanese leaders in various fields. Five Japanese language experts on my staff were mobilized for any necessary interpretation. In this way Dulles and his staff were able to talk lengthily and in confidence with cabinet ministers, political leaders, officers of such organizations as chambers of commerce, bankers, newspaper publishers and editors, radio station executives, university presidents, Diet parliamentarians, trade union leaders, company executives, diplomats, representatives of the imperial household, and others. Opinion ranged from the monarchical court officials and conservative politicians to relatively moderate right-wing Socialists and extreme left-wing Socialists. Through these sessions and an endless series of additional meetings in my office, Dulles acquired every conceivable shading of Japanese thought and could speak authentically on the type of treaty with which Japan could live.

One of the longest and most unsatisfactory of Dulles' private sessions was with two representatives of the Japan Socialist party, the main political opposition to a succession of conservative governments which held power at that time and subsequently. The late Inejiro Asanuma, representing the Socialist party center, and the left-wing leader, Mosaburo Suzuki, outlined their ideas on

behalf of the entire party. In general, they echoed the party platform of "positive neutrality," by which it was contended Japan
could avoid involvement in the cold war by eliminating United
States forces and bases and by remaining totally unarmed itself.
These ideas, particularly in the context of the Korean War and
the Chinese Communist participation, were completely unrealistic. They demonstrated that the Socialist leaders lacked practical understanding of the world situation and of the complexities
in negotiating formal peace with Japan.

Prime Minister Yoshida spent an hour and a half with us, but
again little progress was made, much to Dulles' chagrin and frustration. Yoshida gave the impression that he was unprepared to
discuss even broad principles. Afterward, I spoke to my friend
Katsuo Okazaki, the chief cabinet secretary, urging him to advise
Yoshida to get to work and to stop stalling, since time was too
short for these circuitous methods. The government then named
Sadao Iguchi of the Foreign Office as vice minister in charge of
treaty negotiations. The choice was excellent, for Iguchi had a
clear mind and a broad understanding of the problems involved.
At the next meeting in my office with Yoshida and Iguchi, the
conversations were smoother and more productive. Considerable
progress was made. We found general agreement on broad principles of the proposed treaty, although, of course, there were
certain provisions which were not negotiable, particularly those
pertaining to the disposition of Japan's former territorial possessions.

In his only speech during this visit, Dulles further developed
the concept of a nonpunitive peace which was growing larger and
clearer, despite some lingering objections among the Allies.
Speaking on February 2 at a luncheon of the America-Japan Society, before most top Japanese leaders, Dulles gave this keynote:

. . . We can . . . already say that we seek a peace which will
afford Japan opportunity to protect by her own efforts the integrity of
the full sovereignty which peace will have restored; opportunity to
share in collective security against direct aggression; opportunity to
raise her standard of living by the inventiveness and industry of her

people; and opportunity to achieve moral stature and respected leadership through the force of good example.

Emperor Hirohito received Dulles and his wife in audience February 10, together with my wife and me. Although friendly and courteous, the Emperor seemed somewhat ill at ease. The conversation had ground to a halt until I suggested the Emperor might be interested in learning what the mission had accomplished during its visit. Hirohito replied he would like this very much. Dulles thereupon gave a clear outline of the progress to date, the concept of the proposed treaty, the problems of security, and some of the remaining difficulties. The Emperor soon relaxed and listened with interest, asking a number of pertinent and searching questions.

The Dulles mission left the next day for Manila, Canberra, and Wellington to begin the task of building up Allied support for the treaty. During this trip the security agreement between Australia, New Zealand, and the United States—the Anzus pact—was born. The foundation also was laid for further talks, through which these three key allies eventually gave their full support to the peace settlement. Dulles had instructed me to meet him in Honolulu, where he proposed to confer with Admiral Arthur W. Radford, Commander in Chief of the Pacific Area. With his usual careful preparation, Dulles wanted to be certain that the Pacific commander agreed with the proposed security arrangements for his area of responsibility. These conversations also were rewarding, and the mission left for Washington two days later, February 22. I accompanied it, for further consultations in the capital.

Japan suddenly had become a focal point of world attention and, during my three weeks' stay in Washington, I was besieged for information and impressions. By this time a number of Far Eastern Commission countries had replied to the initial United States treaty proposals, many of them offering suggestions to implement or to alter the planned document.

During the third week of March, 1951, Dulles completed a

provisional draft of the Japanese treaty. Essentially a United States document, it nevertheless reflected to a considerable degree the views of other governments with which Washington had corresponded on the draft. Dulles personally went over the proposed draft treaty thoroughly with the Far East Subcommittee of the United States Senate Foreign Relations Committee on March 19, to acquaint the legislators with its provisions and to solicit their suggestions. Expanding this personal diplomacy, Dulles also called in the diplomatic representatives of the fourteen principal Allies and Korea in Washington, handing each a copy of the draft, with the request for an early expression of their governments' views.

A week after my return to Tokyo, on March 27, I was able to provide General MacArthur with the draft, as instructed by the State Department. The General expressed his gratification at the progress which was being made. He emphasized hope that a treaty would be completed without delay, although new speculation of continued Pentagon opposition had just arisen. This reached us in the form of a Washington news dispatch quoting "well-informed sources" as saying military officials believed the treaty should be delayed. Two days later my British colleague, George Clutton, called to inform me that "the generals" in the Commonwealth Headquarters were opposed to the proposed treaty. The generals, including Lieutenant General Sir Horace Robertson, Commander in Chief of British Commonwealth Forces, contended that the treaty would cause "administrative difficulties in carrying on the Korean War." If this attitude existed in fact, it was minimal and of no apparent effect. And no substantial Pentagon opposition developed.

Three further temporary complications arose without, however, causing the ill effects which many of us, under the stress of this prolonged diplomatic effort, anticipated from any disruption. We had, of course, taken maximum efforts to ensure secrecy. When I gave Prime Minister Yoshida his copy of the draft, I had made special efforts to impress upon him that the document was confidential and that great damage could result from its premature disclosure in Japan. Nevertheless, I was awakened at 1:30 A.M. on April 7 by a telephone call from Dulles in Washington, informing me that the text had appeared there in the morning papers, through a "leak," and asking whether it was likely to appear in Japan. Within a short time I was able to report back that Tokyo papers soon would publish the complete document, having received it from American news agencies. I also was informed in a later telephone conversation with Washington that the leak had occurred in the Indian Embassy there, whether intentionally or not was not clear.

As if this were not enough, I was informed later the same day that British officials were insisting upon the insertion of a "war guilt" clause in the final treaty. They were willing to accept a watered-down version of an original proposal to condemn Japan harshly for initiating the war, but they were determined to obtain some mention of this responsibility in the final document. I argued strenuously against this idea, on the ground it would undermine the entire concept of the nonpunitive treaty as it had been developed. At a minimum, such a clause in my estimation would have created great difficulties in obtaining Japanese acceptance of the treaty as a whole. This was, at the time, a genuine worry, but fortunately the idea was later abandoned.

MacArthur's dismissal created the third, and potentially most serious, complication. When Dulles had said good-by to me at the Washington Airport, before my return to Tokyo on March 18, we both expected to meet next at a formal peace conference, in perhaps five or six months. Instead, Dulles was sent back to Tokyo by President Truman, arriving on the day of MacArthur' departure, April 16, 1951, to shore up the diplomatic situation. This special mission included Earl D. Johnson, Assistant Secretary of the Army.[5]

Shortly after the arrival of the mission, Dulles, Earl Johnson, and I called on Ridgway at his office to discuss the situation. Dulles was greatly concerned that the MacArthur dismissal and the resultant change in the situation would cause a revulsion of feeling among the Japanese which might be difficult to control and which could seriously undermine his efforts to negotiate a peace. The consensus of the meeting was that there must be immediate reassurance to the Japanese government and to the people and that they must be given visual evidence that United States policy had not changed. It was also agreed that the gradual liquidation of Occupation restraints and controls would continue, but at an accelerated pace. Among other steps to augment this policy, Dulles intended giving a major speech and Prime Minister Yoshida was invited to conferences, first, with General Ridgway alone, then with Ridgway and Dulles, and finally with the entire Dulles mission. In this manner we hoped to demonstrate and to highlight what was a fact: that the same easy relationship between the Japanese government, SCAP, and Dulles on peace treaty matters, which had previously existed, would continue.

Dulles' last day in Japan, April 23, was devoted to an intensive review of a British Draft treaty which we had just received. Prime Minister Yoshida, Vice Foreign Minister Sadao Iguchi, and Kumao Nishimura, the knowledgeable head of the Japanese Treaty Bureau and a skilled technician, joined us for a conference lasting several hours in my office. The Japanese, who had been given a copy of the British draft, preferred the American version to the technically precise and comprehensive United Kingdom document. The latter, although not formally agreed upon by the British Commonwealth, was to a large degree the product of overall Commonwealth thinking, evolved through Commonwealth meetings in Canberra, August, 1947, in Colombo, January, 1950, and in London, May, 1950.

The American and British drafts finally were meshed into a single document dated May 3, 1951, by a joint working group in Washington under the chairmanship of John M. Allison. This combined version, however, left unresolved several major policy differences between the United States and United Kingdom governments. Among these were the questions of the disposition of

Formosa, whether Communist or Nationalist China should sign the treaty, and the disposition of Japanese-owned gold and other assets in neutral and former enemy countries.

During April and May most of the governments to which the United States provisional draft had been sent submitted their comments to Washington. A number of the British Commonwealth nations also commented on the joint Anglo-American document which London had forwarded to them. On the other hand, on May 7 the Soviet government submitted a list of comments on the United States draft which were not helpful. The Soviets took exception, at the outset, to the method of negotiating the treaty, insisting that a meeting of the Council of Foreign Ministers, where the veto applied, should be convened to begin preparation of a peace settlement. The United States sent a lengthy reply, taking exception to the Soviet position on almost every point.

In order to resolve the Anglo-American differences, Dulles visited London on June 2. The problem of Formosa was solved readily by agreement that Japan, through the treaty, merely would renounce sovereignty over the island, leaving its eventual ownership unmentioned. South Sakhalin and the Kurile Islands were treated in the same way. Several meetings were necessary between Dulles and Herbert Morrison, the British Secretary of State for Foreign Affairs, to produce a compromise on the question of which China should sign the final document. The two men finally agreed that neither Chinese government should participate and that Japan should decide with which China to conclude formal peace. This agreement, however, was not accepted by the British Cabinet. It was only after strong argument by Dulles that the Cabinet reversed itself and approved the Dulles-Morrison solution.

Nevertheless, the British government reserved its position on several additional points, and final agreement was not reached until July 3. A joint draft then was circulated to the thirteen other concerned governments for comment. It was sent on July 9 to the governments of all other countries which had been at war with Japan, except the two Chinas. Recipient governments were advised that this document was a joint Anglo-American product, based on the United States draft of March, an independently prepared British draft, and the comments on those drafts received from the nations principally concerned.

A slightly revised draft was circulated on July 20, and the various governments were informed that a final text would be distributed on August 13. Each government was invited to a conference in San Francisco, to be convened September 4, 1951, to conclude and sign a final treaty based on the August 13 text.

Considerable correspondence was exchanged at a governmental level between the State Department and the governments involved during the summer of 1951. Communications with the Soviet Union were especially burdensome. It soon became apparent that the Soviets, while attending the San Francisco conference, would use every means to disrupt or, if possible, to wreck it. Of the fifty nations invited to attend the conference, only Yugoslavia, Burma and India—each for a different reason— declined.

12

Problems of Peace and Security

A TREATY OF PEACE, concluded after a long, bitter, sanguinary war, usually is the result of lengthy and difficult negotiation and considerable flexibility by all involved. If the treaty is to have meaning and is to function, the highest attributes of statesmanship in its formulation are necessary. The pact with Japan encompassed all of this, for it was the product of eleven months of diplomacy, of constant revision, and of close consideration and understanding of the views of many countries. But a treaty document, no matter how carefully drafted, is worthless until it is signed by the parties concerned. In normal diplomacy this is done at an international conference where further negotiation and last-minute bargaining may occur, but where ultimate conclusion of the treaty is expected.

The San Francisco Peace Conference was exceptional on two major points. It was, first, a conference called to approve a treaty already completed, not to conduct further negotiations. John Foster Dulles had elected to conclude peace arrangements through bilateral diplomacy, because the Soviet Union had demonstrated it would accept a peace only on its terms. Secondly, the Communist participants—Soviet Russia, Poland, and Czechoslovakia—all clearly were determined to thwart the conference, unless it capitulated to their desires. Therefore, in this case the steps leading to the final signing of the pact were as important and certainly as difficult as the negotiations which led to the conference.

The story of the San Francisco meeting, from September 4 to 8, 1951, has already been recorded elsewhere, and even the bare record of the proceedings provides fascinating reading long after the event.[1] But a conference of this kind does not simply happen. It is the result of careful preparation, needful negotiation, inter-national understandings, and the quick solution of delicate prob-lems before they become unmanageable. For example, what would the United States and the United Kingdom, co-sponsors of the conference, have done if the Japanese government had re-fused to attend, for various reasons of its own? Or what would have happened if the Japanese government, at the last minute, had been unable to agree upon a delegation and had been forced into calling a special election to decide the issue? These prob-lems, which seldom attracted public notice, demanded a consid-erable amount of attention and thought.

In mid-July, 1951, it became necessary to sound out Japanese government opinion before further planning for the conference could proceed. The Japanese had not yet been invited to attend, but no invitation could be proffered until Japanese acceptance was assured; for the political consequences of a refusal would have been significant. Accordingly, I asked Sadao Iguchi, the Foreign Office vice minister handling peace treaty affairs, for an official assurance that an invitation would be accepted. He agreed to provide this and obtained a formal cabinet resolution to that effect. It was after this step that, following instructions from Washington, I was able on July 20 to extend the official invitation for Japanese attendance at the San Francisco meeting.

The Japanese government left no doubt of its sincere desire to conclude peace, for, as Yoshida has recorded in his memoirs, this was its primary goal throughout the Occupation. This desire was underlined, for example, by the rather unusual procedure for a special cabinet meeting on July 13. Members of the cabinet had been invited to a reception for Governor Thomas E. Dewey, at the prime minister's official residence, and while there each was asked to attend a cabinet session to be held in the dining room after the party. The special meeting was called to approve certain proposed legislation regarding claim provisions in the United States draft treaty which had been handed to the government and made public the previous day. Yoshida wanted no delay in carrying out Japan's legislative requirements under what still was an uncompleted peace treaty.

But the problem of selecting a "representative delegation" for Japan, as Dulles had suggested, was difficult, prolonged, and often heated, and was punctuated by bitter partisan politics. At the time of extending the official invitation, I had been informed that Prime Minister Yoshida would head the mission, in his capacity both as head of government and as minister of foreign affairs. The scramble for places quickly involved me, not without some personal embarrassment.

A number of Japanese politicians called on me during the latter half of July to discuss the treaty draft and the composition of the Japanese delegation, probably on the assumption that I would be able to influence the prime minister, or perhaps for more subtle and inexplicable reasons. On July 19 I spent two hours with a group from the Japan Socialist party, including such leaders as Inejiro Asanuma, Kanju Kato, Eki Sone, Seiichi Katsumata, and Eiichi Nishimura. They were critical of several provisions in the draft. I carefully explained the history and background of these particular points, arguing that they should support the treaty instead of placing the Socialist party in opposition to it. Even so, I doubted that any of my arguments would change the party's policy. Rather, it was most probable that the Socialists, in a perverse sort of way, wished to create a public image of fair-mindedness by discussing the treaty with me before bitterly opposing it in the Diet. From these discussions it appeared evident that any pact which the Socialists might have supported would have created endless future difficulties.

Even conservative politicians began to complain that Yoshida's dominant Liberal party was using its appointive power to the peace delegation to obtain major political concessions. In fact, Takeo Miki, secretary of the Democratic party, was extremely bitter about this point and told me the Liberals were waging "guerrilla warfare" against his organization in the Upper House. The Democrats, who later merged with the Liberals, were equally conservative and pro-Western, and I urged Miki to accept a place for his party on the delegation if offered. The contest over this issue was an internal political matter entirely outside my responsibility, I pointed out, adding that failure of the principal Japanese parties to support the liberal peace treaty would be regarded in the United States as a sign of "insincerity"—a useful word in situations of this kind.

The political fight continued, however, much to the concern of the Foreign Office. I called in my friend, Katsuo Okazaki, the secretary general of the Liberal party, told him of the complaints made by my various visitors and strongly urged a compromise effort. He promised to investigate, and apparently took action. On August 4, Iguchi brought me a final list of the delegation. Perhaps political peace was obtained by expanding the group to include five alternate delegates and ten parliamentary visitors, all members of the Diet.[2] The Socialist party boycotted the delegation, however, and continued to oppose the treaty.

There were other half-hidden complications, some minor and some potentially important. The political atmosphere was ruffled not only by partisanship but by the uncertainty of some Japanese regarding the proper procedure in such unfamiliar circumstances. For instance, a member of the so-called "Green Breeze Society" (Ryokufukai), a political grouping in the House of Councillors, asked me whether I thought it would be unreasonable for the society to demand the right to debate the treaty as the price for furnishing a representative on the delegation. I replied with a strong affirmative. It would be unwise to debate a treaty before it was signed, I said, adding that such a debate would only create a poor impression regarding the sense of responsibility of the Upper House.

During this period the United Kingdom advanced a suggestion in Washington and Tokyo that it might be advisable to encourage the Emperor's participation in the treaty signing. It was suggested this could be done indirectly by the issuance of an Imperial Rescript approving the signatures of the Japanese delegation. The reasons for this idea were somewhat obscure. I opposed it, because I felt the Japanese constitutional process must be maintained. Constitutionality would be subverted, I argued, by use of the Imperial Rescript, in much the same way that the Japanese militarists had misused the Throne to sanction aggression, and this could establish a precedent for future subversion of the constitution on one pretext or another. This view finally prevailed.

Washington also continued to demonstrate shortsightedness, despite the vision which had gone into the making of the treaty. In late July, for example, I received a telegram outlining the procedures to be followed at San Francisco, including a suggestion that the Japanese delegation would receive *almost* equal treatment with other representative groups. Upon reading this instruction, I was not only surprised at our lack of political sophistication but incensed at this evidence that we had forgotten the lessons of Versailles. In my comment I strongly urged that the Japanese delegation be received in a spirit of equality, friendship, and understanding and that it be treated hospitably from the moment of arrival in the United States. This approach was adopted, and in so far as I could discover the members of the Japanese delegation were pleased by their official and unofficial reception and treatment during their stay in the United States. Prime Minister Yoshida noted in his memoirs that the atmosphere of the conference "was friendly throughout, without any manifestation of hostility toward us." [3]

In late August the Foreign Office advised me that SCAP Headquarters had informed the Japanese government of its intention to inspect closely the baggage of all members of the Japanese delegation upon departure. It was also proposed, with the prime minister's knowledge, to place a second-generation (nisei) Japanese agent with the party in one guise or another. These extraordinary measures were designed to ensure the security of the prime minister and his colleagues. I, too, was concerned with the safety of this great statesman, but I could visualize the storm of criticism which would erupt if the Japanese press learned about the plan. Immediately I telephoned Brigadier General Riley F. Ennis, Assistant Chief of Staff for Intelligence, for information. He sent over my old friend, Colonel Rufus Bratton to discuss the matter. Rufe told me G-2 was extremely worried and desired to take every possible method of ensuring security. I advised him to tell his boss to relax and to adopt more conventional precautions which would not cause an international incident. I do not know what Rufe reported back or what steps finally were taken, but the Japanese delegation made the round trip without any untoward incident.

The atmosphere in Tokyo at this time was best exemplified, perhaps, by a luncheon given by the America-Japan Society on August 28 in honor of the Japanese delegation. The occasion was unusual, for General Ridgway attended—the first time the Supreme Commander appeared at a public function of this sort. Earl Warren, then governor of California and visiting Tokyo at the time, also was present. The dominant theme of speeches by General Ridgway, Prime Minister Yoshida, Governor Warren, and me was hope that the impending Peace Conference would be successful. This was an uncertain hope at the time, for the Soviet Union had ominously announced a short time earlier that it would participate in the conference. This could only foreshadow difficulties. But it was rather symbolic of the new mood, I thought, that on this same day Yoshida, acting as foreign minister, and I signed the first Fulbright Agreement between Japan and the United States for educational exchanges between the two nations. The importance of this agreement for long-term cultural benefit to both sides cannot be overestimated.

In the bustle and uncertainty of preparing for the climax of Japan's postwar development under American influence, there were many, no doubt, who recalled that one of the key figures, General MacArthur, would be absent from the conference. The subject was raised with particular vigor one night at my residence by the visiting radio commentator, H. V. Kaltenborn. He was highly critical of the State Department for not inviting Mac-Arthur to address the Peace Conference, in view of the General's great service to the United States. I agreed that the proposal had great merit and would constitute a warm gesture toward the General, but I pointed out that the difficulties would probably be too great. General MacArthur was without official status, and he could have been invited only by creating a special precedent. In fact, there would have been no proper role for him, I pointed out, even if he had continued to be the Supreme Commander, an international military position. The peace delegates, on the other hand, were national representatives. This probably was the reason, I surmised, that no consideration had been given to inviting General Ridgway to attend.

My own role in the San Francisco meeting was to act as a senior adviser to the United States delegation, and I had received instructions to arrive at San Francisco about September 1. Prime Minister Yoshida called on me two days earlier to wish me bon voyage and to request assistance in arranging visits to Washington and New York for two members of the Japanese delegation, Finance Minister Hayato Ikeda and Hisato Ichimada, governor of the Bank of Japan. The visits, made after the conference, established the practice of high-level fiscal consultation which has continued to characterize American-Japanese relations.

OVER THE YEARS, I have always felt a sense of exhilaration upon arriving in San Francisco, whether through the magnificent Golden Gate or across the wide, ruffled bay. The significance of the Peace Conference made me doubly eager to plunge into the vibrant atmosphere of the hospitable bay city when my plane landed on August 31, Pacific Coast time. Work began immediately, it seemed, as I stepped into warm, mellow sunshine; for the local State Department representative and an armed MP met me, to assist with a small pouch of classified documents which I was carrying.

At the Palace Hotel, on lower Market Street, where the United States delegation was staying, I was met first by Joe Rosenthal, photographer for the San Francisco *Chronicle* who won international fame for his wartime picture of the Iwo Jima flag-raising. He had scarcely departed with a far less memorable photograph of me when the endless round of conferences, details, arrangements, and small but significant diplomatic encounters which occur backstage and can often determine the course of an international meeting, drew me into an hour-by-hour maelstrom. Dean Rusk, Assistant Secretary of State for Far Eastern Affairs, was the coordinator of the American delegation and briskly handled daily meetings. My specific assignment became that of political liaison officer with the Japanese delegation.

There were airport arrivals to meet on precise schedule—Secretary of State Acheson, suave and confident, and John Foster Dulles, poised and smiling; Prime Minister Yoshida, correctly dressed in striped trousers and carrying a silver-tipped walking stick and gloves. Yoshida, pausing to read an arrival statement as the first postwar Japanese prime minister to stand on the soil of the onetime enemy, obviously seemed pleased by his reception, despite the unseemly tugging and shoving of a herd of Japanese photographers and correspondents. There were private conferences to arrange, such as the first meeting between Acheson and Yoshida, when important questions, like reparations and the proper relations for the Japanese delegation to maintain with other delegations, were discussed in a hotel room. There was the rather awkward moment, on the first night of the conference, when I found Yoshida and his daughter, Mrs. Kazuko Aso, wandering through the Palace Hotel, searching for a reception being given for heads of delegations to meet President Truman. When I escorted them to the proper room, Mrs. Aso and I were unceremoniously ushered out. There were luncheons and dinners and corridor consultations and all the activity during which the actual work of such a conference is conducted.

By coincidence, September 2, 1951, was the sixth anniversary of the surrender ceremony aboard the U.S.S. *Missouri*. Much progress had been made in preparing the world for Japan's readmission as a full member of the society of nations, from which by its own actions it so long had been isolated. Nevertheless, many of the Free World representatives in San Francisco were constantly mindful of the bitterness created among their peoples by the war. They were unsure of the proper relations, both official and unofficial, to maintain with the Japanese at San Francisco. Most of them seemed to prefer a "formally correct" approach. It was, therefore, highly desirable, if the treaty of reconciliation was to be meaningful, that we of the United States, representing the country which had borne the brunt of the Pacific War and as the hosts, set an example which others might follow. This was done by American representatives throughout the conference.

At this late date, however, there remained serious difficulties over the aspects of the treaty which some delegates regarded as a denial of proper restitution for wartime Japanese depredations. Thus, the Indonesian delegation demanded more than mere good faith as a pledge of future reparations. It was with great difficulty that James L. O'Sullivan from the State Department and I were able to suggest a solution which satisfied the Indonesians, was acceptable to the Japanese, and did not violate our principle of a liberal treaty. Letters also were exchanged between the Japanese chief delegate and Dirk U. Stikker, Minister of Foreign Affairs of the Netherlands, on the question of guaranteeing payments to the Dutch prisoners of war whom the Japanese had so badly mistreated in the Netherlands East Indies. These problems—and there were many others—were of great political importance to those concerned. It was evident that, unless some solution satisfactory to the home governments could be reached, they might have refused to sign the treaty.

The obstacles were smoothed over, however, and the conference opened and proceeded with considerable agreement among the non-Communist nations. Its tone was set by the initial speeches at the San Francisco Opera House on the night of September 4. President Truman, voicing the keynote, stressed the need for peace. In his address, the President mentioned the "outstanding leadership of General of the Army Douglas MacArthur and his successor General Matthew Ridgway." He noted the great progress made by Japan in reforming its institutions, and in consequence, he emphasized, the time had arrived to restore full sovereignty to the Japanese people. The peace agreement, said the President, is "a treaty that will work. . . . It is a treaty of reconciliation."

To my mind, however, this mood was voiced best by two quotations from the ancient East which rang through the conference hall. J. R. Jayewardene, Minister of Finance, who as the Ceylonese delegate made a profound and moving speech, quoted Buddha: "Hatred ceases not by hatred, but by love." And the urbane minister of foreign affairs of Pakistan, Zafrullah Khan, added this thought from Mohammed: "The hand that bestows lifts itself higher than the hand that receives."

As the speeches rolled on, from the representatives of the fifty-two nations finally attending the conference, the importance of the Japanese presentation increased. The ceremonies were televised live throughout the United States for the first time, by the completion of a new coaxial cable, and were carried by various means, in sound and picture, to all interested corners of the world. Yoshida would appear to this audience of tens of millions as the personification of the New Japan.

The prime minister proposed to give his speech in English when his turn arrived. I had alerted the Japanese delegation well in advance to be ready. Late on the morning of Friday, September 7, the prime minister's private secretary, Akira Matsui, brought me an English copy of the draft speech, requesting that I read it and suggest any desirable changes. I do not know who wrote the speech, but it was not good. In fact, portions of it would unwittingly have undone much of the good will which already had been engendered by the conference, especially among some of the Asian countries. Something had to be done to change the tone and theme of the speech, and quickly, for there were strong indications Yoshida would be called to speak during the late afternoon or at the start of the evening session.

I suggested to Matsui that he ask the prime minister to give his address in Japanese, with a simultaneous English version to be given by Henry Shimanouchi, the Japanese delegation's bilingual interpreter. My reason was fundamental. Although Yoshida had an excellent knowledge of English, his enunciation like that of many Japanese was poor and at times was difficult to understand, particularly when unfamiliar phraseology was involved. I shuddered at the thought of a badly written speech being delivered in a strange tongue, with poor pronunciation. When I discussed these doubts with the prime minister at his hotel, he readily agreed to make the speech in Japanese.

Meanwhile, several of my colleagues worked hastily on the original draft. They edited where needed, deleted portions which might give offense, and generally polished the language to the point where the speech was good and yet maintained the integrity of what Yoshida wanted to say. Matsui was present during this anguished work, which went on while we munched hastily ordered sandwiches, and he was highly pleased with the result. Matsui dashed off with the revised draft. After approval by Yoshida, it then had to be translated into Japanese. To the everlasting credit of Yoshida and his staff, everything was ready by 8 P.M.—but just ready—when Dean Acheson, as president of the conference, called upon the prime minister to speak.

Yoshida's delivery was something of a monotone, without interruption or break, and sounded flat. In contrast, the simultaneous interpretation, read from the prepared text, flowed in Shimanouchi's cultured and highly articulate and persuasive voice. It was a masterful job. The resounding applause at the end of the speech was clear proof that a good impression had been made upon the delegates and, as I later learned, upon the millions of television viewers.

Throughout most of the conference, Soviet Deputy Foreign Minister A. A. Gromyko maintained continual pressure on Secretary Acheson, as the presiding officer, in an effort to create circumstances through which the Soviets could veto the treaty and thereby destroy the international meeting. Gromyko used various procedural dodges in this endeavor. One was an attempt to force discussion of a number of suggested treaty amendments which were made, out of order, in the course of the prepared Soviet speech. The illicit "amendments" were deliberately provocative and designed to arouse debate, for in the unlikely event of their adoption, the United States would have been driven from the Western Pacific and Japan would have been left helpless within Communist encirclement. Acheson, however, handled the parliamentary challenges with consummate skill, outwitting and outmaneuvering the Communist delgates, yet affording them full opportunity within procedural limits to present their views. On two key votes, the entire conference, except for the Communist nations, supported Acheson in ruling as out of order the Soviet attempt to amend the treaty. This prevented a full-scale debate which might have resulted in endless wrangling and delay.[4]

The treaty finally was signed, on the morning of September 8, 1951, by the delegates of forty-nine countries, including the six representatives from Japan. Only the Soviet Union, Poland, and Czechoslovakia refused to sign. Thus was completed the long diplomatic effort to restore Japan to full standing in the international community.

The next ceremony on our schedule was the formal signing of the Security Treaty between the United States and Japan at 5 P.M. on the same day. This pact had been under quiet negotiation in Tokyo for about eight months, and its text was released to the press only two hours before the scheduled ceremony. The cere-

mony was held at the Presidio in San Francisco, the Army Headquarters for the Western United States, which then was commanded by Lieutenant General Joseph M. Swing, the former
commander of I Corps during the Occupation.

There was to be an exchange of letters between the two signatories. One, from Secretary Acheson to Prime Minister Yoshida,
raised the official inquiry whether, after the peace treaty became
effective, Japan would "permit and facilitate the support in and
about Japan" of a member or members of the United Nations in
an action in the Far East. The second letter was a response by the
prime minister that Japan would so permit and facilitate such
support for the purpose stated. Dean Rusk, who had been holding
the American letter, suddenly discovered that he had left the
signed original at the delegation headquarters. By coincidence,
the Japanese official charged with bringing the prime minister's
reply also had forgotten his copy. Messengers were hurriedly sent
for the letters, and in due course the originals were exchanged.

The Security Treaty was a brief document, containing only a
preamble and five short articles. Referring to the Treaty of Peace
with the Allied Powers, the preamble states that "Japan will not
have the effective means . . . of self-defense." As irresponsible
militarism had not been driven from the world, the preamble
continued, Japan desired a Security Treaty with the United States
"to come into force simultaneously with the Treaty of Peace."
The Security Treaty provided, in Article III, that the disposition
of United States armed forces in and about Japan would be determined "by administrative agreements between the two Governments." Although no time was fixed for the negotiation of these
agreements, it was the consensus of a meeting held in Dulles'
hotel room after the ceremony that this should be undertaken at
the earliest practicable time, so that the Peace Treaty, Security
Treaty, and Administrative Agreement could become effective
simultaneously.

DURING THE Japanese peace treaty negotiations, it was clear that
a number of countries remained deeply and genuinely concerned

about the extent to which the Japanese threat—real or imagined —could or would be contained once Japan's full sovereignty was restored without any external controls or restrictions over armaments. This concern was especially acute in the Philippines, which had suffered such extensive damage during the war, and in Australia and New Zealand, where the feeling against Japan was still high. Dulles met this apprehension by concluding a series of security pacts under which the United States would assist in repelling external armed attack. Accordingly, a bilateral treaty was negotiated with the Philippines and signed in Washington, August 30, 1951. The so-called ANZUS Security Treaty between Australia, New Zealand, and the United States was signed in San Francisco, September 1, 1951. With the bilateral treaty between the United States and Japan the framework for security in the Far East was established.

In due time additional treaties were signed: with the Republic of Korea (in Washington, October 1, 1953); the Southeast Asia Collective Defense Treaty (SEATO—in Manila, September 8, 1954); and the Mutual Defense Treaty with the Republic of China (Washington, December 2, 1954).

It will thus be seen that, through its security treaties in the Far East and Southwestern Pacific, the United States, as the common denominator of this network of agreements, effectively tied together for mutual defense a number of otherwise disparate nations. It should be remembered that, at least during the period of negotiating the Japanese peace treaty, it was inconceivable that Korea, the Philippines, Australia and New Zealand, or even the Republic of China on Formosa, would have joined with Japan in a common action for mutual defense. Based upon the security relationships with the United States, however, and, of course, assisted by the ameliorative effects of time, common action in concert with the United States is no longer impossible.

UPON MY RETURN TO TOKYO from San Francisco on September 12, I was met at the airfield by a large number of friends including the Japanese treaty experts, Sadao Iguchi and Katsuo Okazaki. The inordinately complicated nature of a final peace settlement was underlined by the fact that I was to be in almost daily contact with these two outstanding men during the next six months, completing additional agreements on the basis of the triumph at San Francisco. And there was no doubt in my mind, as I told General Ridgway later that day, that San Francisco had been a major triumph for the Free World. Summarizing the conference for the General, I emphasized that the Soviets had suffered a severe diplomatic defeat. Gromyko and his colleagues were inept and completely outclassed by the American delegation, aided by a number of our close allies.

A few additional notes on the conference, which I outlined to Ridgway, illustrated the atmosphere of that period. Even after the San Francisco meeting, I reported, it was unclear why the Soviets attended the conference, since presumably they intended to boycott the treaty in any event. Perhaps they had hoped to build a record for future action, but if so, they have been unable to capitalize upon it. Fortunately, the Free World demonstrated complete solidarity when vital issues were to be decided. This was shown particularly by the solid vote in adopting rules of procedure which effectively blocked the Soviet attempts to throw the conference open for treaty amendments. Secretary Acheson gained immeasurable prestige for his skillful handling of the conference.

All this resulted from careful preparation, and was not merely spontaneous. The United States delegation worked long and hard, with a surprising unity of purpose and complete bipartisanship. The Japanese delegation handled itself with tact and restraint. The Soviet moves were anticipated and careful advance strategy was well-planned and smoothly executed.

Yoshida returned to Japan two days later looking tired, as well he might after two busy and vital weeks which would have taxed a far younger man. But, with his remarkable recuperative powers, he appeared fresh and cheerful later in the day when he attended a large reception given in his honor by General and Mrs. Ridgway at the American Embassy. Some two hundred Americans and Japanese were present, and it was obvious that the Japanese guests were pleased by this manifestation of the change in their status, upon conclusion of the peace treaty. Moreover, at this same time there was considerable evidence that Occupation authorities also accepted the new stature of the Japanese. SCAP was engaged in liquidating the Occupation controls as rapidly as circumstances would permit. There was promise that this process would be accelerated, but much remained to be done before it could be said that Japan had again regained full sovereignty.

The long and difficult task of augmenting the San Francisco treaty with additional bilateral peace agreements now became a major project in our office. My deputy, Niles Bond, for example, suggested the eventual compromise formula to break a long impasse over formal peace between Japan and Italy. This solution was timely, as tempers were growing short and negotiators for the two nations were beginning to show signs of anger.

The problem of the peace treaty between Japan and the Republic of China was more difficult. It engaged my close attention for some months. There were, unfortunately, some domestic political overtones to this problem in the United States. A number of influential senators had let it be known that ratification of the San Francisco treaty would be difficult to obtain in the United States Senate unless Japan beforehand gave satisfactory evidence that it intended resuming relations with the Chinese government at Taipei, instead of the Chinese Communist government.

The Japanese, however, appeared reluctant to proceed with any China treaty, and there was no progress for some time. The reason for this reticence was explained in this way to me by Hollington Tong, the well-known Chinese official who later became ambassador to the United States: A number of knowledgeable officials in the Japanese Foreign Office contended that, if Japan concluded a treaty with Taipei, the Chinese people on the mainland would be whipped into a frenzy of anti-Japanese feeling.

This might have been part of the Japanese reasoning, for popular Chinese opposition had been an important influence on Japan's pre-Pearl Harbor foreign policy. Perhaps, also, the question of "face" contributed to the delay; which government would first approach the other? In the Asian view, the country making the first move might lose face. Further, there was the dilemma of conflicting American and British policies. I suspected at the time, without clear evidence, that my British colleagues were advising Yoshida and his aides to follow the British lead in recognizing the Chinese People's Republic. Whether this was true or not, the divergent Anglo-American China policies gave Japan ample scope for playing one country against the other, or so it seemed in Tokyo. But this also posed a great problem for Yoshida himself. He was fundamentally pro-British in his personal views, but for many practical reasons he had strengthened the pro-American posture of his government. Yoshida often complained to me about this dichotomy of policy by Japan's two principal postwar friends.

Little was accomplished on the matter of a China peace treaty until John Foster Dulles and Senators H. Alexander Smith of New Jersey and John J. Sparkman of Alabama arrived in Tokyo on December 10, 1951. At a news conference the following day Senator Sparkman said in answering a question: "If Japan should open relations with the Peiping government, such action would raise a very considerable roadblock in the Senate." This statement and its implications were widely publicized in the Japanese press. Later Dulles and I met with Iguchi and pointed out how essential it was for the Japanese government to realize the importance of the China problem to the United States. Dulles said pointedly that American officials wished to know *now* whether Japan's foreign policy would parallel that of the United States or would be inimical to it. Parallel policies, he said, would simplify the solution of many problems. Divergences, however, would force the United States to review its position. The China problem was further explored in a later meeting between Dulles and Yoshida, and

Dulles gave this outline of his fundamental position: Japan should conclude a treaty with Taipei relating only to the Chinese territory over which that government had *de facto* control— Taiwan and its adjacent islands. Relations over other Chinese areas which the Republic of China did not control, principally the mainland, would be left for later determination. This formula, like other elements of the peace settlement, postponed a final solution to the indefinite future when the Communist attitude might change, while affording Japan an opportunity to resume relations with Taipei.

On December 18 Dulles and I again called on Yoshida. One result of this meeting was the preparation of a letter by the prime minister outlining Japan's policies along the above lines. The letter, addressed to Dulles, stated that the Japanese government had no intention of concluding a treaty with Communist China. It cited, in support of this position, two of the anti-Japanese actions which Peking had initiated. The first was the Sino-Soviet defense treaty of 1950 which was specifically aimed at Japan and all nations allied with it. The second action was continuing support given by Peking to the Japan Communist party, which had been fully documented. The signed original of this letter was brought to me by Iguchi under date of December 24, 1951. It was released to the press in Tokyo on January 16, 1952, and was quoted in full in the report of the Senate Foreign Relations Committee's hearings on the Japanese peace treaty. At the time of the press release, I was told that a section of the Japanese Foreign Office was concerned over the possible reaction in the United Kingdom, although the immediate response within Japan was good.

This did not settle the differences between Tokyo and Taipei, however, and I was increasingly in the middle of these complicated problems until the end of February, 1952, when the negotiations were transferred to Taipei. Washington asked for my advice at this time and I replied that the two nations could themselves resolve the question. The Chinese, I said, were old hands at diplomacy and would take care of their own interests.

The Japanese, I added, would carry out their commitments under the Yoshida-Dulles letter of December 24, 1951.

Early in March, 1952, I made one final call on Yoshida in relation to this problem. I thought he should know that in some Washington circles there was growing belief that the Japanese were not negotiating in good faith with the Chinese and would break off the discussions when the United States Senate had ratified the peace treaty. After hearing this, Yoshida replied with a chuckle: "We are not that clever!" However, he promised to instruct his negotiator, Isao Kawada, to be more reasonable in the Taipei discussions. During the following week the prime minister sent Eiji Wajima of the Foreign Office to Taipei with more liberal instructions. Yoshida told me on March 14 that he foresaw no difficulties in the negotiations with China, and they were finally concluded and the treaty signed on April 28, 1952. It came into force on August 5, 1952.

Another "peace" effort which caused many difficulties and some embarrassment was the Korean-Japanese conference to settle some of the outstanding difficulties between those two nations. This was convened, with SCAP's approval, on October 20, 1951. It seemed incongruous to me for Japan and Korea, neighbors with long historical ties, to be unreconciled and, in fact, not even on speaking terms. The initial meeting, held in the conference room of the Diplomatic Section as a neutral location, brought together Sadao Iguchi, the chief Japanese negotiator, and the Korean representative, You Chan Yang, then the ambassador to the United States. Yang was an American-educated Korean doctor from Honolulu who had been selected by President Rhee to become his newly independent country's representative to Washington.

At the outset I made it clear that I was not a mediator and that the two diplomats should negotiate in their own way. Nevertheless, I urged them to be reasonable, particularly in their opening statements, which were to be made public. The situation was complicated, of course, by the effects of Japan's long domination of Korea and by Rhee's intransigent attitude toward the Japanese. With more hope than optimism, I made an opening statement designed to encourage both sides to take a broad approach toward solving their many outstanding problems.

Iguchi followed with a conciliatory and friendly statement, calling for give-and-take on both sides. Yang then proceeded to deliver a scorching indictment of Japanese actions in Korea for the previous forty years. He included demands for payment of an indemnity so huge that it would have bankrupted Japan. As soon as the Korean representative had finished I adjourned the meeting. Iguchi was obviously troubled and annoyed. I spoke to Yang about his statement, pointing out that he could not obtain Japanese cooperation through intemperate language. I also attempted to soothe Iguchi. At the time I believed I had made progress with both sides. I had, but only for a few weeks. The conference slowly collapsed after futile attempts to agree upon an agenda. Talks were revived later and periodically were pursued, but the issues still remained unresolved at the end of 1964.

No DATE HAD BEEN FIXED to negotiate the United States–Japan Administrative Agreement which, under Article III of the Security Treaty, would provide for the maintenance and manning of United States bases in independent Japan. Japanese political parties began in October, 1951, however, to use the eventual agreement as an element of bargaining in domestic politics. Katsuo Okazaki told me on October 24 that the Democratic party had demanded "proper answers" by Yoshida to five major questions as the price of the party's support for the Security Treaty when it came up for Diet approval. The most important of the questions concerned Article I, regarding the use of Japan-based United States forces for service outside the country in the Far East. Would there be consultation with the Japanese government before these forces were sent elsewhere in Asia? When Okazaki asked this question, I replied that close coordination between the two governments could be assumed on matters of this kind. The other queries raised by the Democratic party were speculative and related to costs, specific bases, jurisdiction, and similar details which still had to be negotiated.

General Ridgway, acting as SCAP, handed Prime Minister Yoshida the United States draft Administrative Agreement, to serve as the basis for negotiation. I was present when this took place, on January 24, 1952. I had prepared an *aide-mèmoire*, explaining the purpose of the draft and discussing its main points. Katsuo Okazaki, who eventually headed the Japanese negotiators, accompanied the prime minister for this little ceremony.

Dean Rusk, the chief United States negotiator, and his delegation reached Tokyo on January 26, and formal negotiations on the Administrative Agreement opened three days later in the conference room of my offices. The completed agreement was not signed until February 28. The length of the negotiations is a fair indication of the thorough exploration which was made of all the questions raised by this rather complicated arrangement. At the conclusion I was certain that both sides felt "a hard negotiation resulted in a good agreement."

My staff and I had anticipated this. Before the arrival of the Rusk delegation, we had prepared studies of possible Japanese attitudes toward the full range of problems under the Security Treaty and the subsidiary Administrative Agreement. This was a normal procedure in advance of most international meetings. We foresaw a stiffened attitude by our Japanese friends, producing demands for absolute equality and the recognition of Japan's full and independent sovereignty. Unless the United States in some way recognized this attitude, at least implicitly, we concluded that there could be no agreement. We felt that the new Japanese attitude was natural and justifiable, although it might be difficult for United States authorities to understand, since they had been accustomed to giving orders for so long a period.

When I read a paper outlining these points to a meeting in GHQ, prior to Rusk's arrival, its soundness was questioned. But not for long. The Japanese comments on the draft agreement, received on January 29, confirmed our advance analysis. They included the demand that all language which might give the appearance of dictation be omitted from the agreement. Further, the Japanese requested that all facilities occupied by Occupation authorities be returned to the Japanese government, which would then assign to the United States forces the installations necessary to carry out the Administrative Agreement. This was based on the theory that the Japanese had been *compelled* to furnish the facilities at the command of the Occupation; once peace was in effect, there no longer would be an Occupation to command. Finally, in Okazaki's opening statement at the conference, a clause touched on another Japanese grievance: ". . . while technically speaking, you are not here because we have invited you," he said. This referred to the fact that the United States delegation had determined the schedule for the conference without reference to the convenience of the Japanese, a frequent practice at that time.

During the ensuing month, however, the negotiations, while hard and sometimes seemingly in impasse, were conducted in friendly spirit, businesslike manner, and with growing respect and understanding. I felt that a conference of this kind was salutary, for ourselves and for the Japanese, because ample opportunity was afforded to both sides to learn some of the difficulties inherent in the relationship that was about to be established. It was not easy for either side to abide by the new rules; each country was giving up something in order to produce understanding and cooperation in the face of the irresponsible militarism still rampant in the Far East.

It was on this note of mutual respect and realistic toughness that the Occupation closed and a new facet of Japanese-American relations began. I doubt if anyone could have foreseen such a denouement when Allied forces first marched into Japan in the angry aftermath of the war. Under tremendous pressures, a peace had been forged with great ingenuity and skill and understanding. When my own role in this great undertaking—the Occupation of Japan—ended a short time later, I felt proud of what had been accomplished.

13

Evaluation

PREPARATIONS FOR DISMANTLING the elaborate SCAP organization were well under way some months before the peace treaty was ratified. By early 1952 an informal planning group was operating in Headquarters to anticipate the multitudinous questions involved in the transfer of authority back to the Japanese government. Among other matters, this group accepted my recommendation that General Ridgway move as soon as possible out of the American Embassy, so that it could be restored for use as an embassy. When the Imperial Hotel, that strange and gloomy billet for senior officers in the center of Tokyo, closed for redecoration and eventual reopening under Japanese control, the changeover had already made considerable progress.

My own departure from Japan conformed to this precipitate change. When transfer orders arrived on March 10, I was given eight days to complete all arrangements for permanent departure from Japan. I was offered the ambassadorship to Burma and promptly accepted it as another exciting challenge. My transfer had been rumored for some time, and I had received fairly substantial indications that the first post-treaty United States ambassador to Japan would be Robert D. Murphy, a distinguished career officer with a record of unusual achievement in special wartime missions in Europe and North Africa. He then was serving as ambassador to Belgium. Still, even with this forewarning, I could not bring myself to believe that the stimulating, trying, and often exciting days of the Occupation were about to end. No doubt, this feeling was shared by many others in SCAP Head- quarters.

Our departure followed the usual whirlwind of packing, offi- cial and personal farewells, and the poignancy of breaking up our happy household establishment. At 2:30 P.M., March 18, 1952, Edith and I took off from Haneda Airport for Washington. The sky was overcast with lowering clouds, and there was a feel of rain or snow in the air. At the field to see us off were many of our friends, including: General and Mrs. Ridgway, Mr. and Mrs. Katsuo Okazaki, Mr. and Mrs. Sadao Iguchi, most of the diplo- matic corps, press correspondents with whom I had worked so closely over the years, almost all the personnel of the Diplomatic Section, and those of our weeping household staff who were brave enough to face the ordeal. Precisely on time we taxied to the runway, and in a matter of minutes were on our way.

Comfortably settled in our plane, I pondered over my situa- tion. Upon my return to Washington there would be much to do—not only in briefing Bob Murphy to the extent that he de- sired, but also going through the customary process of "de- briefing" for the benefit of the numerous United States govern- ment agencies interested in Japan. There would also be consulta- tion before undertaking my new assignment. With this in mind, I began to reassess and evaluate my ideas and impressions of the previous six years. It seems almost odd that the notes entered into my Journal at that time correspond, upon recapitulation, to my views today on the accomplishments and failures of the Occupa- tion.

I recalled that at the outset the ultimate objectives the United States laid down for the Occupation were, firstly, to ensure that Japan would not again become a menace to the United States or to the peace and security of the world; and secondly, to bring about the eventual establishment of a peaceful and responsible government, although it was not the policy of the Allied Powers to impose upon Japan any form of government not supported by the freely expressed will of the people.[1]

The first of these two objectives was achieved quickly, as we have seen, and with reasonable surety, through the physical and spiritual demilitarization and total disarmament of Japan, including the complete abolition of the military services and destruction of all the weaponry of war. Its lasting effect is demonstrated by the fact that even though Japan, in less than two decades, has become the economic giant of Asia once more and is economically far stronger than at any period during its thrust for empire, there has not been a single legitimate complaint that Japan has again menaced its neighbors.

As to the second objective, the early adoption of the Occupation-inspired constitution paved the way for the establishment of democratic and responsible government. The people became sovereign, and overwhelming power now rests in the Diet, responsive to the freely expressed will of the people. That this government is peacefully inclined is assured by the inhibitions against war as a sovereign right of the nation contained in Article 9 of the constitution.[2]

A third goal, originally unanticipated, was the clear United States objective of keeping Japan out of the Communist orbit. Paradoxically, a relatively short occupation would almost surely have resulted in a Communist Japan, for it is extremely doubtful that the nation, militarily defenseless and economically prostrate, could have withstood Communist aggressive pressures. It was a realization of this dangerous situation that brought about a change of direction in the philosophy of the Occupation, from an attitude that SCAP surveillance was the sole function of the victors to a new approach which provided vast financial assistance for Japan's economic reconstruction. This change of policy also provided the impetus, in many ways, for the removal of fiscal, political, and psychological barriers to the economic rehabilitation of the talented Japanese. Through this help, most of it

American, Japan added fresh inventiveness to the postwar epoch. The Korean War also brought home to the Japanese the extent of the danger in the divided world to which they were to be readmitted.

The achievement of these three major objectives was in large measure the result of the initiative of General MacArthur. On the Japanese side, major credit must belong to Shigeru Yoshida who, as prime minister during much of the Occupation period, often defied powerful public opinion on major issues, particularly in implementing unpopular SCAP directives which were constructive in intent. These two men towered over a difficult and complex period in Japan and, no doubt, they will both long be remembered for their contributions.

But even MacArthur might have been impotent in the challenging situation he faced if Washington had failed to recognize in time that the pressures of events had outdated many of the carefully prepared advance plans for conducting the Occupation. With all the inescapable bureaucratic problems and disagreements involved in backstopping the Occupation, the United States government eventually threw its great resources, with remarkable unanimity of purpose, into the unpopular task of transforming an enemy—one bitterly remembered—into a viable ally.

In retrospect, perhaps the most remarkable aspect of the Occupation was the fact that, from the outset, it was benevolent and nonvindictive, despite the overtones of the Potsdam Declaration and the harshness of initial policy statements. Seldom has a conquering army moved into a fallen country with more absolute power and less venom. This attitude was translated into policy largely on United States initiative, to the mutterings of several Allies. Fortunately, there was no conscious effort to inflict undue punishment on the Japanese people as a whole, and this, alone, made the Occupation singularly unique. That it worked as well as it did was probably due, in the final analysis, to the fact that the United States arrogated the definitive voice to itself, and thereby eliminated the indecisiveness which characterizes most international enterprises.

Against these considerations, a balance sheet of the specific accomplishments and failures of the Occupation necessarily becomes secondary. It would be purely academic to discuss the merits of land reform, for example, if Japan had come under control of either the Communists or resurgent military autocrats. Therefore, in my opinion, a further evaluation of the Occupation must be placed against the fact that, certainly in major achievements, it was a success.

On the debit side, the Occupation tinkered too deeply and often needlessly with Japan's social and institutional life. The attempt to destroy the so-called Zaibatsu was foredoomed, for, as was later demonstrated, the Japanese preferred economic centralization and cartelization and quickly restored them. The unwarranted severity of the purges likewise deprived the country of experienced leaders and skills at a period when these assets were desperately needed. It should have been obvious that Japan required the strength of cohesion, not weakening fractionization, during the early years of economic revival. Not only did the war-shattered industrial establishment need rebuilding, but the Japanese were far behind and had much to learn in industrial techniques, knowledge, and skills developed in the West during their wartime isolation.

Socially, many Occupation measures resulted only in the weakening of spiritual values and restraints, without contributing new values, amid the already grave uncertainties produced by war and defeat. Enforced revisions of the civil code practically eliminated the family system, the foundation of society for centuries. In abolishing Shinto as a state religion, SCAP also undermined it as a philosophy. The Emperor was made "human," in the process of democratization, but the Throne lost much of its authority as a disciplinary restraint for large numbers of Japanese. SCAP abolished the extraconstitutional bodies, such as the Privy Council, through which in practice the Japanese drew into political life the wisdom and experience of previous leaders. To a people struck so deeply by the sacrifices of a decade of war, the elimination of military monuments and mementos and, particularly, the discreditation of shrines to the war dead was deeply unsettling.

With restraints thus weakened, opposing pressures consequently became unduly strong. Immorality spread by war grew into license and pornography under an Occupation which, while practicing political censorship, otherwise permitted uninhibited publication and generally turned its back to ill-mannered behavior. Freed youth embraced Americanism, as many in SCAP had hoped, but it sought the ugly more eagerly than the solid virtues of American tradition. Politically, elements in SCAP Headquarters appeared to the Japanese as protectors, for far too long, of the Communist party and the excesses it preached. When labor was encouraged to organize, in one of the positive Occupation achievements, it assumed inordinate power, and the process of adjustment is still incomplete. Through its social experimentation, the Occupation left Japan a legacy of ferment which, perhaps, was unwarranted and unnecessary.

On the positive side, however, the assets left by the Occupation doubtless could not have been achieved without deep SCAP intervention in the nation's daily life. Only the power of Headquarters, for instance, was capable of enforcing the extensive land reform program which, to a large measure, freed the downtrodden peasantry and barred the Communists from any important position in what once was their most promising field of exploitation. In the cities, the Communists and other extreme leftists, distorting the freedoms enforced by SCAP, have exercised a disruptive influence in politics. Japan's farmers, with an eye on the land they acquired under the Occupation, continually have provided the main support for the conservative political parties.

A long list of other social and political changes, which most Japanese appear to welcome and support, resulted only from direct SCAP order. The constitution, largely an Occupation product, provides such basic rights as habeas corpus and, equally important, contains safeguards against their abrogation. Under SCAP prodding the civil and criminal codes were overhauled, tax laws revised, civil government and prison administration improved, and numerous other half-seen changes were made. It is an unforgettable experience for one accustomed to the harsh ways of the prewar Japanese police to observe their restraint today, despite the frequent provocations of extremist demonstrators. The army, navy, and air force—however they may be called—no longer display the arrogance and narrow fanaticism of the prewar services, an attitude which reflects American basic training. Moreover, American officials during the Occupation contributed a wide variety of other innovations—ranging from simplification of the written language to improved dietary habits, expansion of the public health service, and medical practice. Japanese today are better fed than ever and have the lowest death rate in their history.

The Japanese themselves have rejected some of the Occupation-inspired changes, as illustrated by the revival of cartelization. Repeated attempts to overthrow land reform have been made, but have been defeated by the SCAP-strenghtened Supreme Court, thus illustrating a new majesty of the law. Other SCAP "reforms" are still in the process of adjustment, and partial changes may yet be made. It is possible, for instance, that the power of labor may be curtailed but, significantly, it is highly doubtful that the right of labor to organize again would be eliminated. Under SCAP protection, labor became too strong. And yet, most Japanese have accepted the principle of organized labor while rejecting many of the excesses it has permitted.

In general, it might be said that the adaptive Japanese already have incorporated into their lives those aspects of the SCAP legacy which clearly benefit the Japanese people. As time goes on, a reversion to the pre-Occupation practices of an ingrown and basically parochial Japan becomes more unlikely. Today's rapid communications—telstar, TV, jet planes, radio—and the uninhibited exchange with the Free World of information, culture, and experience have effectively ended Japan's isolation. The growth and dependence upon foreign investments and the impact of vital foreign trade, especially with the United States, have made Western influences a permanent and highly constructive and stabilizing factor.

Politically, until the Security Treaty with the United States was signed in 1951, Japan was given the choice of alignment. John Foster Dulles insisted throughout the peace treaty negotiations, both privately and publicly, that Japan was free to make its choice: to join the West, remain politically neutral, or join the Communist bloc. However, established trade patterns already constituted a powerful influence for pro-Westernism; the validity of neutralism had been destroyed for most Japanese by the lessons of the Korean War; and, except for a vociferous minority, there was no perceptible desire by the overwhelming majority of Japanese for political or even, at that time, economic, links with communism.

Prime Minister Yoshida, therefore, accepted the logic of Japan's situation when he anchored his country firmly to the United States and the West by concluding the Security Treaty, braving a political outcry at home by a loud and disruptively influential minority. The wisdom of this decision has been endorsed repeatedly by the majority of the Japanese people at the polls and by their deep undercurrent of friendship for the United States.

There are at present those who, especially in Japan, maintain that the world situation has so changed that the Security Treaty with the United States is no longer required or desirable. To accept this view would be to ignore the need for a balance of power in Northeast Asia, a balance that over the years has kept Soviet pressures against Japan to a nuisance level, such as the harassment of Japanese fishing vessels. These advocates of a neutral Japan might well take heed of the political unrest and disturbances in so many of the countries of Asia during the past fifteen years.

Whatever its shortcomings, the Occupation, for better or for worse, has left its imprint, and there is much of America in evidence in the Japan of today. Aside from the noteworthy rise in the standard of living, the rapid growth in physical wealth throughout the country, a healthier and seemingly happier people, and a general Westernization of life and mores in the larger cities, some of the influences left behind by the Occupation are less obvious. A few of these I have already mentioned. But it is interesting to note that the most vocal critics among the Japanese of the present system of government—the left-wing elements, such as the far left of the Socialist party, the Communists, and the more radical labor unions—owe their very existence and capability of demonstrating to those rights of assembly, free speech, and permissible political agitation gained during the Occupation.

The war, the Occupation, and indeed the times in which we live all have created problems with which the Japanese people and their chosen governments will long have to deal. And yet, in the light of Japan's past, the disruptive pressures to which it has been subjected, and the turmoil in much of Asia of which it is an indivisible part, the adjustments have been remarkable. As I have attempted to portray in this book, it is my belief that Japan is a valuable asset of the Free World.

In September, 1951, after my return from the San Francisco Peace Conference, I delivered an address to the America-Japan Society in Tokyo. My closing remarks were the following:

I believe that the Japanese people are endowed with the unity of purpose which will enable Japan to become a respected, free, independent and self-supporting member of the Free World. I believe that Japan will add its strength to the growing forces of freedom. And, finally, I believe that as Japan again becomes capable of contributing its just share to the forces of Freedom, it will never again dissipate its strength in aggressive adventure, but will find its greatest satisfaction within the principles of the United Nations Charter.

We have ahead of us an unparalleled opportunity to witness here in the Pacific area a great experiment of two sovereign and free nations sharing their energies in the interests of peace and security. We shall learn from you as you shall learn from us. The times are too critical, the forces of evil are too great, to allow of petty suspicions or want of mutual faith and trust. To stand still is to invite disaster. We must go forward in the interest of world peace.

Today, thirteen years later, I know of no words which would more clearly express the present-day hopes and aspirations of what I believe is United States foreign policy for the far reaches of the Pacific.

Appendix A

RESOLUTION

Regarding the Waiving of Japan's Claims in the *Awa Maru* Case

Japan, sensible of the sympathetic understanding of Allied Powers, is now emerging out of the ravages of war and clothing herself with a new existence dedicated to peace and to the high principles of freedom and democracy;

And whereas, it is the United States of America who as the principal occupying power, has assumed a major role in the formulation and execution of that policy, and the Japanese people owe to the American government and people an incalculable debt of gratitude for their generous aid and assistance toward her recovery and rehabilitation;

Be it resolved:

(1) That Japan spontaneously and unconditionally waives all her claims arising out of the sinking of the S.S. *Awa Maru* by a U.S. naval craft on April 1, 1945; and

(2) That the government shall speedily commence a negotiation with the government of the United States through the good offices of the Supreme Commander for the Allied Powers and shall amicably settle the case on the basis of waiving the above claim; and

(3) That, as an internal measure, the government shall take appropriate steps to provide adequate solatium for the bereaved families;

(4) That the government shall speedily report to this House the results of the measures carried out in accordance with this resolution.

> Adopted by the House of Councillors
> at the Fifth Session of the Diet,
> this 6th day of April, Nineteen-Hundred and Forty-Nine.

Appendix B

AGREED TERMS OF UNDERSTANDING

The signatories to the Agreement signed this date for settlement of the *Awa Maru* claim have confirmed on behalf of their respective Governments the following:

It is understood that Occupation costs and loans and credits extended to Japan by the Government of the United States of America since the time of the former's surrender are valid debts owed by Japan to the Government of the United States, reducible only by the decision of the Government of the United States.

Executed in duplicate, in the English and Japanese languages, at Tokyo, this fourteenth day of April, 1949 (24 Showa).

For the Government of the United States of America:

[SEAL]

_____
(*signed*) WILLIAM J. SEBALD
Acting United States Political Adviser for Japan

For the Japanese Government:

_____
(*signed*) SHIGERU YOSHIDA
Minister for Foreign Affairs

Attest:

_____
(*signed*) DOUGLAS MacARTHUR
General of the Army
United States Army
Supreme Commander for the Allied Powers

Appendix C

PROCLAMATION
DEFINING TERMS FOR JAPANESE SURRENDER,
July 26, 1945

(1) We—The President of the United States, the President of the National Government of the Republic of China, and the Prime Minister of Great Britain, representing the hundreds of millions of our countrymen, have conferred and agree that Japan shall be given an opportunity to end this war.

(2) The prodigious land, sea and air forces of the United States, the British Empire and of China, many times reinforced by their armies and air fleets from the west, are poised to strike the final blows upon Japan. This military power is sustained and inspired by the determination of all the Allied Nations to prosecute the war against Japan until she ceases to resist.

(3) The result of the futile and senseless German resistance to the might of the aroused free peoples of the world stands forth in awful clarity as an example to the people of Japan. The might that now converges on Japan is immeasurably greater than that which, when applied to the resisting Nazis, necessarily laid waste to the lands, the industry and the method of life of the whole German people. The full application of our military power, backed by our resolve, *will* mean the inevitable and complete destruction of the Japanese armed forces and just as inevitably the utter devastation of the Japanese homeland.

(4) The time has come for Japan to decide whether she will continue to be controlled by those self-willed militaristic advisers whose unintelligent calculations have brought the Empire of Japan to the threshold of annihilation, or whether she will follow the path of reason.

(5) Following are our terms. We will not deviate from them. There are no alternatives. We shall brook no delay.

(6) There must be eliminated for all time the authority and influence of those who have deceived and misled the people of Japan into embarking on world conquest, for we insist that a new order of peace, security and justice will be impossible until irresponsible militarism is driven from the world.

(7) Until such a new order is established *and* until there is convincing proof that Japan's war-making power is destroyed, points in Japanese territory to be designated by the Allies shall be occupied to secure the achievement of the basic objectives we are here setting forth.

(8) The terms of the Cairo Declaration shall be carried out and Japanese sovereignty shall be limited to the islands of Honshu, Hokkaido, Kyushu, Shikoku and such minor islands as we determine.

(9) The Japanese military forces, after being completely disarmed, shall be permitted to return to their homes with the opportunity to lead peaceful and productive lives.

(10) We do not intend that the Japanese shall be enslaved as a race or destroyed as a nation, but stern justice shall be meted out to all war criminals, including those who have visited cruelties upon our prisoners. The Japanese Government shall remove all obstacles to the revival and strengthening of democratic tendencies among the Japanese people. Freedom of speech, of religion, and of thought, as well as respect for the fundamental human rights shall be established.

(11) Japan shall be permitted to maintain such industries as will sustain her economy and permit the exaction of just reparations in kind, but not those [industries] which would enable her to re-arm for war. To this end, access to, as distinguished from control of, raw materials shall be permitted. Eventual Japanese participation in world trade relations shall be permitted.

(12) The occupying forces of the Allies shall be withdrawn from Japan as soon as these objectives have been accomplished and there has been established in accordance with the freely expressed will of the Japanese people a peacefully inclined and responsible government.

(13) We call upon the government of Japan to proclaim now the unconditional surrender of all Japanese armed forces, and to provide proper and adequate assurances of their good faith in such action. The alternative for Japan is prompt and utter destruction.

Appendix D

FULL TEXT OF THE REVIEW

The following is the text of General MacArthur's Review of the War Crimes sentences:

No duty I have ever been called upon to perform in a long public service replete with many bitter, lonely and forlorn assignments and responsibilities is so utterly repugnant to me as that of reviewing the sentences of the Japanese War Criminal defendants adjudged by the International Military Tribunal for the Far East. It is not my purpose, nor indeed would I have that transcendent wisdom which would be necessary, to assay the universal fundamentals involved in these epochal proceedings designed to formulate and codify standards of international morality by those charged with a nation's conduct. The problem indeed is basically one which man has struggled to solve since the beginning of time and which may well wait complete solution till the end of time. In so far as my own immediate obligation and limited authority extend in this case, suffice it that under the principles and procedures prescribed in full detail by the Allied Powers concerned, I can find nothing of technical commission or omission in the incidents of the trial itself of sufficient import to warrant my intervention in the judgments which have been rendered. No human decision is infallible but I can conceive of no judicial process where greater safeguard was made to evolve justice. It is inevitable that many will disagree with the verdict, even the learned justices who composed the Tribunal were not in complete unanimity, but no mortal agency in the present imperfect evolution of civilized society seems more entitled to confidence in the integrity of its solemn pronouncements. If we cannot trust such processes and such men we can trust nothing. I therefore direct the Commanding General of the Eighth Army to execute the sentences as pronounced by the Tribunal. In doing so I pray that an Omnipotent Providence may use this tragic expiation as a symbol to summon all persons of goodwill to a realization of the utter futility of war—that most malignant scourge and greatest sin of mankind—and eventually to its renunciation by all nations. To this end on the day of execution I request the members of all congregations throughout Japan of whatever creed or faith in the privacy of their homes or at their altars of public worship to seek Divine help and guidance that the world keep the peace lest the human race perish.

305

Notes

CHAPTER 3

1. Harry S. Truman, *Memoirs* (Garden City, N.Y.: Doubleday & Company, Inc., 1955), vol. I, pp. 440–441.
2. *Ibid.*, p. 443.
3. The hearings are recorded in a bound typewritten copy in the files of the Senate Foreign Relations Committee. Committee officials say the transcript has not been formally published.

CHAPTER 4

1. Truman, *Memoirs,* p. 441.
2. Terms of reference of the Far Eastern Commission, Moscow Communiqué, Dec. 27, 1945.

CHAPTER 5

1. Quoted in Courtney Whitney, *MacArthur—His Rendezvous with History* (New York: Alfred A. Knopf, 1956), pp. 300–301.
2. Government Section, GHQ, SCAP, *Political Reorientation of Japan—September 1945 to September 1948* (Washington: U.S. Government Printing Office, 1949), p. 18.
3. *Ibid.*, p. 553.
4. *Ibid.* These letters are reproduced as Appendix 5h.
5. The legal basis for control of the economy was contained in a number of laws passed by the Diet early in the so-called China Incident of 1937. I translated and published the key statutes under the title: *A Selection of Japan's Emergency Legislation.* The preface, written on Nov. 20, 1937, opened with this statement: "Recent events in China have caused the enactment of a considerable number of laws, the purpose of which obviously is to place full control of the national economy into the hands of the Government."
6. See GHQ, SCAP, *Selected Data on the Occupation of Japan* (Tokyo, 1950).
7. Yoshida recounts this story in a less favorable light to himself in his memoirs. *The Yoshida Memoirs* (Boston: Houghton Mifflin Co., 1962), pp. 64–65.

CHAPTER 6

1. The principal functions of the Far Eastern Commission were the following:
    1. To formulate the policies, principles, and standards in conformity with which the fulfillment by Japan of its obligations under the Terms of Surrender may be accomplished.

2. To review . . . any directive issued by the Supreme Commander for the Allied Powers or any action taken by the Supreme Commander involving policy decisions within the jurisdiction of the Commission.

3. To consider such other matters as may be assigned to it . . .

CHAPTER 7

1. Truman, *Memoirs*, vol. I, p. 441.
2. Allied Council for Japan, Verbatim Minutes, Second Meeting, April 19, 1946, pp. 10 ff.
3. By a curious twist of fate, Gen. Derevyanko spent his last days as military commander of the Vorkuta Prison complex located at the northern end of the Ural Mountains. See Joseph Scholmer, *Vorkuta* (New York: Henry Holt and Co., 1954), pp. 239 ff.

CHAPTER 8

1. The judges were the following:

Sir William Webb, *Australia*
Edward Stuart McDougall, *Canada*
Ju-ao Mei, *China*
Henri Bernard, *France*
Radha M. Pal, *India*
B. V. A. Roling, *Netherlands*
Erima Harvey Northcroft, *New Zealand*
Delfin Jaranilla, *Philippines*
Ivan Micheyevich Zaryanov, *U.S.S.R.*
Lord Patrick, *United Kingdom*
John P. H. Higgins, succeeded by Maj. Gen. Myron C. Cramer, *United States*

2. The following were the prosecutors at the outset of the trial. Some of them left Japan when they had finished their part of the case, leaving a substitute. A few returned to Japan at intervals; others did not return. Some remained on the job throughout the trial.

NAME AND COUNTRY	TITLE
Joseph B. Keenan, *United States*	Chief of Counsel
Che-chun Hsiang, *China*	Associate Counsel
A. S. Comyns Carr, *U.K.*	—do—
S. A. Golunsky, *U.S.S.R.*	—do—
A. J. Mansfield, *Australia*	—do—
H. G. Nolan, *Canada*	—do—
Robert Oneto, *France*	—do—
W. G. F. Boegerhoff Mulder, *Netherlands*	—do—
R. H. Quilliam, *New Zealand*	—do—
Govinda Menon, *India*	—do—
Pedro Lopez, *Philippines*	—do—

3. The following are the sentences given to the Class A war criminals:

AGE	NAME	SENTENCE	FORMER POSITION
71	Sadao Araki	Life imprisonment	Ex-War Minister
65	Kenji Doihara	Death by hanging	Ex-General
58	Kingoro Hashimoto	Life imprisonment	Ex-Director-General Imperial Rule Assistance Assn.
69	Shunroku Hata	Life imprisonment	Ex-War Minister
81	Kiichiro Hiranuma	Life imprisonment	Ex-Prime Minister
70	Koki Hirota	Death by hanging	Ex-Prime Minister
56	Naoki Hoshino	Life imprisonment	Ex-Governor of Planning Board
63	Seishiro Itagaki	Death by hanging	Ex-War Minister
59	Okinori Kaya	Life imprisonment	Ex-Finance Minister
59	Koichi Kido	Life imprisonment	Ex-Lord Keeper of the Privy Seal
60	Heitaro Kimura	Death by hanging	Ex-War Vice Minister
68	Kuniaki Koiso	Life imprisonment	Ex-Prime Minister
70	Iwane Matsui	Death by hanging	Ex-General
56	Akira Muto	Death by hanging	Ex-Chief, Military Affairs Bureau
58	Takasumi Oka	Life imprisonment	Ex-Chief, Naval Affairs Bureau
62	Hiroshi Oshima	Life imprisonment	Ex-Ambassador to Germany
53	Kenryo Sato	Life imprisonment	Ex-Chief, Military Affairs Bureau
61	Mamoru Shigemitsu	7 years' imprisonment	Ex-Foreign Minister
65	Shigetaro Shimada	Life imprisonment	Ex-Navy Minister
61	Toshio Shiratori	Life imprisonment	Ex-Ambassador to Italy
60	Teiichi Suzuki	Life imprisonment	Ex-Governor, Planning Board
66	Shigenori Togo	20 years' imprisonment	Ex-Foreign Minister
64	Hideki Tojo	Death by hanging	Ex-Prime Minister
66	Yoshiro Umezu	Life imprisonment	Ex-Chief of General Staff
74	Jiro Minami	Life imprisonment	Ex-War Minister

4. 338 U.S. 197.

CHAPTER 9

1. Tang Tsou, *America's Failure in China* (Chicago: 1963), p. 316.

2. *New York Times*, March 2, 1949.

3. The following works were found especially useful: Field, *United States Naval Operations, Korea* (Washington: 1962); Roy E. Appleman, *South to the Naktong, North to the Yalu* (*U.S. Army in the Korean War*) (U.S. Government Printing Office: 1961); Robert Leckie, *Conflict, A History of the Korean War* (New York: G. P. Putnam Sons, 1962); T. R. Fehrenback, *This Kind of War* (New York: Macmillan Co., 1963).

4. For an excellent, detailed, and well-written account of the appalling difficulties encountered in planning and mounting this operation, see Field, *op. cit.*, chap. VII.

5. *Ibid.*, pp. 291, 381.

6. On Sept. 29, 1950, Gen. George C. Marshall, Secretary of Defense, sent MacArthur a personal and private message, which President Truman had approved, giving him complete tactical freedom for the northward advance across the 38th parallel. MacArthur notified the Joint Chiefs of Staff on Oct. 1 that, unless they objected, he would instruct all United Nations commanders the following day that "the field of our military operations is limited only by military exigencies and the international boundaries of Korea." Appleman, *op. cit.*, p. 608.

7. Truman, *Memoirs*, vol. II, p. 365.

CHAPTER 10

1. Quoted in Whitney, *MacArthur—His Rendezvous with History*, p. 374.

2. Cf. Robert L. Eichelberger, *Our Jungle Road to Tokyo* (New York: Viking Press, 1950), pp. 165–167.

3. The General was accompanied by Brig. Gen. Courtney A. Whitney, one of his closest advisers; Col. Laurence E. Bunker, his personal aide; and Lt. Col. Charles C. Canada, his personal physician.

4. Truman, *Memoirs*, vol. II, pp. 438–439.

5. *Ibid.*, pp. 440–442.

6. *Ibid.*, pp. 445–448.

7. *Ibid.*, p. 446.

8. *Ibid.*, p. 449.

CHAPTER 11

1. See particularly Frederick S. Dunn, *Peace-Making and the Settlement with Japan* (Princeton University Press, 1963).

2. *Political Reorientation of Japan*, p. 765.

3. Other members of the Dulles party were: John M. Allison, Dulles' State Department assistant; Miss Doris Doyle, secretary; and two unofficial newsmen-companions, William R. Mathews of the *Arizona Daily Star*, and Carl W. McCardle of the Philadelphia *Evening Bulletin*.

4. The members of the Dulles Mission were the following:

John Foster Dulles, *Ambassador*
John M. Allison, *Minister*
Robert A. Fearey, *Foreign Service Officer*
Earl D. Johnson, *Asst. Secretary of the Army*
Maj. Gen. Carter B. Magruder, *Department of the Army*
Col. C. Stanton Babcock, *Department of the Army*
John D. Rockefeller, III, *Cultural representative*
Doris Doyle, *Secretary*

5. Other members of the party were Mrs. Dulles, Foreign Service Officer Robert A. Fearey, Col. C. Stanton Babcock, and Mrs. Bernita O'Day, secretary.

CHAPTER 12

1. See *Conference for the Conclusion and Signature of the Treaty of Peace with Japan* (U.S. Government Printing Office, 1951).

2. For a complete list of the entire Japanese Delegation, see *ibid.*, p. 6.

3. Yoshida, *Memoirs*, p. 255.

4. For an admirable description of this maneuvering, see Dunn, *Peace-Making and the Settlement with Japan*, chap. VIII.

CHAPTER 13

1. See the United States Initial Post-Surrender Policy for Japan, *A Decade of American Foreign Policy, 1941–49* (Washington: 1950), p. 627. The substance of these two objectives was adopted by the Far Eastern Commission on June 19, 1947.

2. Article 9 of the Constitution of Japan reads as follows:

Aspiring sincerely to an international peace based on justice and order, the Japanese people forever renounce war as a sovereign right of the nation and the threat or use of force as means of settling international disputes.

In order to accomplish the aim of the preceding paragraph, land, sea, and air forces, as well as other war potential, will never be maintained. The rights of belligerency of the state will not be recognized.

Index

Index